RELIGION AND THE POLITICS OF IDENTITY IN KOSOVO

In memory of my father

GER DUIJZINGS

Religion and the Politics of Identity in Kosovo

Columbia University Press
New York

Columbia University Press
New York
© 2000 by Ger Duijzings
All rights reserved.
Printed in Malaysia

Library of Congress Cataloging-in-Publication Data
Duijzings, Gerlachlus, 1961–
    Religion and the politics of identity in Kosovo / by Gerlachus Duijzings.
        p.   cm.
    Includes bibliographical references and index.
    ISBN 0–231–12098–2 (cloth : alk. paper) — ISBN 0–231–12099–0
    (pbk. : alk. paper)
    1. Serbia—Religion—20th century. 2. Kosovo (Serbia)—Religion —20th
    century. 3. Kosovo (Serbia)—Ethnic relations. I. Title.

    BL980.Y83 D85 2000
    305.6'094971—dc21   00 –023834

C 10 9 8 7 6 5 4 3 2 1
P 10 9 8 7 6 5 4 3 2 1

CONTENTS

v

ILLUSTRATIONS

PREFACE AND ACKNOWLEDGEMENTS

This book is not the one I initially intended to write. Due to the events in the former Yugoslavia, the doctoral research that I was conducting in Kosovo in the early 1990s took an unexpected turn. During the autumn of 1992, within a few months after the beginning of my fieldwork in Letnica (a Croat enclave near the border with Macedonia), research was made virtually impossible because most of my subjects became refugees. The turbulent developments in Croatia and Bosnia-Hercegovina triggered off sudden and radical processes of ethnic fermentation, which resulted in the end of the community that I was planning to study. Although at that time there was no war going on in Kosovo, between July and December 1992 more than three-quarters of the Croat population of Letnica and surrounding villages decided to abandon their homes, leaving their possessions behind. They went to Croatia, where most of them were resettled in Western Slavonia, in empty villages that carried the undeniable marks of war, in houses that had belonged to Serbs.

It is clear that these events greatly affected my research. I was forced to abandon my original project: the community was in a state of complete turmoil, and doing fieldwork there under those conditions was becoming more and more dangerous – and questionable from both the practical and the ethical viewpoint. The present book is in many ways an attempt to pick up the pieces, the debris that the Yugoslav wars left behind in the minds and lives of ordinary people, but also in my own work. The book clearly bears the marks of the vicissitudes of my research: since I was unable to produce the anthropological monograph that I had planned at start, I decided to compile papers worked on during the years of my involvement with the area from 1986 onwards (beginning with a MA thesis written in 1989, which forms the basis of Chapter 5 of the present work). It has grown into a collection of ethnographic case-studies on Kosovo, all dealing with subjects that at some stage have caught my interest. My choice of topics has been led by intuition rather than by any clear preconceived concept, yet all the case studies share certain themes and ways of approach. Although the focus is on Kosovo, the scope is much wider, covering developments in Croatia, Bosnia, Albania, Macedonia and Serbia. The rationale behind this is that it is almost impossible to understand developments in Kosovo without discussing them in a larger Balkan context.

The chapters can be read separately since they describe different, usually local, arenas and contexts. All are meant as separate case-studies, with emphasis on the historical and ethnographic detail. However, the chapters all deal with interconnected themes, and each exhibits a general interest in the tension between conflict and symbiosis in this part of Europe, and the role played by religion in the local, regional and national politics of identity. The themes revolve around the ways identities are formed and transformed, as a result of wider political developments, and how religion and ritual help, on the one hand, to establish forms of community across ethno-religious boundaries and, on the other hand, to create divisions, draw borders and delineate (ethnic) identities. In spite of all the variety, these chapters share certain theoretical assumptions which are sketched out in the introduction. The conclusions attempt to transcend the particularity of these case-studies, and sums up the research findings in more general terms.

Some of the chapters included here have been published pre-viously in some form. Although most of them have been revised and rewritten considerably, they still reflect the development of my thinking. In my latest work, approach and style are probably more mature than in my oldest chapters (3 and 5) which were written before the start of the wars in the former Yugoslavia. Chapter 2 was first published in Croatian ('Egzodus iz Letnice. Hrvatske izbjeglice sa Kosova u Zapadnoj Slavoniji. Kronika', *Narodna umjetnost* (Zagreb), 32/2, 1995, pp.129-52) and then in English (as 'The exodus of Letnica: Croatian refugees from Kosovo in Western Slavonia. A chronicle', in Renata Jambrešić Kirin and Maja Povrzanović (eds), *War, exile, everyday life: Cultural perspec-tives*, Zagreb: Institute of Ethnology and Folklore Research, 1996, pp.147-70); Chapter 3, now considerably revised, was first pub-lished in Dutch ('Van het rechte pad geraakt. Gezamenlijke pelgrimages van moslims en christenen in Joegoslavië en Albanië', in Willy Jansen and Huub de Jonge (eds), *Islamitische pelgrimstochten*, Muiderberg: Coutinho, 1991, pp.113-26) and then in English (as 'Pilgrimage, politics and ethnicity. Joint pilgrimages of Muslims and Christians and conflicts over ambiguous sanctuaries in Yugoslavia and Albania', in Mart Bax and Adrianus Koster (eds), *Power and prayer: Religious and political processes in past and present*, Amsterdam: VU University Press, 1993, pp.79-90). Chapter 5, also much revised, is based on my MA thesis ('Derwisjen in Joegoslavië. Religieus nonconformisme onder Albanese moslems in Kosovo', ICSA, University of Nijmegen, 1989), and subsequently presented at the conference 'The anthropology of ethnicity – A critical review', held in Amsterdam on 15-19 December 1993 ('Islam and ethnicity: Dervish brotherhoods in Kosovo', Workshop V: Ethnicity, language and religion, pp.53-62). Chapter 6 was first published in Dutch ('De Egyptenaren in Kosovo en Macedonia', *Amsterdams sociologisch tijdschrift*, 18, 1992, pp.24-38) and then in an updated English version almost identical to the one in this book ('The making of Egyptians in Kosovo and Macedonia', in Cora Govers and Hans Vermeulen (eds), *The politics of ethnic consciousness*, Basingstoke: Macmillan, 1997, pp.194-222); recently this paper was also published in Serbian ('Egipćani na Kosovu i u Makedoniji', in: *Filozofija i društvo*, 14, 1998, pp.119-46). Chapters 1, 4, 7, 8, and 9 have not been published before.

Many people and institutions were helpful to me during the subsequent stages of my research. It is impossible to thank them all, but I will nevertheless mention a few: first, the Roman Catholic charity Church in Need, which at the initial stage of my doctoral research enabled me to start with fieldwork in 'mixed' pilgrimage sites in Kosovo during the summers of 1990 and 1991. The Amsterdam School for Social Science Research financed most of the subsequent research, and I thank both staff and students of the School for offering a stimulating environment. Throughout the years I have also benefited from regular meetings with a group of fellow anthropologists, Karin Bijker, Gerard Hersbach, Dina Siegel and Sjef Vissers, all involved with research on pilgrimage. Most chapters have been scrutinised separately by experts on the specific issues that are dealt with, and for comments and suggestions I am grateful to Peter Bartl, Xavier Bougarel, Wendy Bracewell, Nathalie Clayer, Robert Elsie, Victor Friedman, René Grémaux, Willy Jansen, Anastasija Karakasidou, Denisa Kostovičová, Aleksander Lopasic, Noel Malcolm, Christos Mylonas, Alexandre Popovic, Mattijs van de Port, Maria Todorova, and Mitja Velikonja. Wendy Bracewell has offered invaluable help in correcting the

English. I am also grateful to the School of Slavonic and East European Studies, University College London, for allowing me some extra time to finish my manuscript, and to my students who have helped me to formulate my ideas in a much clearer and more coherent way. Finally I must express special gratitude to my three supervisors, Mart Bax, Henk Driessen and Bonno Thoden van Velzen, who played a crucial and indispensable role in helping me to construct my argument and sharpen my ideas. Unfortunately, my informants and friends in Kosovo and other parts of the former Yugoslavia need to remain unnamed here for obvious reasons. The best way to thank them has been writing this book, which may contribute – if only a little – to a better understanding of the Kosovo (and Balkan) conundrum.

Postscript

This manuscript was finalised before the start of NATO actions against Serbia in March 1999, and the events that have followed in Kosovo and Serbia. Although these developments have put my work in a completely different light, I could not include them in my account. It is sad that this book now bears testimony to a world that may have ceased to exist.

December 1999   GER DUIJZINGS

MAPS

SERBIA

SERBIA

MONTENEGRO

Mitrovica

Devič

Peć
Peja

PRIŠTINA
PRISHTINA

Gračanica

Janjevo

Dečani

Gnjilane
Gjilan

Junik

Orahovac
Rahovec

Zočište

Uroševac
Ferizaj

GORNJA
MORAVA

Djakovica
Gjakova

Suva Reka
Suharekë

Vitina
Viti

Stublla

KARADAG

HAS

Zjum
Zym

Prizren

Letnica

Dunav

SREDAČKA ŽUPA

SKOPSKA
CRNA GORA

ALBANIA

0   25
km

GORA

Tetovo
Tetova

SKOPJE
SHKUP

MACEDONIA

1

INTRODUCTION

Kosovo is an area which has become known as a conflict-ridden and segregated society in which Albanians and Serbs live completely divided in two 'parallel' societies.[1] The region is often seen as a kind of frontier where – since the famous Battle of Kosovo fought between the Ottoman Turks and Balkan Christian forces in 1389 – Muslims and Christians have met and clashed. In the 1980s these divisions have turned the province into one of the most dangerous hot-spots of Eastern Europe. Since the end of the war in Bosnia and the signing of the Dayton Peace Agreement (in November 1995), the situation in Kosovo has escalated, especially since the Albanians have started a guerrilla war after years of political stalemate. In light of these recent developments it is logical that the rift between Albanians and Serbs is perceived as being definitively divisive. Yet Kosovo also has a history of co-existence with considerable movement across its ethnic and religious frontiers, through trade, cultural diffusion, religious exchange and conversion. Many cultural traits were and still are shared across group boundaries, and throughout its history the ethnic and religious barriers have been anything but watertight. Instead of two 'ethnic' societies, I prefer to speak here of one single 'frontier' society, in which periods of confrontation alternate with periods of contact and co-operation across ethnic and religious boundaries. Although the war in Kosovo may cause us to think in terms of irreconcilable differences, one should not forget that boundaries – the territorial as well as the cognitive ones – have often faded in more quiet periods. Everyday realities in small communities,

---

[1] A note on the spelling used in this book is necessary for the reader. I have decided to use the name Kosovo, which is the one generally employed in Western literature. The Albanian term for the province is Kosova. For other (geographical, personal, and other) names I alternatingly use Albanian, Serbian or Croatian spelling, i.e. the one which is most appropriate depending on context.

2   *Introduction*

which are usually the field of analysis for the anthropologist, suggest that in a distant and not so distant past things have sometimes – though certainly not always – been quite different. This tension between conflict and symbiosis, particularly in the field of religious life, is one of the main themes of this book. Since 1991 I have done research on ethnically and religiously 'mixed' pilgrimages in Kosovo (in such places as the Serbian-Orthodox monasteries of Gračanica and Zočište and the Roman Catholic shrine of Letnica), which offer good examples of this contact across religious and ethnic boundaries. At present this seems unimaginable, but Muslims and Christians of different ethnic backgrounds have visited each other's sanctuaries, worshipped each other's saints and ignored the evident theological objections of religious orthodoxies. Ethnographic studies of the area show that ethno-religious border-crossing and syncretism have been widespread (see especially F.W. Hasluck 1929).[2] Particularly in the field of popular religion, which religious authorities traditionally control least, formal boundaries are most often disregarded (Badone 1990). There are numerous examples – in Kosovo, Albania, Macedonia, Montenegro and Bosnia – where Muslim and Christian forms of pilgrimage and saint veneration have amalgamated and formal religious divisions have become blurred (see Chapter 3).[3]

[2] I am aware of the present scepticism about using the term syncretism. It is defined here as the process of religious synthesis, of hybridisation and 'mixing', that occurs at the interface of different religious formations. It refers to practices that are not sanctioned by the church, i.e. institutionalised and backed up by forms of ecclesiastic power and authority (Badone 1990; Stewart and Shaw 1994). However, what is syncretic at one point in time may become part of religious orthodoxy later. Orthodoxy (and orthopraxy) are thus always situationally defined and linked to relationships of dominance and authority (Eickelman 1989:287). For ethnographic accounts of syncretism in the Balkans see Dawkins (1933), Barjaktarović (1950), Skendi (1967), Bartl (1967), and Bartl (1968:87-98).

[3] Victor and Edith Turner's claim that '[w]ith rare and interesting exceptions, pilgrims of the different historical religions do not visit one another's shrines, and certainly do not find salvation *extra ecclesia*' (Turner and Turner 1978:9) does not seem to hold true for the Balkans and probably also for many other parts of the world (see for instance Ben-Ami 1990; Oberoi 1994; van de Veer 1994:33-43; Tambiah 1986:62-3). Famous shrines of one particular religion are often visited by members of other faiths as well, e.g. Lourdes, the most famous Roman Catholic shrine in Europe, which has also attracted Muslims from Bosnia (Oršolić 1978).

Gypsy pilgrims in Letnica, August 1991.

Though ethno-religious differences need not be an impediment to a certain degree of *communitas* (Turner 1974), harmony and tolerance do not always reign in these pilgrimage sites. *Communitas* is a highly precarious matter which, under certain political conditions, can turn into precisely the opposite. I experienced this shift from relative symbiosis to conflict most drastically during the research I did in Letnica, a Catholic and Croat enclave in Kosovo. In Kosovo and beyond, it is a well-known 'ecumenical' Marian shrine visited by thousands of pilgrims, not only by local Catholics (Croats and Albanians), but also by members of other groups living in the region (Muslim Albanians, Orthodox Serbs, and Gypsies). Relations between these groups were the focal point of my research, and I was primarily interested in the role ritual plays in the formation and delineation of ethno-religious identities. I viewed the pilgrimage as a laboratory of identity, where one can see both these dimensions of ethno-religious conflict and symbiosis, of fission and fusion, 'at work'. Letnica was a fascinating place to do this research because the municipality of which it is part has always been one of the most heterogeneous in Kosovo. The area forms an ethnic and religious microcosmos, consisting of a complicated patchwork of groups (Muslim and Catholic Albanians, Albanian crypto-Catholics, Orthodox Serbs, Catholic Croats and Gypsies).

In the summer of 1991 (when I first visited Letnica to observe the pilgrimage) the war which just had started in Croatia was already throwing its shadow on the 'ecumenical' character of this event: tensions between local Croats and Serbs were mounting; pilgrims did not come in their huge numbers as in former days and went home much earlier; Serbs from neighbouring villages were boycotting the shrine; and other pilgrims seemed not to enjoy themselves as fully as in previous years, feeling vaguely insecure and made anxious by the war that was raging a few hundred miles to the north. Somehow war was in the air in these parts as well, and many felt that it was unsafe to spend the night outside as pilgrims usually do. As far as my research was concerned, I initially did not feel too discouraged by these rising tensions; after all, I had anticipated them, asking questions such as: How does the deterioration of ethno-religious relations affect the 'ecumenical' or mixed character of this pilgrimage? Do people of different ethnic and religious backgrounds still gather in relative harmony, or is the shrine transformed into an arena in which ethno-religious boundaries are increasingly marked off and dramatised? And to what extent do shrines become the focal point of ethno-political mobilisation and competition?[4] Yet I did not expect relations between local Serbs and Croats, which had never been burdened with historical antagonism, to deteriorate so rapidly. The end of this story was that within a few months – while I was doing fieldwork – the vast majority of the Croat inhabitants of Letnica fled to Croatia (see chapter 2). This Croat village, which I had thought was too remote and isolated to be affected by an eventual escalation of the conflict between Serbs and Albanians, did not offer the calm and peaceful environment

---

[4] These questions were mainly inspired by the work of Sallnow (1981 and 1987), Bax (1987), and Eade and Sallnow (1991). For a similar view on pilgrimage as both a vehicle for social integration and a source of conflict, see Bax (1995).

– almost a *sine qua non* of normal anthropological research[5] – which I had expected.

Kosovo as an ethnic shatter zone

As I have pointed out earlier, due to these developments I was forced to change my plans, and I decided to transform my doctoral thesis from a local monograph into a compilation of loosely connected ethnographic case studies that go beyond the confines of village society. Before I turn to those case studies, I would like to provide a short ethnographic and historical sketch of the area, in which I will try to pinpoint a number of features which I think are central to this society. In addition, I would like to offer a general theoretical framework which will link all these case studies together.

Kosovo is an example of a poor, peripheral and conflict-ridden society, where the central authority of the state has been nominal for much of its modern history. Like most other Balkan areas which were part of 'Turkey in Europe' until the very end of Ottoman rule (1912), it is an area with an undeveloped economy. The French social geographer Michel Roux, who has produced one of the very few serious studies on Kosovo, has called it the Third World within Europe, 'véritable périphérie de la périphérie' (Roux 1992:238).[6] For its majority rural population life commonly means a struggle for survival: the average Albanian (and Serb) peasant tries to make a living out of a small plot of land, aiming

---

[5] Historically, modern anthropology and its methods (fieldwork, participant observation) have largely developed in colonial contexts, where anthropologists did their research in the relatively pacified conditions that were created by the colonial state. It is only after the end of colonialism that anthropologists have become more aware of the historicity of the societies they study (cf. Blok 1977; Cole 1977; Marcus and Fischer 1986). As a result anthropological methods have broadened in order to include these elements of change and process (for instance through archival research), although I think that common anthropological training still does not equip anthropologists well enough for research in situations of profound and violent change. It is only in the last decade or so that anthropologists have started to work under such conditions. See for instance Nordstrom and Robben (1995).

[6] In 1987 the BNP in Kosovo was on the level of the Ivory Coast and Honduras (Roux 1992:299). For an analysis of Kosovo's longstanding social and economic problems see also Büschenfeld (1991).

Albanian peasant at
Prizren's Wednesday
market, summer 1986.

to ensure some minimal level of subsistence, and sending sons
away (often abroad) to supplement the meagre income of the
household. Since life conditions are harsh and highly competitive,
the extended family provides not only a kind of safety net (as is
the case in Western Europe), but is also the major source of
group solidarity and the primary defensive-and-attack unit, strictly
organised along corporate and patriarchal lines.

These conditions are not unfamiliar to many other parts of
the Balkans. One can find various features which match the conditions of existential insecurity that have reigned elsewhere: a
strong fixation on the family or lineage; distrust towards those
who are not one's kin; a strong pressure to protect the family's
integrity and to avenge infringements upon its reputation; a tendency to conceal information or to mislead or deceive others,

which corresponds to an instrumental view of relations outside the family. In this type of atomised society, in which the struggle for survival dominates life and violent conflict is a recurring phenomenon, loyalties beyond one's own family are highly unstable, changeable and fluid.[7] In Kosovo, blood feuds between Albanian clans were only halted – as recent years have shown – after an external (Serbian) threat became serious.[8] It is clear that lack of social and economic integration has inhibited the development of stable, wider identifications.

In Kosovo the final period of Ottoman rule was marked by chronic disorder: violent rebellions of Albanians against the Ottomans were followed by equally violent reprisals by the Turkish forces. The Christian (particularly Serbian Orthodox) populace in villages suffered most from the lack of protection and the constant abuse by unruly (mostly Muslim Albanian) elements.[9] Kosovo became a frontier region, contested between the Ottoman empire and independent Serbia. The border between these two states was established earlier, at the Congress of Berlin in 1878, and this resulted in large population movements and a considerable rise of ethnic and religious tensions: Serbs massively expelled Albanians from Serbia to Kosovo, while many Kosovo Serbs fled to Serbia as a result of that. For the first time in Kosovo's history, a clear ethnic divide emerged between the Albanians, the majority

[7] For ethnographic accounts see for instance Dinko Tomasic (1948) and Juliet du Boulay (1976). I realise that I might be reinforcing a rather simplified and stereotypical image of the Balkans (see Todorova 1997a), but I would like to stress that I strongly oppose the view that these elements of poverty, violence and existential insecurity should be seen as the fixed and unchangeable facts of Balkan life. I would like to advocate an approach which tries to contextualise and historicise these elements, through anthropological, sociological, and historical analysis.

[8] For analyses of feuding in Kosovo see particularly: Zurl (1978), Karan (1985), Djuričić (1994), and Djurić (1997).

[9] See for instance Durham (1904) for an account of the dismal situation of insecurity, oppression and desperate poverty in Kosovo at the turn of the century. It is not my intention to offer a complete picture of Kosovo's history here. This has been done in two recent publications: Malcolm (1998) and Vickers (1998). As an introduction into Kosovo's troubled past (and present), one can also read a book I co-edited (Duijzings, Janjić and Maliqi 1997). This collection of articles includes Serbian and Albanian viewpoints on the Kosovo issue.

population, and the Serbs, who laid claims on Kosovo's territory as the cradle of the medieval Serbian empire.

During the Balkan Wars (1912-13), Kosovo was conquered and incorporated into Serbia, albeit without losing its frontier characteristics. During the long-awaited 'liberation' of Kosovo by the Serbian army, it was the Albanians' turn to become the primary victims, which contributed much to a further deterioration of relations. The Albanians remained openly antagonistic towards Serbia (and later the kingdom of Yugoslavia), which transformed Kosovo into a colony administered from above. Serbia regarded political and cultural hegemony in Kosovo as an inalienable and sacrosanct Serbian right, and treated the Albanians as a hostile element that needed to be pacified and neutralised, or even expelled. In short, these years between 1878 and 1914 were crucial for Kosovo's recent history, turning the division between Christians and Muslims into an ethnic divide between Serbs and Albanians (Malcolm 1998:xxix).

What predominates now in the minds of most Serbs and Albanians, as well as of most outside observers, is the image of a deeply rooted and unbridgeable rift between Serbs and Albanians, more 'ancient' and clear-cut than the divisions in Bosnia. This ethnic frontier between Slavs and (non-Slav) Albanians is reinforced by the old religious gap that divides them which makes this image indeed compelling. As Noel Malcolm, author of two recent histories of both Bosnia and Kosovo, has noted: 'At first sight this looks much more like a genuine "ethnic" conflict. The basic division is, in the first place, an ethnic one in the full sense. [...] Serbs and Albanians are linguistically quite separate. Together with the differentiation in language goes a range of other cultural differences, many of them linked to religion. [...] With both language and religion setting people apart, all the conditions seem to be present for a primary conflict of peoples' (1998:xxvii). Yet the author rightly points out (and illustrates throughout his work) that the characterisation of Kosovo's history in terms of 'ancient ethnic hatreds' is grossly misleading; many individual Serbs and Albanians nevertheless now fully endorse this type of thinking.

Mainstream Serbian historiography claims that since the Battle of Kosovo (1389), Serbs have suffered centuries of oppression by a Muslim empire and have fought a never-ending battle for the resurrection of their great medieval empire. The Kosovo myth still sets the tone in most Serbian historiography, in which Serb suffering and martyrdom, and conflict and incompatibility between Islam and Christianity is stressed (see Chapter 8). Most contemporary Serbian historiography, notably the books written by respected scholars like Djoko Slijepčević (1983), Dimitrije Bogdanović (1986), and Dušan Bataković (1992), provide an image of inherently conflictual relations, especially after Albanians adopted Islam. In a similar vein, most Albanians, among them some historians and intellectuals of great reputation, like Skënder Rizaj (1992), Ismail Kadare (1994), and Rexhep Qosja (1995), draw a similar picture of continuous Albanian anguish under Serbian hands. The Serbs are alleged to have an almost genetically predisposed and thus immutable racist and violent attitude towards Albanians. Kosovo is referred to as the 'ethnic territory' of the Albanians which has been occupied by the Serbs. The claim that Albanians constitute ('more than') ninety per cent of Kosovo's population, which is being replicated in most Western publications, serves to underline this assumption, although this percentage is probably too high.[10]

If we adopt a long-term perspective, we do not need to go far back into history to see that Kosovo was essentially a pluralistic society, where various ethnic groups coexisted, many languages were spoken and all major religions of the Balkans were represented. Although the Albanians have formed an absolute majority probably from the first half of the nineteenth century onwards (Malcolm 1998:196), Serbs and Montenegrins, as well as other groups like Gypsies and Turks, have formed substantial minorities, even during most of this century.[11] Therefore, instead of perceiving Kosovo as Albanian 'ethnic' territory, I rather prefer to see it historically

[10] This percentage does not take into account the fact that during some of the post-war censuses minorities like Gypsies, Muslim Slavs and Turks have tended to declare themselves as Albanians for reasons which I will explain later (see Chapter 6). I would like to stress that in my view a smaller and more accurate percentage of Albanians (let us say 85%) basically does not undermine the legitimacy of the Albanian demands in Kosovo. It just signals that the area is demographically not exclusively 'Albanian': it is inhabited by other groups as well which deserve to be taken into account.

[11] According to the census of 1961, 67% of Kosovo's population was Albanian, while 27.5% was Serb and Montenegrin, and 5.4% was registered as Turk, Muslim, Gypsy, etc. In 1981 the percentages were respectively 77.4%, 14.9% and 7.7% (Krstić 1994: 267-8).

as an ethnic shatter zone, largely the product of incorporation into the Ottoman state, which embraced and preserved a great variety of ethnic and religious groups (Cole 1981:116-17). Although at first sight Kosovo is perhaps less of an ethno-religious patchwork than pre-war Bosnia, its ethnic, linguistic and religious diversity has been more profound. In Bosnia, Serbs, Croats and Muslims speak basically the same language (religion being the main marker of distinction), whereas in Kosovo Albanians and Serbs – or for that matter Turks and Gypsies – all speak different languages. In addition among Albanians there is a threefold religious divide into Muslims, Catholics, and a substantial community of Shi'a oriented dervish orders, whereas Serbs are Orthodox.

As Roux has noted, before the war started, only half (or even less) of the territory of former Yugoslavia was ethnically homogeneous. Except for Serbia (without the 'autonomous' provinces Kosovo and Vojvodina) and Slovenia, which were the two largest chunks of ethnically homogeneous territory, most other parts of former Yugoslavia had a composite population. Bosnia and Vojvodina were probably the most heterogeneous, followed by Macedonia, Kosovo and Croatia. This did not mean that these areas could be characterised as 'melting pots'. Roux points out that the element of mixture often only applied to the region as a whole: the habitat and 'lived spaces' (*espaces vécus*) of different ethnic groups were always quite separate and segregated, especially at the village level. In most general terms, one can see a pattern of juxtaposition in rural areas – ethnically 'pure' villages forming an absolute majority – whereas mixture is more characteristic of urban areas. But even in towns, ethnic groups are concentrated in particular quarters (*mahale*). For instance, in Kosovo, Serbs and especially Montenegrins usually live in the town centres, whereas the new suburbs are dominated by Albanians mainly as a result of recent rural-urban migration. Therefore, the process of the gradual Albanianisation of Kosovo since the 1960s applies more to the rural and suburban areas than to the town centres (Roux 1992:129-37).

Although I do acknowledge that Kosovo is a segregated society riven with conflict, I would nevertheless like to challenge the assumptions that only conflict counts, that conflicts have always evolved around ethnic categories, and that ethno-religious categories are bounded and clear. Instead, in a frontier area like Kosovo it is not conflict *or* coexistence that is the hallmark of society; both elements have a history combining in a variety of ways over time. If we accept that in periods of relative peace ethnic relations may carry an element of strife (if only to mark difference), we also should look for signs of co-operation and cross-cutting loyalties in times of conflict. Ethno-religious relations, whether characterised as peaceful or conflictual, are usually much more multifaceted and subtle than these dichotomous labels suggest. This is especially true for frontier societies, which are usually characterised as more conflictual: they are governed by different sets of rules as far as processes of identification are concerned those of most ethnic core societies.

To start with the first, although Kosovo is a society marked by perennial conflict, we should not focus exclusively on conflict and separateness, because we might be ignoring signs of coexistence and symbiosis. As the predominant image of the Balkans is now one of conflict, this book will demonstrate how boundaries between ethnic and religious groups have often faded in more quiet periods, and that many cultural traits were and still are frequently shared across group boundaries. Despite conflict, there has been intimate and varied contact. The classic study of Serb-Albanian 'osmosis' is probably Milan Šufflay's book *Srbi i Arbanasi* (1925), which offers an interesting historical perspective on Serb-Albanian relations. Malcolm also stresses that for instance in Montenegro and northern Albania, relations between Albanians and Serbs were far from only conflictual: 'The Montenegrin *Brdjani* (Highlanders) and the Albanian *Malësori* share many characteristics – customs, traditional laws and forms of social organisation. In past centuries, there were strong links between Albanian and Montenegrin clans, some were longstanding allies in war, others had traditions of each taking brides from the other clan, and some had legends of common ancestry. Long-term patterns of what might be called ethnic osmosis took place: some of the Montenegrin clans may originally have been off-shoots from Albanian families, and some of the Albanian ones may have Slav ancestry too' (Malcolm 1998:10). Although divisions in Kosovo seem to be more clear-cut, we should be cautious about analysing social life only in terms of conflict.

Other studies of frontier societies have emphasised these aspects of symbiosis and contact. In his stimulating study of Melilla (the

Spanish enclave in Morocco), Henk Driessen stresses that periods of confrontation alternate with ones of intense contact and co-operation across boundaries. Interestingly Driessen also points out the wide gap that exists between the central state ideology and frontier practice. State and religious centres always emphasise the fixity and impenetrability of the barrier which is largely cast in religious terms, and they do much to maintain this ideological divide. But in daily life the frontier is a zone of interaction and interchange rather than division (Driessen 1992:190). Another example is Wendy Bracewell's study of the sixteenth-century Hapsburg-Ottoman frontier, which demonstrates the complexity of frontier societies where loyalties cross religious and imperial boundaries. Bracewell also points out the discrepancies between frontier practice, where people of both sides often co-operate and communicate, and the attempts of the state to create clear-cut divisions: 'In spite of the bloody combats and confrontations between Christian and Muslim, conflict was not the only element that shaped border life. More peaceful activities brought the two worlds together. [...] Where there was daily contact, acquaintance and friendship could follow, despite the watchful eyes of church and civil authorities' (Bracewell 1992:33).[12]

Secondly, it is important to stress that, in Kosovo, ethnic divisions have not always been the most salient ones. Much of the conflict and tension that permeates Kosovo society has evolved along lines of division other than the ethnic ones. In the eighteenth and nineteenth centuries, the main lines of division were between Albanian landlords and the rest of the population, and all groups suffered greatly from the conditions of existential insecurity and violence, regardless of their ethnic or religious background (Malcolm 1998:182-3). In fact other divisions have been much more salient in daily life and local contexts than the ethnic one, such as clan or tribal loyalties, religion, the urban-*versus*-rural dichotomy, language (which is not always coterminous with ethnic divisions) or gender. One may also include political or ideological divisions, for instance between communists and 'counter-revolutionaries', which poisoned much of political life in Kosovo in the 1980s. It is worth noting that in this period most Albanian

---

[12] For a recent (and excellent) theoretical survey of the anthropological study of borders, borderlands and frontiers see: Wilson and Donnan (1998).

'irredentists' were sentenced and jailed by fellow Albanians, and not by Serbs.

Thirdly, and perhaps most importantly, group identities are not set in stone. This work will challenge the idea that explosions of violence in crisis zones like Kosovo or Bosnia evolve around clear-cut, fixed, and bounded ethnic groups, and that the recent wars were caused by centuries-old antagonisms dormant under socialism. When we take a closer look at what happens on the ground over a prolonged period of time we see that identity shows many ambiguities in areas like Kosovo, Macedonia, and Bosnia. Contact between different groups (such as between Serbs and Albanians) has been marked by cases of reciprocal assimilation and (incomplete) conversion. If we look at the effects of Is-lamicisation, which has been the major direction of religious con-version in the region, we often see that the Christian element is retained and Christian features (like baptism, the veneration of saints, and the use of icons) coexist with Muslim ones.[13] And in the case of ethnic assimilation, previously used languages are per-petuated, sometimes for a considerable period.[14]

My research shows that ethnic and religious identities are not as fixed as our experience in Western Europe suggests. One can have more than one 'exclusive' identity, and one can change identity more easily and more drastically. In addition, frequent migrations throughout the region have greatly contributed to a blurring of ethnic and confessional boundaries. It shows that in these circumstances of flux and existential insecurity, identities are often unstable and weakly defined, and that shifts or transfers in identity occur frequently. In ethnic 'core' zones, where the centres of power are located (such as central Serbia), identities have been more firmly established. In these areas the state has had a more enduring presence, and therefore the scope for manipulation is less.

There are historical antecedents to this situation of unstable and shifting identifications: for many centuries the Balkans have

[13] See for instance Vryonis (1972). Until recently one could still find bi-con-fessional extended Albanian families in Kosovo, some members being Catholic and others Muslim (Barjaktarović 1950).

[14] The Slavophone Albanians in Rahovec (Orahovac in Serbian) are a good example of this phenomenon (see Chapter 3).

formed the frontier between East and West, initially divided between the Western Roman Empire and Byzantium (395), which was later reinforced by the schism between Eastern Orthodoxy and Roman Catholicism (1054). For most of the Middle Ages, the Roman Catholic and Eastern Orthodox churches tried to gain influence at the expense of the other, and in areas like Albania, Kosovo, Bosnia and even Montenegro and Serbia, ecclesiastics and aristocrats exploited this situation by shifting their allegiances from Constantinople to Rome and vice versa (along with their subjects).[15] This situation of religious rivalry and shifting loyalties was exacerbated with the arrival of a third major religion, Islam. Islamicisation especially affected those borderlands between Eastern Orthodoxy and the Roman Catholic church.[16] After that, the Balkans remained a battlefield for competing churches which tried to enhance their influence or win back souls that were once lost to a rival (see Chapter 4).

Conversion (and reconversion) has been quite a normal process, especially in areas where church infrastructure was weakly developed. In areas where a stable ecclesiastical organisation was absent (as in Bosnia and Albania), populations easily switched from one rite to the other. In such conversion processes, usually both pull and push factors played a role; it was rarely imposed by violent means only, although this also happened. Yet there were considerable variations in the relative importance of those two elements. If we confine ourselves again to the process of Islamicisation, in Bosnia a substantial part of the population converted to Islam soon after the local aristocracy did; they did so more or less on a voluntarily basis and were attracted by the splendour of a growing and magnificent empire. In Albania and Kosovo, however, Islamicisation remained largely confined to the towns, while leaving the countryside untouched for a long time. The rural populations (especially in mountainous areas) converted later, in the seventeenth century, when the wars between the Ottoman empire and the Christian powers became more frequent, and Ottoman persecution of Christians (especially Roman

[15] For Albania, see for instance Skendi (1956).

[16] There is a huge literature on the process of Islamicisation in the Balkans. For recent and concise overviews see Lopasic (1994) and other contributions to the special Balkan issue of the *Journal of Islamic Studies*, 5(2), 1994.

Catholics) led to waves of forced Islamicisation.[17] Nonetheless, or rather because of this, Islamicisation went further than in Bosnia, eventually encompassing seventy per cent of all Albanians. However, because in Albania and Kosovo Islam was imposed in a much more violent manner, most converts were only nominally Muslims. Here, syncretism and heterodoxy were much more widespread than in Bosnia, where an influential school of *ulema* (religious scholars) and a much denser religious infrastructure ensured a higher degree of orthodoxy. In Albania and Kosovo, converts only fully Islamicised after several generations. Women, traditionally confined to the private domain, continued to foster Catholic customs and beliefs, while the men (in keeping up an acceptable public face) tended to embrace the new faith more easily (Skendi 1956:315-16). In some remote and inaccessible mountain areas ambiguous religious identifications and practices have continued to exist until the present day.

People have often changed their ethnic identity or converted to another religion without completely abandoning and forgetting the legacy of previous identities. Because of these historical experiences of conversion and 'mimicry' (the outward adoption of an identity for the sake of survival), and the consciousness of mixed and composite origins, there is often a high awareness among Balkan inhabitants that most identities should not be taken for granted: they are often regarded as 'guises' or 'constructs' that may be accepted or rejected. The phenomenon of contesting the identities of others is widespread, and is even part of the political game. Kosovo is just one example of this phenomenon.[18] Albanians

---

[17] Since the Orthodox were less subject to Ottoman persecution, some Albanian Catholics converted to Orthodoxy as well, for instance in Montenegro (Bartl 1968:31).

[18] One can easily expand this list looking at other areas of the Balkans. In the course of the nineteenth and twentieth centuries a whole series of contesting claims have been made. Croats have been labelled 'Catholic Serbs' by Serbs, and Serbs 'Orthodox Croats' by Croats. Many Serbs and Croats regard the Bosnian Muslims as an 'artificial' creation, as a phantom nation *tout court*, claiming them to be either 'Islamicised' Serbs or Croats. Many Montenegrins consider themselves to be a separate nation, while most Serbs (and also some Montenegrins themselves) see them as fellow Serbs. Identity in Macedonia is probably most liable to contestation because its population is one of the most mixed and amorphous in the Balkans, and because state structures demanding and facilitating

claim that many Serbs are 'really' Albanians by origin, who during the Serbian Empire were converted to Orthodoxy and were Serbianised thereafter. Historical sources indeed suggest that Albanians adopted Serbian names, especially in villages that were part of the estates of a Serbian monastery. Being part of this social, economic, and religious environment probably encouraged a closer identification with Serbian Orthodoxy, and as Malcolm has pointed out, on the basis of this, 'Albanian historians have suggested that many of the bearers of those Serbian Orthodox names were actually Albanians, a hidden ethnic mass whose re-emergence in the early Ottoman period explains an otherwise puzzling "Albanianization" of the area' (Malcolm 1998:55-6). The Serbian answer to these claims is that many Albanians are 'really' Serbs, and there seems to be some historical truth to that as well: in Kosovo the process of Albanianisation, i.e. the continuous migration of Albanians from the tribal areas of northern Albania into Kosovo, coincided with the process of Islamicisation. The great majority of Albanians converted to Islam in the course of this process. Also many Serbs converted, subsequently adopting Albanian, the dominant language of their environment. These processes of Islamicisation and Albanianisation were still in full swing in the nineteenth century.[19]

Supported by this evidence, Serb historians, geographers and ethnographers developed the *Arnautaši* thesis, claiming that many Albanians are 'really' Serbs by origin, a point of view which enjoyed great support among Serbian scholars at the end of the nineteenth century and thereafter. Jovan Tomitch (1913) was a

---

homogeneous identities have only recently been in place. Serbs claim that the Macedonians are southern Serbs, Bulgarians that they are western Bulgarians, and Greeks that they are northern Greeks (Mojzes 1995:15). See also Poulton (1995).

[19] However, some compact and isolated Slav settlements adopted Islam without losing their mother tongue, like the Muslims from Sredačka Župa and Gora (both near Prizren). It is said that the people from Gora converted to Islam in the second half of the eighteenth century, when the (Orthodox) Ecumenical Patriarchate in Constantinople started to appoint Greek-speaking priests to Serbian villages after the Serbian patriarchate of Peć was abolished in 1766 (Malcolm 1998:195). Similar processes took place in (western) Macedonia where part of the Slav population converted to Islam and was later assimilated into the Albanian majority. Others retained their Slav identity and became known as *Torbeši* (western Macedonia) and *Pomaks* (eastern Macedonia and Bulgaria).

main proponent of this thesis: he argued that the so-called Great Exodus of Serbs from Kosovo in 1690 had actually not been so massive as most Serbian historians believe; instead the destruction of the Serbian ecclesiastical structure in the second half of the eighteenth century had resulted in a process of Islamicisation and Albanianisation of Serbs.[20] Although the assumptions were plausible in themselves, they were abused politically, as Roux notes, since they were made subordinate to a nationalist agenda. The aim was to undermine Albanian ethnic identification, i.e. to 'de-Albanianise' as many people as possible and to make 'Serbs' of them, which of course was intimately linked with Serbian territorial claims on Kosovo. At the end of the Ottoman reign, areas like Kosovo, Albania, Macedonia and Bosnia were a *territoire à prendre* for the several neighbouring states (Serbia, Bulgaria, Greece).

One element that accompanied these projects to claim and re-claim the identity of certain populations was the notion that some forms of ethnic engineering were practicable. Many Balkan nation-state builders believed that it was possible to make or break the identities of others, to shift the ethnic orientation of subjects or to assimilate populations by force or otherwise. Since then, contending nations and religions in the Balkans regard assimilation and conversion (next to expulsion and extermination) as a legitimate means to homogenise society, to neutralise enemies and pacify certain newly acquired territories.[21] Many have speculated about bringing about these kinds of shifts in identification through state power. After World War I Serbian policy-makers hoped that Albanians could be changed into Muslim Slavs or 'Serbs', in order to replace the growing ethnic divide between Serbs and Albanians by a (less problematic) confessional one (see Roux 1992:181). Indeed, after 1918 the Serb-dominated Yugoslav government allowed Albanians to receive education in Serbian from Muslim Slav teachers (Roux 1992:207). This programme

---

[20] Another ardent proponent of the *Arnautaši* thesis was Jovan Hadži-Vasilijević who gathered ethnographic evidence to support it (1924, 1939). See also Malcolm (1998:196-9).

[21] Probably one of the most ambitious (and notorious) projects of this kind in this century was the expulsion, extermination and forceful conversion of Orthodox Serbs to Catholicism by the Ustaše in the Independent State of Croatia during World War II.

was part of a policy to reverse Albanianisation of the province through assimilation and colonisation. More radical projects of ethnic engineering aimed at the massive expulsion or forced religious conversion of Albanians.[22] More recently, in the 1970s, the Belgrade authorities promoted Turkish identity in order to counterbalance the political ascendance of the Albanians in Kosovo and Macedonia (Bartlett 1980).

The concept of identity

In order to understand these bewildering ethnographic data on a more general and theoretical level and to incorporate these elements of symbiosis and division and of ambiguous and contested identities into one theoretical framework, I will use the concepts of identity, state and politics, religion and religious regimes, and core and periphery.

In my view, identity (as a sociological concept) represents primarily a link between the individual and a specific category or group of people. It is based on perceived sameness which at the same time implies difference from others: identity is therefore about classification and the process of associating or equating oneself (or others) with someone or something else (Jenkins 1996:3-4). If a category (which is the result of an act of classification) becomes a principle of group formation, then identity represents primarily a social bond between the individual and a collectivity or community, which may vary according to time and place, and may be accepted or contested by both outsiders and insiders.[23] On

---

[22] In 1937, the Serbian academic Vasa Čubrilović presented plans to expel the Albanians from Kosovo, in order to homogenise Yugoslavia ethnically. In 1913 Montenegro tried to bring about mass conversions of Muslims to Orthodox Christianity in regions it had just acquired. In the spring of 1914 this led to an exodus of Muslims to Albania and Serbia (see Roux 1992:188 for further references).

[23] Identity is often fluid and changeable – or 'conjunctural' in James Clifford's words (1988:10-11) – and because of this the use the more dynamic terms 'identification' or 'identification processes' may be equally appropriate. These terms emphasise the processual character of these allegiances. Even though some identities, like gender, kinship, and ethnic identity (so-called primary identities in Jenkins's terminology), are usually more fixed and stable than others, they still need to be constantly re-enacted and reinforced.

the level of the individual person, identity is always multi-layered: every person maintains a variety of identities, i.e. belongs to several categories and groups of people at the same time.

In my view, the concept of identity is more open and flexible than the more narrow concept of ethnicity which tends to over-emphasise only one particular type of bond, i.e. the ethnic one, as the paramount marker of group identity. As it is shared language that is usually implicated in ethnic identities as the *sine qua non* of their existence – mutual intelligibility seen as a fundamental prerequisite for any ethnic group (Jenkins 1997:10)[24] – it pushes other relevant and sometimes even more important criteria of collective identification (such as those based on religion, tribal distinctions, class, the rural-*versus*-urban opposition, etc.) to the background. I do not claim here that ethnic or national identity are unimportant. As Jenkins notes, 'ethnicity is a collective identity which may have a massive presence in the experience of individuals' (Jenkins 1996:65), and that is certainly true for most of the Balkans nowadays. I would only like to argue that local, regional, and religious identities, to name only a few types of identity that are based on non-ethnic criteria, have remained very important, in spite of the fact that now more inclusive (ethnic and national) identities are being superimposed. The stress on ethnicity tends to make us blind to other processes of identification and social affiliation. Thus, my preference for the concept of identity is a *programmatic* one. Seen from the heuristic and analytic point of view, ethnic or national identities should not be treated as more 'basic' or more 'authentic' than others; they are only one among several other possible ways of articulating us-them sentiments (cf. Eriksen 1993:156-158; Banks 1996:142-9; Cohen 1985).

---

[24] In western Europe, many (also scholarly) approaches to ethnicity and national-ism are often based on the assumption that language is the central unifying element of ethnic and national groups, without which they are somehow not 'complete' (this has for instance created problems for the Bosnian Muslims wishing to be acknowledged as a nation in its own right). It is especially the German philosopher Johann Herder's understanding of nations which has put language at the centre of ethnic and national identities. His argument is that the distinctiveness and uniqueness of each nation lies in its language and oral traditions. As Hann writes, Herder's 'romantic equation of language, culture, people and state' has led to the idea that 'language provides the most natural basis for the existence of nations' (Hann 1997:121-2). See also Banks (1996:135).

Some observers have for instance pointed to the urban–rural dichotomy as an important factor in understanding the specific features of the war in Yugoslavia (see especially Bogdanović 1994).[25] In my opinion, it is indeed necessary to incorporate these elements in our analysis to explain what has happened in the former Yugoslavia. We need to go beyond the 'ethnic' discourse, the dominant discourse produced by nationalists in most parts of the former Yugoslavia, which has been too easily adopted by journalists and scholars from abroad. For a better understanding of the violence one needs to incorporate elements of conflict that derive from other (more 'traditional') contexts: religion, family and kinship, tribalism, gender, etc. Mart Bax has demonstrated this very well in his work on Bosnia, where he has focused on the local dimensions of the war (Bax 1995).

An important reason to use the concept of identity instead of ethnicity is that different principles of affiliation and identification (ethnicity, gender, religion, class etc.) usually correlate and overlap. An example is ethnicity and gender: women and men, or the culturally specific categories of 'female' and 'male', are used to express the distinctiveness of ethnic groups and nations; ethnic differences are often perceived in gendered terms (Yuval-Davis 1997). At another level, women (especially mothers and virgins) may symbolise the nation, and in times of war they may be perceived as part of the (symbolic) territory that needs to be

---

[25] The town of Prizren (where I did research in 1986) provides a good example of the importance of the urban–rural dichotomy. Since Ottoman times, Prizren is the symbol of a respected urban tradition in Kosovo, although nowadays Prishtina, a conglomerate of futurist buildings and socialist housing estates, is the capital of the province. The inhabitants of Prizren, in particular the families who have lived there for many generations, take pride in their urban identity which cuts across ethnic lines. The original townsmen of Prizren cultivate their polyglot urbanity to distinguish themselves from newly arrived peasants, mostly Albanians, who have massively settled here since the 1960s. This means that they easily switch languages in the course of one conversation and moreover, have an outspoken preference for Turkish, the *lingua franca* of self-respecting townsmen. Most urban Albanian families even speak Turkish at home, learning Albanian as a second language at school. Among the Serbs of Prizren, the younger generation has lost the capacity to speak Turkish, while elderly people still know it. For all of them, Turkish was and still is an adequate way of marking themselves off from peasant newcomers, who in their view have turned Prizren – once renowned because of its cleanliness – into a garbage dump.

defended or conquered.[26] Not least, the ability of men to check and protect their women becomes a measure of strength of the ethnic group or nation in question. This is very much reminiscent of the traditional gender patterns in 'Dinaric' society as described by Tomasic (1948). A similar type of argument can be developed for ethnic and religious identification, which in the Balkans are very often intertwined.

Even though identities converge, they do not always overlap entirely. Gender relations may vary substantially within the boundaries of an ethnic group (for instance along the urban-rural axis), or they may be identical across group boundaries. Not all religious differences are at the same time ethnic (although in Kosovo they often tend to become perceived as such), nor are all ethnic boundaries underpinned by religious ones. Therefore, gender and religion should be regarded as separate principles of identification, which have a momentum of their own. Gender relations may be of such a nature that they can potentially undermine the cohesion of the group (Denich 1974), just as religious divisions may threaten the unity of a nation as has been the case for instance with the Albanians. Although Albanian nationalist ideology claims that religion was never important to the Albanians – their only true religion being 'Albanianism' – religion has caused deep divisions within Albanian society (see chapter 7). Among Albanians in Kosovo a certain degree of animosity based on religious difference certainly exists, as between Sunni Muslims and Catholics, or between Sunni Muslims and Shi'ite oriented dervish orders.

In this context it is worth quoting Eriksen, who ends his overview of the study of ethnicity and nationalism (1993) with a critical note on the problems and limitations of the ethnicity concept: '...the choice of an analytical perspective or "research hypothesis" is not an innocent act. If one goes out to look for ethnicity, one will "find" it and thereby contribute to constructing it. For this reason, a concern with non-ethnic dimensions of polyethnic societies can be a healthy corrective and supplement to analyses of ethnicity' (1993:161). He further adds: '... we ought to be critical enough to abandon the concept of ethnicity the moment it becomes a straitjacket rather than a tool for generating

---

[26] For an interpretation of nationalist rape and its cultural 'meanings', see: Sofos (1995) and Bracewell (2000).

new understanding' (1993:162). Eriksen sympathises with the French anthropological approach which – instead of treating ethnic phenomena as a separate field of study – generally tends to deal with political ethnicity and ethnic identity under the more general headings of the study of politics, identity and ideology (Eriksen 1993:161; cf. Lévi-Strauss 1977).

In sum the concept of ethnicity does not always help to understand the nuances and complexities of group conflict. Where ethnicity appears to be the dominant emic (native) discourse, we should not simply take that discourse for granted. In order to improve our understanding, a more general and inclusive view is needed which allows us to be alert to lines of division other than the 'ethnic' ones. Apart from ethnic distinctions – which seem to set the tone in most Western analyses of Balkan society – it is crucial to give more attention to other principles of identification and affiliation which govern much of ordinary social life, such as kinship, gender, the urban-rural dichotomy and religion. All these criteria are important in establishing bonds of loyalty and assigning social roles.

States and the politics of identity

A corollary to identity is the decisive role played by the state. As this book tries to demonstrate, the formation and transformation of ethnic and religious identities is determined by wider political developments. Many social scientists and historians have already pointed out the importance of the state for the development and sustenance of ethnicity and nationalism. Gellner has shown how modern nation-states (through the standardisation of language, the introduction of a uniform education system, the creation of national labour markets, etc.) have gradually forged nations out of diverse human material (Gellner 1983). Another classic is Eugen Weber's historical work on the formation of French national identity (1976).[27] However, most studies within the field of ethnicity and nationalism have been based on empirical examples of more or less fixed and stable groups, with the primary focus on

---

[27] As far as the Balkans is concerned, the best and most recent study is probably Karakasidou's book on the making of a Greek national identity in Greek Macedonia (1997).

mechanisms of boundary maintenance (Barth 1969). The only exception to this rule is perhaps Benedict Anderson (1991) who demonstrates the changeability and arbitrariness of identity categories in the Southeast-Asian colonial context. He shows how administrative penetration of the colonial state has made categories created or invented by the state increasingly real. The smooth functioning of modern bureaucratic states requires certain 'simplifications' by which they can master their physical space and populations. Above all, modern states need to develop un-ambiguous delineations of ethnic identity, with clear criteria for inclusion and exclusion. These simplifications are inadequate rep-resentations of reality, but because they are backed by state power, they transform the real world – as James Scott (1995) has put it – in ways that make it more closely resemble the simplified and legible grid of their observations.

In my view, it is Katherine Verdery (1994) who has worked out this idea most interestingly by pointing out the marked fixity of ethnic identities in Western Europe: 'The kind of self-consistent person who "has" an "identity" is a product of a specific historical process: the process of modern nation-state formation' (1994:37). It is one of the most essential requirements of the state that a person has only one identity: 'one cannot keep track of people who are one thing at one point, another thing at another' (ibid). Modern state-making presses toward single identities out of a situation of multiple and often diffuse identities. Verdery uses the example of the disintegration of Yugoslavia to illustrate her point: 'Although the 19th and 20th century national movements had produced single identities for people defined as "Croats", "Serbs", "Macedonians", etcetera, in Yugoslavia overall, this process, while advancing, had not gone so far as to preclude holding multiple identities. Within the states of Yugoslav succession, however, this is no longer true. Persons of mixed origin – those who once declared themselves "Yugoslavs" – are being forced to elect a single identity. "Ethnic cleansing" does not mean only that people of the "other" group are being exterminated: it also means the extermination of alternative identity choices' (Verdery 1994:38).

Although anthropological studies generally stress that ethnic identities are not necessarily fixed and permanent but malleable, it seems that the scope for the manipulation of ethnic identities is much narrower in Western Europe than in other parts of the

world. Verdery says : 'Such identities will be less flexible wherever
the process of modern nation-state formation has the greatest
longevity and has proceeded the furthest; wherever long-standing
nationalist movements have effectively inculcated the sentiment
of a single kind of belonging; and wherever colonial states had
more extensive and deeper rather than shallower roots' (Verdery
1994:37). By implication this means that in peripheral societies,
identities are more fluid and ambivalent; they can be made and
unmade more easily than in modern and industrial societies.

That the conscious development of stable, fixed and unam-
bivalent identities is much weaker in peripheral settings has been
confirmed by recent ethnography. In his monograph on the Spanish
enclave society of Melilla, Henk Driessen shows how most categorical distinctions (of ethnicity, religion, gender etc.) become blurred
in the margins of society (1992:177-88). Also Wilson and Donnan
note that because of the liminal and contested nature of borders,
identities there are often shifting and multiple; this is not only
true of national identities, but also of other identities such as
those based on ethnicity, class, gender, and sexuality (1998:13).
Of similar theoretical relevance is Connell's observation that working class men who live at the economic margin are often much
more pragmatic and flexible in gender relations, in spite of their
symbolic display of an aggressive masculinity (1996:168-72). In
Kosovo, due to its longstanding position at the peripheries of
subsequent states (in the Ottoman empire as well as afterwards),
group boundaries tend to be more fluid and less institutionalised,
and identities are more ambiguous and situational. The establishment of clear labels is a more recent phenomenon, although
this process is far from finished in present-day Kosovo.

That this is the case is exemplified by the existence of ethnic
and religious anomalies, small ethnic and religious minorities that
do not fit into the neat system of the dominant Serbian-Albanian
opposition, for example the Croats, Turks, Gypsies, Circassians
and Slavic Muslims (*Goranci*), as well as the Catholic Albanians,
the Turkophone Albanians (particularly in Prizren) and the Slavophone Albanians (in Rahovec). Their identity can be considered
as 'neither-nor' or 'both-and'. They are 'betwixt and between'
and tend to mess up any neat system of contrast in ethnic classification (Eriksen 1993:156). They remind us of the fact that
group boundaries are not unproblematic, and that there is always

friction between the ideal ethnic and religious models or ideologies, produced by states and religious regimes, and the social reality to which they refer.[28] It is primarily the state, which in its efforts to categorise and administer its populations makes these cases into anomalies. As they threaten existing demarcations states (as well as religious regimes) usually aim at reducing their ambiguity and ambivalence, either by absorbing them into the main groups, or by expelling or eliminating them. 'Nationalist and other ethnic ideologies hold that social and cultural boundaries should be un-ambiguous, clear-cut and "digital" or binary. They should also be congruous with spatial, political boundaries. This [...] is an ideal which is very difficult to uphold in practice. Some violent nation-alisms may try to eradicate the anomalies. [...] In most cases, however, complex realities are coped with more gracefully' (Eriksen 1993:114). As far as Kosovo is concerned, the exodus of Kosovo Croats and other minorities is an example of what these processes can lead to (see Chapter 2).[29]

It is often these anomalous groups which, pressurised by political developments, change their identity and shift their loyalties (see Chapters 4 and 6). However, in spite of the fact that they are numerically and politically marginal, they should not be thought of as merely the passive recipients of wider developments but as active agents trying to maximise opportunities within the limits that are provided. They sometimes demonstrate a high degree of inventiveness and creativity in this respect. In general their space to manoeuvre depends on the dominant classificatory system, which they can do little to change, but nevertheless they try to exploit

[28] These anomalies, which tend to defy the fundamental categorical distinctions, do not only exist in the sphere of ethnic and religious identity, but also in the field of gender. Although Kosovo is a patriarchal society where gender segregation is very profound, examples can be found of women who defy or subvert the 'natural' gender order by becoming social men, adopting the male social identity with the (tacit) approval of the family and the wider community (Grémaux 1994).

[29] A current example of the elimination of such an 'anomaly' is that of the Circassians. According to a BBC news report (2 August 1998), the Circassians (or Adygs) are leaving Kosovo, fleeing to their historic homeland in the Caucasus. The report states that Albanians consider the (Muslim) Circassians to be too supportive of the Serbs; the Kosovo Liberation Army is thought to have threatened them.

their ambiguous position to their own advantage. Only in some cases do groups seem to vanish completely, but even then they may reappear. The Vlachs are a good example: through processes of assimilation they virtually disappeared in most of the Balkans but have now reappeared in Albania (Schwandner-Sievers 1999).[30']

In the twentieth century, one can find many examples of identity shifts (*transferts identitaires* as Roux calls them) in Kosovo, usually as a result of political changes. These shifts often occur between groups who share some important characteristics such as language or religion, and use that common trait to bridge the gap. These processes may result from political pressure, much as was the case for instance with the (Slavophone) Albanians in Rahovec in the 1920s: during the census of 1921, most of them were registered as Serbs (Krasnići 1957:125). But apart from push factors there may be pull factors in play as well, such as the desire to conceal an inconvenient identity and adopt a better one. In the 1950s, for instance, tens of thousands of Albanians declared themselves as Turks to be able to emigrate to Turkey.[31] And in the 1970s, Muslim Slavs in Kosovo declared themselves as Albanians, then later turned back to their original Muslim (Slav) identity.[32]

Sometimes groups with a weakly defined or ambiguous identity become a bone of contention between more powerful groups. The latter claim such groups and dispute the 'authenticity' and 'credibility' of claims made by the groups themselves or others; the identity of such small groups is not in the first place established by the group itself, but determined by other more powerful actors as well. An interesting example are the *Goranci*, Muslim Slavs in

[30] During the Yugoslav census of 1948 there were 103,000 people registering as Vlachs, and during the census of 1981 only 32,000 (Roux 1992:46). Nevertheless, it is worth pointing out that the first figure was inflated because the term 'Vlach' in the 1948 census was also used to include the Rumanian-speaking population of north-eastern Serbia – people who were not considered to be Vlachs in the common use of the term (Noel Malcolm, personal communication).

[31] During the 1948 census there were 98,000 people declaring themselves as Turks, and five years (1953) later that number had almost tripled to 260,000 (Roux 1992:155).

[32] The main example is Sredačka or Sredska Župa, near Prizren: during the census of 1971, 80 per cent of the population of these nine mountain villages declared themselves as Albanians, while in 1981 92 per cent as (Slav) Muslims (Roux 1992:420-1; Vukanović 1986-I:208-11).

Gora (a mountainous region near Prizren at the Albanian border).
Before World War II (1939) the Yugoslav authorities subsumed
the *Goranci* under the category of 'non-Slavs', probably because
of their religion, which they share with the Albanians and Turks
(Roux 1992:202). After 1945, their names were Albanianised (e.g.
Hasanović to Hasani). In the mid-1980s the Macedonian press
claimed that they are actually Macedonians (i.e. *Torbeši*), even
though they learn Serbo-Croat at school (Roux 1992:421-2). In
spite of the fact that the inhabitants of Gora declared themselves
as ethnic Muslims (like those in Bosnia) during the censuses of
1971 and 1981, they seem to prefer the local term *Goranci* as the
most appropriate label.[33]

Religion and religious regimes

Apart from the state, I think it is important to look at the role
religious regimes have played in the creation and (trans)formation
of identities. Instead of regarding religion and politics as separate
domains of human societies, I would like to see them as intimately
connected, as expressed in Mart Bax's concept of religious regimes:
religious regimes can be regarded as formations of power and
dependence operating at times in tandem with, as well as in
opposition to states (Bax 1987, Wolf 1991).[34] This is especially
relevant in the Balkans, where the Ottoman state, as a force of
integration, was weakly developed, assigning an important role
to religious formations as the main vehicles of communal iden-

---

[33] A quite similar case is that of the *Pomaks* in Bulgaria, who have been zigzagging
between a 'Turkish' identity (because of religion) and a 'Bulgarian' identity
(because of language). To bring an end to confusion and uncertainty, quite a
large portion of 'Bulgarian' *Pomaks* in the Rhodopes mountains have converted
to Christianity, while other *Pomaks* have opted for Turkish identity (Todorova
1997b).

[34] Bax has defined a religious regime as 'a formalised and institutionalised con-
stellation of human interdependencies of variable strength, which is legitimised
by religious ideas and propagated by religious specialists'. As the concept is an
'open' one, it is applicable to all kinds of religious phenomena at various levels
of societal integration. Bax stresses that religious regimes are power constellations,
or political constellations, which implies the formulation of ideologies. 'It [...]
induces us to investigate religion in terms of cultural content, structural form,
and the interplay between these two aspects' (Bax 1987:2).

tification: due to the Ottoman *millet* system the politically relevant identities were defined in religious terms.[35] The *millet* system nurtured a strong sense of belonging which was determined by religious affiliation rather than ethnicity or language (Poulton and Taji-Farouki 1997:3). In fact, ethnic identification in the Balkans still very much relies on religious affiliation, which explains the frequent use of the term ethno-religious identities.

What is important to point out is that the *millet* system did not put all religious communities on an equal footing. It created a situation of what Roux calls 'hierarchised pluralism' (1992:60-1): although the non-Muslim religious communities were fully recognised they were also subordinated. Despite their legal subordination, the *millets* enjoyed considerable autonomy provided they accepted the inferior status of a tolerated religious community. Though one may object to the systemic inequality, the system nevertheless guaranteed the continued existence of certain groups, protecting them against assimilation or complete elimination (Roux 1992:61-2). In the second half of the nineteenth century, the Ottoman *millet* system made way for the European concept of the nation. New perceptions of (ethnic and national) identity emerged, and the Christian *millets* became the kernels of new national communities. This is especially true for the Christian-Orthodox nations (Greece, Serbia, Bulgaria), where the *millet* system produced a very strong link between national and religious identity (Arnakis 1963; Petrovich 1980). The Orthodox churches adopted a central role in various Balkan nationalist movements, while religious ideas and doctrines were important in articulating nationalist discourse. Only at a later stage, at the end of the nineteenth century, did a similar tendency develop among Balkan Muslims: a shift occurred from a communal identity based solely on Islam to one where

[35] The term *millet* refers particularly to the non-Muslim religious communities, designating the organisation of each group under its ecclesiastical leaders. The Ottoman *millet* system was perhaps not a system, but rather a form of indirect rule through the existing church organisations. Muslims were under direct rule of the sultan's bureaucracy and enjoyed a privileged position. The Orthodox and Armenian *millets* were by far the largest, whereas the Jewish *millet* was much smaller compared to the other two. The Roman Catholic *millet* was only established in 1839, at the start of the Tanzimat reforms. Whereas the Orthodox church was an accepted institution of the empire, the Catholic church was regarded with deep suspicion (Malcolm 1994:55).

Albanians in front of the mosque, Prishtina, summer 1986.

ethnicity became an important factor (Poulton and Taji-Farouki 1997:242). And, attempts were made to inject national identities with religious elements, as in Albania (see Chapter 7).

Though ethnic and national identities have become primary identities in most of the Balkans, the religious dimension has remained strong. The old *millet* concept of a community primarily based on religion and religious affiliation is still perpetuated. Religion continues to play an important if not a decisive role in processes of group identification and demarcation. As Todorova shows for the *Pomaks* in Bulgaria, the *millet* consciousness has been most resilient among certain groups of Balkan Muslims who have retained a fluid consciousness as far as their 'ethnic' or 'national' allegiances are concerned (1997b:75). However, more generally, religious identification has been made subordinate to ethnic identification, and religious rivalry has been transformed into ethnic and national antagonisms. In Kosovo itself, for instance, the current Serb-Albanian conflict has replaced the old confessional divide between Muslims and Christians.[36] Ethnic lines of division have

[36] Davison notes, however, that the religious divide was not all-embracing: the Muslim peasant was generally no better off than the ordinary non-Muslim.

become more important than religious ones, in spite of the fact
that the latter continue to play a crucial role in defining the
former. Also, within religious communities as such (the Orthodox
church, the official Islamic Community, and the Roman Catholic
church) ethnic differences have become more significant, and the
sense of a collective identity across ethnic lines of division has
eroded. Before the former Yugoslavia fell apart this had already
led to a compartmentalisation of the organisation of the different
churches along ethnic lines (Pavlowitch 1988:107). These developments have also been reflected at the level of communal ritual.[37]
The fact that Albanian Catholics, including many prominent clergy,
have actively participated in the movement for an independent
Kosovo has had the inevitable side-effect of alienating the Catholic
Croat minority in Kosovo.

Yet as a criterion of identity religion has remained very important, although most people are not great believers and do not
comply with religious precepts. Religious symbols and customs,
though often only cultivated in vague and residual forms, have
become part of the national heritage and as such help to delineate
ethnic boundaries. In Bosnia-Hercegovina in particular, religious
affiliation defines and delineates ethnic identities since all groups
speak the same language.[38] There, it is enough to know the

'He was as much in need of reformed government as the Christian, but he
had neither treaty, foreign power, nor patriarch to protect him, and his lot was
generally unknown in Europe. The line of basic demarcation ran, therefore,
not between Muslim and Christian, Turk and non-Turk, but between ruler
and ruled, oppressor and oppressed' (1973:63). Those on top were often Christians
who closely co-operated with the Ottomans: merchants, bankers, land owners
and higher ecclesiastics.

[37] In Kosovo these divisions resulted in the formation of a separate suffragan
diocese for Albanian Catholics (in Ferizaj, or Uroševac in Serbian) within the
Skopje bishopric, and the creation of the Community of Dervish Orders (in
Prizren) next to the Sarajevo-based Islamic Community (see Chapter 4). Whereas
Letnica was for a long time the only Catholic Marian pilgrimage centre in
Kosovo, a parallel 'Albanian' shrine was created in Zym, a Catholic Albanian
village near Prizren.

[38] It is this close equation between religion and ethnicity that in my view
justifies the separate status of Muslims in Bosnia as a nation. Although religion
is usually mentioned as a key marker of ethnic identity, it is often not considered
sufficient, at least not in everyday parlance. As stated earlier, language is usually
seen as the most decisive element in defining nationhood. Many outside observers

confessional background of an individual to determine his or her ethnic identity. Ethnic identities are primarily expressed in religious customs, symbols and emblems, for instance in the way a person crosses oneself (using two or three fingers), or, as in the case of Muslim men, in bodily marks like circumcision.

Several authors have, therefore, in one way or another stressed the importance of the religious element in explaining the conflicts in the former Yugoslavia, especially since churches and mosques were major targets of destruction during the war. Paul Mojzes was one of the first scholars to point out that the religious dimension should not be ignored: 'The concrete historical embodiments of religions in the Balkans did contribute religious traits to the present warfare, usually in combination with ethnic and other aspects' (1995:126). Although he disagrees with the view that religious differences are at the heart of the violent clashes in the Balkans, he emphasises that these conflicts have been imbued with religious meanings. The use of religious symbols and emblems does not say much about the level of actual religiosity of those individuals who use them; they function like 'clan totems' and create 'tribal' distinctions between otherwise very similar and related groups that have common cultural and historical roots (Pavlowitch 1988:94-111). In more general terms religious ceremonies and symbols induce feelings of belonging, and provide the means to sacralise the nation and demonise its enemies, to reduce complex social and historical realities to a clear and simple distinction between the forces of good and evil. Much of this can be observed in Bosnia-Hercegovina: religious labels were used to enforce ethnic loyalty both by political and religious leaders, while priests tolerated and stimulated the use of religion for ethnic or national purposes, presenting themselves as national leaders and hoping in this way to enlarge their following. Many of them were enthusiastically supporting a militant type of nationalism before the war (Mojzes 1995:125-51), and during it, quite a number of them joined the

---

have therefore had difficulties in acknowledging the Bosnian Muslims as a nation in its own right, viewing the status of a religiously defined group insufficient to justify the political claims that 'real' nations like the Serbs and the Croats can make (a view shared by Serbian and Croatian nationalists). It is significant in this context to note that Bosnian Muslims now prefer to use the term *Bošnjaci* (Bosniacs) for themselves and have started to cultivate 'Bosnian' as a separate language alongside Serbian and Croatian.

frontlines, offering moral support and even fighting at the side of soldiers.

All of this shows that, although nationalism is a modern phenomenon, it frequently draws on 'traditional' values and symbols, borrowed particularly from kinship and religion, to instil feelings of belonging to the wider and more abstract collective that is represented by the nation. Membership of the national community is often imagined in terms of (metaphoric) kinship, in which notions of shared blood and common descent are stressed. The nation is depicted as one large 'family', or symbolised as a mother (or a virgin) which expects men to protect her against those outside forces who want to violate and desecrate her. Similarly, the nation is often seen as a 'sacred community', for which individual members of the nation should be ready to die. Death, sacrifice, and martyrdom are usually important nationalist values, which make nationalist ideology more often than not quite violent in character (Eriksen 1993:107).[39] However, as I will show in the last two chapters there are clear variations in the role religious ideology plays in Balkan nationalism.

Violence, identity and the nation-state

Violence is a main force behind the formation or transformation of ethnic and national identities, either as a way of bolstering the nation (which is most common), or as a force which impels people to change their identity or dissimulate one (which is rarer but not uncommon). War has often been the engine of nation-building, and the Balkans seems to be no exception. In short, the war fought in former Yugoslavia and the processes of national homogenisation and 'ethnic cleansing' that have accompanied the war seem to have been primarily motivated by the necessity to forge single and unambiguous identities out of a population that is very much mixed and of diverse origins, and to erase the elements of mixture, 'pollution' and ambiguity that are threatening

---

[39] The importance of religion as a main ideological source and force in present-day nationalism has started to receive the attention it deserves. See for instance the work of Stanley Tambiah (1986) and Bruce Kapferer (1988) on Sri Lanka, and Peter van der Veer (1994) on India. For present-day European nationalism the subject still needs to be explored (but see Hastings 1997).

the newly established national states. It seems that the violence in former Yugoslavia is in the end not only the *result* of opposite and incompatible identities, it is perhaps even more the *means* to achieve them.

Violence is not only functional in creating new realities on the ground, such as gaining control over territories and expelling and 'exchanging' unwanted populations, processes which can be subsumed under the term 'ethnic unmixing' (Brubaker 1995:204). It also helps to deconstruct and disentangle the legacies of shared life and common existence in the minds of victims and perpetrators alike, and establish unambiguous identities and undivided loyalties. By constructing solid and impenetrable boundaries, violence creates purity out of impurity. It is therefore helpful, or sometimes even essential, to create new identities and loyalties: 'Violence may achieve results that cannot otherwise be achieved' (Sorabji 1995:81). Through its ability to engineer new situations, it also helps to produce self-fulfilling prophesies: it makes reality resemble the ideological constructs that underpin the violence.[40]

In Bosnia, as Sorabji notes, violence was central to altering local understandings of the category of the 'nation' (*narod*), and to narrowing down the complexity of pre-war collective identifications to just one: that of the ethnic nation. Violence changes the perceptions held both by victims and perpetrators about the very nature of group relations and boundaries. Especially brutal and personalised violence is a kind of 'counterpoint to culture' (Daniel 1996:194-212): it is capable of creating 'blank spaces', erasing old memories, and altering mental categories and beliefs (Sorabji 1995:91-2). In such situations victims as well as perpetrators lose the images of previous coexistence and are made to forget how things used to be. Apart from negating the familiar, violence helps to construct something new: it functions as a rite of passage to a new type of situation, new consciousness, statuses, loyalties and identities. As anthropological studies on primitive warfare

---

[40] This has been shown in the case of the Bosnian Muslims. Continuous Serbian propaganda, depicting Muslims as fundamentalists embarking upon a *jihad* against the Serbs, combined with the subsequent use of massive military power to counter the alleged Muslim threat, has made reality more and more resemble propaganda. Fundamentalist tendencies of some wider significance have indeed emerged in Bosnia after the start of the war.

have shown, violence and violent initiation rites may serve to create bonds among a group of men, and the more violent the rites the more effective they are. War itself is probably the most effective way to bring about these changes, by blood, sacrifice and suffering, which have an indelible effect on the collective memory. Therefore, in nationalist discourse violence and war are often considered positive forces, as a means to regenerate and purify the nation, and as a matter of societal 'hygiene': in the never-ending Darwinian battle between the nations of the world only the fittest will survive. Periodical violence and war contribute to the preservation of a healthy nation (Pick 1993).[41]

Apart from being an engine of identity construction, integration and homogenisation, violence is also a force which impels the odd individual and small minorities to change their identity or dissimulate one. In the Balkans, violence and existential insecurity have always been important forces behind these processes of identity transformation. Flexibility with regard to identity is in many ways crucial for survival, and under these circumstances, non-dominant identities tend to become increasingly insecure, changeable and fluid. Religious conversion, the adoption of another ethnic identity, or forms of ethnic or religious mimicry, are all strategies of adaptation or survival (see especially Chapters 4 and 6).[42] In cases of necessity, when sheer physical or social survival is at stake, forms of ethnic and religious dissimulation and identity transformation may be the only way to avoid death or deportation. In a situation in which the state monopoly of violence is weak or eroding, the identity of those who can organise an effective physical or military defence is most steadfast and dominant, and even tends to acquire a certain 'absorbing' capacity towards other less powerful groups.

[41] This is why during the Bosnian war nationalist politicians from Republika Srpska (for instance Biljana Plavšić and Sonja Karadžić), spoke of the healthy environment that existed for Serbs in wartime Bosnia. In their view, life in wartime Bosnia evolved from vital instincts, which has contributed to the Bosnian Serbs' vitality, whereas Serbia (and especially Belgrade) has degenerated (Čolović 1994:33-9).

[42] Bi- or multilingualism can also be seen as a strategy of this kind. In the case of Kosovo it is interesting to note that, at the end of the nineteenth century, bilingualism was much more widespread among Serbs (at that time the weaker group) than among Albanians (Roux 1992:205). This situation has been reversed in the twentieth century.

In this way Serb families in some parts of Kosovo (for instance in Orahovac) were incorporated into Albanian tribes or clans, where they enjoyed full protection (Krasnići 1957:123).[43] During the recent wars in the former Yugoslavia, there were similar examples: for instance Bosnian Muslims who converted to Serbian Orthodoxy in Republika Srpska, or Serbs in Croatia who changed their names to Catholic ones and even demanded withdrawal from the Serbian Orthodox church in order to become Catholics. Keeping a low profile and demonstrating loyalty to the state has been the only way to secure a more or less normal existence (*Vreme News Digest*, 12 June 1995).[44]

Dissimulation is a universal phenomenon. Erving Goffman (1959) has shown that in any social situation people try to engineer a convincing impression, which he compares with 'acting' and the putting up of masks. In situations of gross inequality and violence the tendency to dissimulate is even stronger or, as James Scott writes in his book *Weapons of the Weak*, 'the more menacing the power, the thicker the mask' (Scott 1990:3). Barnes has also noted that lying can be expected foremost in highly competitive contexts (like warfare and politics), and in relations of domination and subordination (Barnes 1994:20–35 and 83–6). If the necessity is there, people may tell lies or falsify their identity in order to protect themselves. Among minority religions or religious sects, dissimulation may even become an accepted strategy to prevent persecution.[45] In the Balkans, deceit, telling lies, and other forms

---

[43] The incorporation of non-kin into kin-groups is a more common phenomenon in marginal regions of Europe. The household tries to strengthen its position vis-à-vis other clans through recruitment of others and spiritual kinship ties. Cf. Claude Lévi-Strauss's concept of 'house societies' (Hann 1995:103).

[44] Processes of realignment with another ethnic group may also be the result of rivalries in the group of origin. As a result ethnic stigmatisation may take place, and individuals can be 'expelled' from their own ethnic group and 'pushed' into absorption by the enemy group. In his recent book on Medjugorje, Bax describes how the members of a Croat clan, involved in conflicts with two other Croat clans, align themselves with Serbs in the region as a result of which they are identified as 'little Serbs'. They were finally cleansed from the area by Croat forces (Bax 1995:101–18).

[45] See for instance the strategies of religious dissimulation among Protestants (during the Counter-Reformation), and among *Marranos* or crypto-Jews in Spain (during the Inquisition), and the concept of *taqiyah* among the Shi'ites (Zagorin

of dissimulation have also been widespread strategies of protection and evasion in the face of superior and hostile powers.[46] The archetypal South Slav hero is not Prince Lazar or Miloš Obilić (who, because they die for a higher cause, represent a purely moral position) but Kraljević Marko, the Turkish vassal who co-operates with the Ottomans but at the same time deceives and outwits them in his defence of the Christian population. As Tatyana Popović writes: 'In the oral tradition the Balkan people lived the imaginary heroic life of Prince Marko. As they changed him from a vassal in the Sultan's service into a fighter of the Turks, so they transmuted themselves from the reality of slavery to the spirit of active national resistance and the struggle for justice' (Popović 1988:140).

In modern political terms people often tend to identify or at least to align themselves nominally with those in power at a particular point in time. At the end of World War II and in the post-war period, many people in Yugoslavia became communists for many reasons, but usually not out of ideological commitment. Now many people have become nationalists: as Ivan Čolović has formulated it, as soon as the 'political traffic light' switches, people change their political allegiances to those who are currently in power, at least outwardly. In the era of television and other mass media this means that they carefully emulate what the 'most' authoritative voice tells them to think and believe (Čolović 1994:57–62). It seems that this situation will only be overcome when conditions of economic stability and existential and legal security can be established in all parts of the former Yugoslavia.

1990). The Bektashis (in Albania and elsewhere in the Ottoman empire) also employed *taqiyah* as a means of defence and survival (Birge 1937:78). More generally religious esoterism (the concept of secret religious knowledge), which is central to the religious doctrines of many heterodox Sufi orders and other religious sects, can also be seen as a form of dissimulation (Zagorin 1990:11). Another example in the Ottoman Balkans was that of the *Dönmeh,* a crypto-Jewish sect that was concentrated in Salonica (present-day Thessaloniki) (Ross 1982:83–98).

[46] See for instance du Boulay (1976), who deals with forms of lying and deceit in a Greek village.

2

THE EXODUS OF KOSOVO CROATS
A CHRONICLE OF ETHNIC UNMIXING

The wars in the former Yugoslavia, and the transformation of this multinational state into a number of new national states, has resulted in large-scale population movements across the newly established borders. Through ethnic cleansing and other, less violent but equally efficient forms of ethno-demographic 'engineering', the war has resulted in a seemingly irreversible process of ethnic 'unmixing' (Brubaker 1995), which has radically altered the ethno-demographic picture of the whole region. Yugoslavia, which, as Roux has noted, was perhaps the only country in East-Central Europe where a complex ethnic picture had not been 'simplified' during the great wars of the twentieth century (Roux 1992:30) is now sharing the dubious fate of many other European states. Many areas in Croatia, Bosnia-Hercegovina and Serbia which have had mixed populations for many generations and longstanding traditions of ethnic coexistence, have now been exclusively appropriated by one or the other group (Serbs being the main land grabbers, closely followed by the Croats, while Muslims have largely picked up the pieces that were left behind). Besides removing those who do not belong to the nation, the procedure of ethnic cleansing also has involved the appropriation and 'cultural' purification of the landscape, destroying churches and mosques, and eliminating the cultural heritage of the 'Other(s)'.

The most drastic and painful consequence of this process of ethnic unmixing and national homogenisation has been the enormous flow of refugees, who were either dumped in the West, or were 'sent home' to their respective 'native' countries. While Muslims in Bosnia have carried the heaviest burden of human suffering, we should not forget that numerous Serbs and Croats have also been expelled from their homes. This chapter describes my own experiences with this process while I was doing fieldwork

in Letnica, a Croat village in Kosovo on the present-day border
with Macedonia. Although there was no war going on in Kosovo,
within a few months (between July and December 1992) the
majority of the Croat population of Letnica and the surrounding
villages decided to flee, abandoning their houses and their possessions. They went as refugees to Croatia, where most of them
have been resettled in Western Slavonia. As I was in a position
to witness and observe these events first hand, I have attempted
to describe and document these events as factually and as faithfully
as possible, my first aim being to save them from oblivion. While
writing this, I have put most (if not all) of my anthropological
preoccupations in the background, although I would stress that
it still reflects primarily my own point of view. It is an account
which I hope does justice to the chaotic and distressing experiences
of the people most concerned.

An ethnographic sketch of Letnica

Letnica is a small and remote mountain village hidden away in
the Black Mountains, or Skopje's Montenegro,[1] at the very fringe
of present-day rump Yugoslavia. This mountainous area is still
also known under the old Turkish name *Karadag*. Letnica is situated
at the upper end of a long and narrow valley, surrounded by
green and flattened mountains which form a natural frontier with
Macedonia. The new Yugoslav-Macedonian frontier is within a
stone's throw, only half an hour's walk up hill or along the brook
which goes through the village. Not very long ago the border
did not have the importance which it has now gained. When I
first came here in the summer of 1991 it was an unguarded
administrative border between Kosovo and the Yugoslav Socialist
Republic of Macedonia. Letnica's residents were able to cross
the border freely, for example those pilgrims who used to walk
to Skopje every year in June, to visit the Catholic Church there.
However, in 1992 the border was 'upgraded': it became the new
state border between the republics of Yugoslavia and Macedonia.
    Letnica is – or I should say was – the geographical centre of a
number of villages and hamlets, which together form a Croat

[1] Mali i Zi i Shkupit in Albanian, or Skopska Crna Gora in Serbian and
Croatian.

and Catholic enclave in an area that is mainly inhabited by Muslim Albanians. Letnica was not the largest Croat settlement here, but thanks to its central geographical position (in the valley), its importance in the economic, administrative as well as religious sense surpassed that of nearby Šašare, which had twice as many inhabitants as Letnica. The church of Letnica had long been the only Catholic church in this area, and on Sundays – when people used to go to church – a market was held around the village green. Letnica was also the administrative centre of this Croat enclave, housing the *mesna zajednica* (local community office) where for instance the municipal registers were kept. But Letnica earned its reputation primarily as a pilgrimage site, visited every year by thousands of pilgrims of various ethnic and religious backgrounds.[2] The huge white church of Majka Božja Letnička (the Madonna of Letnica) is built on a hill, and dominates the whole village.[3] It was erected more than sixty years ago on the site of a nineteenth-century church which had been damaged by a landslide (Turk 1973:18). In the mid-1980s, in Vrnez and Vrnavokolo – two nearby villages that border on one another – a second modern church was built, dedicated to the Croatian saint Leopold Mandić (canonised by Rome in 1982).

Stublla, one of the few Catholic Albanian villages in the province, is 5 km. away high and splendidly situated on a mountain terrace overlooking the plain of Kosovo. Stublla is larger than any Croat settlement, and since the beginning of the twentieth century it has had its own church, forming a separate Albanian parish. Prior to this it was part of the parish of Letnica, like all other Catholic settlements in Karadag. Stublla has a special historical reputation as the village of the 'Albanian martyrs'. In the middle of the

[2] This sanctuary was visited not only by (Croat and Albanian) Catholics, it was and still is also extremely popular among Gypsies, who are predominantly Muslim. Letnica was also – but to a lesser extent – visited by Orthodox Serbs and Muslim Albanians. Already between the two World Wars, Letnica was the main Catholic Marian centre in the south of Serbia, visited by Catholics, Orthodox and Muslims from Kosovo and beyond. Letnica was of such a crucial importance to the diocese that the first eucharistic congress of the Skopje bishopric was organised in Letnica, in 1931 (Urošević 1933:161).

[3] The Madonna of Letnica is popularly called *Letnička Gospa* (by Croats) or *Nëna e Letnicës* (by Catholic Albanians). One also encounters the names *Majka Božja Crnogorska* (Croatian) and *Zoja Cërnagore* (Albanian).

Catholic church at Letnica, 1992.

nineteenth century many Albanian families from Stublla were
deported to Anatolia after they had publicly declared themselves
to be Catholics. Until then they had been *laramans* or crypto-
Catholics, who had feigned to be Muslims, especially in contact
with the Turks and neighbouring Muslim Albanian clans (Turk
1973:33-47). Many Catholics in Stublla claim to be the direct
descendants of these *laramans*, and some of them still carry names
of an irrefutable Islamic origin. In the mountainous hinterland
of Stublla, in some remote and almost deserted hamlets, there are
still some crypto-Catholic families left. As some informants told
me, they have kept their Muslim appearance because of traditional
marital ties with Muslim clans. As far as I know, at least until
1925 many *laramans* let their children be baptised by the Catholic
priest of Letnica or Stublla, who gave them a Catholic name apart
from the Muslim name which was the one used in public (the
church mostly referred to them as *occulti*). However, most of the
laraman families moved to the plains, where many of them gave
up their double religious identity. Some openly converted to
Catholicism, while others became full-fledged Muslims, depending

on which of the two religions was dominant in their new environment.

Stublla, Letnica and all other Croat settlements are part of the municipality (*opština*) of Vitina, where political power is now entirely in Serb hands, although Serbs comprise no more than seventeen per cent of the total population of the municipality. Their most important stronghold is Vitina itself, a small town situated on the plain, some twelve km. from Letnica. In this town, which only has a few thousand inhabitants, Serbs form the absolute majority.[4] Since 1990 they have assumed complete control over the administrative bodies of the municipality, expelling all the Albanians – and to a lesser extent the Croats – from all important and less important positions. Apart form Vitina, there are two other Serb settlements on the road to Letnica, the two villages Vrbovac and Grnčar. When from the summer of 1991 tensions between local Serbs and Croats were on the rise, due to the war in Croatia, the strategic position of these two Serb villages – at the very entrance of the valley that leads to Letnica – was seen as a potential danger. In the event of violent clashes, which the people of Letnica increasingly feared, the Serbs had a very important strategic advantage: they were able to cut off the main communication road. For the Croats in Letnica, as well as for the Albanians in Stublla, this was their only connection to the outside world.

Listening to the stories of my informants, I realised Serbs and Croats had been on friendly terms with each other until quite recently. Often, Serbs would offer shelter and meals to those

---

[4] According to the census of 1981, the municipality of Vitina had 47,839 inhabitants. Almost three quarters were Albanians (35,105 persons), Serbs accounted for 17% (8,369) and the Croats for 8% (3,722) of the total population. The last census of 1991, which was massively boycotted by the Albanians of Kosovo, shows the following results. In that year the Croatian community of Vitina (including the settlements Letnica, Šašare, Vrnez, Vrnavokolo and the predominantly Croat hamlet Kabaš) numbered 4,324 persons, of a total (and estimated) population of 57,290 inhabitants. Šašare was by far the largest Croat settlement with 1,606 inhabitants, while the villages Letnica (808), Vrnez (835) and Vrnavokolo (885) were more or less of the same size. Almost all residents were Croats. The mixed Croat-Albanian settlement of Kabaš, near Vitina, numbered 351 inhabitants, of which the vast majority (248) were Croats. Most inhabitants of Kabaš had settled there recently, and had largely come from Albanian and Croat villages in Karadag.

Croats from Letnica who possessed land near Vrbovac and Grnčar, and who went there to work their land or to reap the harvest. Every year in the middle of August, many Serbs would visit Letnica during the Assumption Day pilgrimage. Some of them would come primarily for trading or to sell their agricultural surpluses. Others, especially women, would visit Letnica for religious reasons as well. Even Serbs from more remote places like Gnjilane (30 km. away) were eager to visit Letnica; young people in particular considered going there was one of the main opportunities for fun and courtship in this part of Kosovo. A young Serb politician from Gnjilane (a member of Milošević's Socialist Party) told me with nostalgia in his voice how during one of his visits to Letnica he had fallen in love with a Catholic Croat girl. His passionate attempts to marry her failed since the parents of the girl disapproved of a marriage with a non-Catholic. Though intermarriage seems to have been unusual, the relation between Serbs and Croats was one of affinity and mutual support, since both were very much aware of their shared position as an ethnic and religious minority among a vast majority of Albanian Muslims. During my fieldwork in 1992, many Croats from Letnica told me that relations with Serbs had deteriorated only in the last two to three years. Traditionally, as older people remembered, there had been more problems with Muslim Albanians, who used to raid houses, steal cattle and start blood feuds.

What I found most striking in this area was the ambiguity and convertibility of identities. I was often asking myself 'Who is actually what, and what were they originally?' The Albanians in Stublla are Catholics at present, but they were Muslims before, or to be more precise they were Catholics and Muslims at the same time. Depending on the particular requirements of a situation, they would choose one or the other option. The Catholic women of Stublla still wear *dimije*, harem trousers that nowadays worn only by Muslim women, and other Muslim habits have been preserved as well. However, some individuals from Letnica claim that the Albanians in Stublla are Catholic Croats by origin, who in Turkish times were Islamicised and subsequently Albanianised.[5]

[5] This claim seems to be untenable in the light of historical evidence provided by Urošević. On the basis of his own research Urošević concluded that the ancestors of Stublla's inhabitants were Catholic Albanians who came from Topojane

At the time of my fieldwork in 1992, the inhabitants of Vrnavokolo, a village next to Stublla which is now almost deserted, were Croats. But I heard many of them speak perfect Albanian, in contrast to other Croats, who normally did not know and simply did not want to know Albanian. They had traditional marital ties with the Albanians in Stubla, and were much more oriented towards Stublla than the Croat parish of Letnica, to which they formally belonged. Most women also wore *dimije*, whereas literally two houses further on – in the adjoining village of Vrnez – the women dressed in the typical red-white costume that is considered the traditional Croat costume of the area.[6] Some inhabitants of Letnica sneered at the people of Vrnavokolo for their old-fashioned and patriarchal way of life, which they claimed was very similar to that of the Albanians. I started to wonder whether or not the Croats of Vrnavokolo were perhaps Albanians before, who had been Croatised as a result of being under the jurisdiction of the parish of Letnica. This was at least the view held by some Albanian Catholics from Stublla.[7]

The 'Croat' identity of the inhabitants of Letnica and Šašare was not completely beyond doubt. Although local tradition says that they are Croats who many centuries ago came from Dalmatia, they were formerly called *latini* instead of 'Croats' by most other groups (Urošević 1933). This term, which is still used for (Albanian and Croat) Catholics in Kosovo, but less frequently than before, shows that they were seen in the first place as followers of the

---

in northern Albania in the middle of the eighteenth century (Urošević 1933:165).

[6] The border between Vrnez and Vrnavokolo was once indicated to me by a inhabitant of Vrnavokolo, who drew a imaginary line between two houses that were built next to each other. There is no better example to show how boundaries are primarily constructed in people's heads.

[7] Processes of osmosis and mutual assimilation between Catholic Croats and Albanians in Kosovo have been noted by Rizaj (1987:378). In 1922 Baerlein pointed out that the Austrians tried for thirty years to Albanianise the Catholic Croats in Janjevo, and that the *Janjevci* resisted this, boycotting church and school. Their priest, called Lazar, who defended Slav national consciousness, was forced to flee to Serbia. After Kosovo was conquered by Serbia in 1912, he became mayor of Janjevo. The Austrians were afraid that Slav identity could bridge the gap between Catholicism and Orthodoxy, which occasionally happened: if no Catholic priest was available in a Catholic village his place would be taken by an Orthodox priest from a neighbouring Serbian village (Baerlein 1922:42-3).

Croat wedding, Šašare, spring 1992.

Roman Catholic Church (which until the 1960s used the Latin liturgy here like elsewhere in the Catholic world). Some Croats, especially those living in Šašare, are believed to be partially of Saxon origin, while Serbs, on the other hand, have claimed that the Croats in Letnica are actually Catholic Serbs who have forgotten their original Serb identity. They maintain that the Croats of Letnica observe some old Serbian habits, in particular the *slava*.[8]

[8] For instance, in the 1930s, the Serbian ethnographer Atanasije Urošević labelled them as '*Srbi katolici*', Catholic Serbs, hardly mentioning the fact that, at that time, some (if not most) regarded themselves as Croats. Only in one place he writes: 'There are also those who because of their Catholic religion want to call themselves Croats' (Urošević 1993:144). As far as the village of Šašare is concerned, he suggests that some inhabitants are of Orthodox origin. There are some Orthodox families in other nearby villages which trace their origins from Šašare, although there are no Orthodox left in Šašare, he writes. His main source is the nineteenth-century Russian consul Jastrebov, who claimed that there were a number of Orthodox families in Šašare which had been Catholicised. This is confirmed, according to Urošević, by a legend which says that a rich inhabitant from Letnica was the driving force behind this conversion process. The tradition adds that this was also caused by the marital ties that existed between Catholics and the Orthodox (1993:114-15).

In short, nobody was what he seemed to be at first sight, and everybody was contesting the identity claims of others.

Letnica 1992

The wars in Croatia (since the summer of 1991) and in Bosnia–Hercegovina (since the spring of 1992) clearly pushed the complexities and ambiguities of these local identities to the background. National and international events started to dictate daily life, while local peculiarities lost their immediate importance. When I visited Letnica in April 1992 (the first time after a short field trip in August 1991), most village men were listening interminably to their transistor radios, in particular during the evenings and nights, when they could catch Radio Zagreb most easily. They devoured the countless reports on the war in Bosnia-Hercegovina and Croatia and I was impressed by their detailed knowledge of fights, frontlines and weaponry, as well as of the main leading figures that were orchestrating the Yugoslav drama. They were completely absorbed by the events of the war, and with good reason. Every move of Tudjman, Milošević, Izetbegović, or any international actor or mediator, was bound to have immediate repercussions for them. When I arrived, I also feared finding Yugoslav army units, which had just started to retreat from the Republic of Macedonia (in the spring of 1992). Their presence at this new and delicate border would have made my work difficult if not impossible. In addition, the Yugoslav People's Army (JNA) did not have – to say the least – a very good record of conduct in non-Serb areas. But in April 1992, life in Letnica had still not been affected by a Yugoslav army presence; apparently, events evolved sometimes too fast for the JNA itself; the first soldiers did not arrive until August 1992. At this time there were indeed reports of misdemeanours by Yugoslav army personnel, of which the Croats in Letnica became the main victims.

Most Croats in Letnica identified strongly with the independent Croatia of Franjo Tudjman and its difficult struggle for survival at that time. Nevertheless, there had been mixed feelings towards Croatia. On the one hand people regarded it as the land of milk and honey, where life was easier and more affluent. On the other hand it was also a place where secularisation and modern Western influences, especially mass tourism, had led to decadence and an erosion of the traditional Catholic family values. Nonetheless, in these times of hardship, people forgot their usual prejudices and felt solidarity with their co-nationals who were suffering the consequences of war. Many feared that a similar tragedy could happen in Kosovo, possibly sweeping Letnica from the map.

The Croats from Letnica had some reason to be afraid. Prior to the war in Croatia, they had not concealed their enthusiasm for Tudjman. His victory during the elections of April 1990 had led to positive and even euphoric reactions. Tudjman's image and other Croatian national symbols could be seen in many houses, in shops and on the streets. However, when the war started in 1991 these expressions of sympathy for Croatian nationalism began to cause serious trouble. The Croats of Letnica were all of a sudden 'on the wrong side': they began to be seen by the Serbs as quislings and the local fifth column of the Croatian Ustaše or 'fascists'. The Serbian police started to remove Croatian national symbols, posters of Tudjman had to be taken from the walls, and some people started to hide other paraphernalia that could easily be interpreted as expressions of Croatian nationalist sympathies.[9] Some houses were searched by the police, who hoped to find weapons and propaganda material. Some 'loyal' Croats continued to work together with the Serbs, but they came to be increasingly regarded as collaborators of the Milošević regime.

One of the most immediate consequences of the war was the flight of many young men to Croatia, especially those who had still not served in the Yugoslav People's Army and expected to receive a call at any moment. When staying in Letnica, they risked being sent to the front in Slavonia or elsewhere. If they had to fight at all, they preferred to join the Croats on the other side of the frontline. A critical event, I was told, had been the death of a young Croat soldier from nearby Vrnavokolo, who had served in the army and was brought home in a coffin. The official cause of death was suicide, but most people believe he had been killed by Serb recruits. When I visited Letnica in August 1991, most young men had already left the village. I was told that they had fled Kosovo in a rush at the outbreak of the war in Croatia. Most of them went to Skopje, where they found shelter in the

---

[9] One of my informants told me that as a precautionary measure he destroyed an old Croatian banknote, a 'relic' from the Independent State of Croatia (1941-5).

parks of the Macedonian capital, waiting for an opportunity to go to Croatia. During my next visit to Letnica, in April 1992, a new element was added to an already tense situation. Just a few weeks before Vojislav Šešelj, leader of the ultra-nationalist Serbian Radical Party, publicly declared that Croats from Serbia should be deported to 'their' Croatia. There were only a few people who did not take this threat seriously, as Šešelj was (and still is) considered a man of his word (for which he was openly lauded at that time by Milošević). Since April 1992, the Croat minority from Vojvo-dina experienced what this meant. Serbian Radicals exploited the vengeful feelings of Serb refugees from Croatia, and together with them started to raid Croat houses. In many cases the Croat residents were 'offered' houses in Croatia, i.e. those that the refugees had been forced to leave. In anonymous threats they were urged to leave immediately in order to avoid more serious measures. And in some cases bombs were thrown into the yards of their houses. As the authorities did next to nothing to prevent these threats and incidents or to prosecute the perpetrators, many Croats were forced to flee to Croatia. The most notorious example – and the one that has attracted most attention – is the small town of Hrtkovci in the area of Srem (Srijem in Croatian), where almost all Croats were expelled by the spring of 1992. Serb refugees from Croatia and local nationalists, who took over local power, gave Hrtkovci (which somehow sounds like '*Hrvatski*', 'Croatian') a new 'Serbian' name: Srbislavci. When I arrived in Letnica, Šešelj's threats to the Croats in Serbia were on everyone's lips, causing a great deal of fear and desperation. 'They are going to deport us, we will have to leave here', was the first thing I was told by my hostess on arrival. On May 17 Šešelj paid a visit to Vitina for an election meeting, and some Croats from Letnica claim to have seen him in their village, anonymously, in a car accompanied by bodyguards. From that moment on, fears in Letnica rose to a unprecedented level.

The exodus

Following Šešelj's threats and his visit to Vitina, panic started to spread among the inhabitants of Letnica. Shortly after Šešelj's visit a few houses and sheds were burnt down by unknown persons.

Most people assumed that this was the work of Serb extremists who had felt encouraged by Šešelj's statements. There was also a widespread rumour that the arsonist was a mentally ill Croat from Letnica who had been pushed by the Serbs. As some residents from Letnica – those few who had stayed behind – suggested to me in August 1994, it might as well have been the work of Croat nationalist fanatics who wanted to spread fear among the inhabitants of Letnica in order to incite them to leave for Croatia. In any case the men of the village started to organise an armed guard which patrolled during the night and was equipped with no more than a few hunting rifles. Shortly after these first incidents panic rose again in the village: a small group of armed Serbs arrived by car in the middle of the night and moved into the forests around Letnica. They left their car in the centre of the village, where the inhabitants of Letnica started to gather and to discuss what should be done. In the morning when the Serbs returned from their night excursion, they told the crowd that they had been drinking the previous evening and had very much felt like going on a night hunt. They had chosen Letnica – Croat territory – for this. Their message left little room for doubt.

There were also concerns about the possibility that Letnica might be cut off from the outside world by the Serbs in nearby Vrbovac. There were all kinds of wild rumours circulating that these Serbs – with whom relations had always been quite cordial – were heavily armed and that extremists were planning to carry out a massive carnage among the Croats of Letnica. Although I did not take these rumours very seriously, I still listened with pricked ears when people were discussing escape routes through the nearby mountains to Macedonia. In short, life in Letnica became disrupted by fear and insecurity, and many people started to consider the possibility of leaving Kosovo and going to Croatia. Obviously, some had already taken that decision: two days after Šešelj's visit to Vitina, I saw a big lorry parked on the village square in which some families were already packing furniture and other belongings.

The reasons to leave became more pressing. Apart from the incidents mentioned before, which caused great anxiety among the population, life was made increasingly difficult by problems and 'inconveniences' that were partly the result of the UN-sanctions against Serbia. Electricity was cut off almost on a daily basis, usually for several hours, and often there was no water for days. The Serb authorities in Vitina were held responsible for this, especially when it happened on Catholic holidays such as Easter or Christmas. There were shortages of almost everything: petrol, soap, flour, edible oil and other basic foodstuffs. The most essential medicines and medical appliances, like tetanus injections and antibiotics, were completely lacking. Already in 1991, the medical centre (*ambulanta*) of Letnica had been closed down, forcing people to go to Vitina for whatever small check-up or vaccination they or their children needed.

Economic conditions also became more and more wretched. The possibilities of making a living had always been quite limited in Letnica itself. In the past many men had sought their luck elsewhere, often finding jobs as construction workers in the Macedonian capital of Skopje or in Belgrade, or even further away in Germany or Switzerland. Not so long ago, some men even went to the United States, most of them not returning for years. In most cases, however, they continued to foster their ties with Letnica, normally leaving behind their wives and children and returning once or twice a year. The money that was earned abroad was invested in building a new home or a small shop. For those who were working abroad nothing changed, at least in the economic sense, but for those who had a job in Skopje or Belgrade, wages were reduced drastically, especially after the war began. Most of them were left with almost nothing, earning no more than 10 to 20 Deutschmarks a month, while prices were rocketing due to war inflation. Prospects were even worse for the many young jobless men in an area where non-Serbs could hardly hope for a job. Pensioners saw their sources of income dry up more or less completely; pensions did not arrive, and if they did, their value had greatly diminished due to inflation.

The departure of most of the young men – usually followed by their families – as well as the exodus of the population of Janjevo (a small Croat town not far from Prishtina) intensified the emigration fever. As early as Christmas 1991, I was told, more than half the inhabitants of Janjevo had left for Croatia, where most of them ended up in the famous Dubrava quarter of Zagreb, already a bastion of Croats from Janjevo many years before the war started. This had a major psychological effect on the population of Letnica, since the presence of the *Janjevci,* who used to make a living by the production and trade of plastic trinkets and other kitsch objects,[10] was for most people a reassuring thought. Although there were clear rivalries between these two Croat communities – the simple peasant folk of Letnica regarded the Croats from Janjevo as arrogant, impulsive and impudent – the *Janjevci* were regarded as smart and world-wise, which was some kind of safeguard if things got worse.[11] Their massive departure was seen as a bad omen, inciting others to follow their example. Some individuals had more pressing reasons to leave; the only baker of Letnica for instance fled from the Serbian police after they had learned that he had hidden a weapon at home. In general terms, the war prevented people making plans for the future. They continued to work the land, harvesting what they had sown in spring, but other more demanding activities like the construction of a new house came completely to a halt.

The calls to leave became louder, especially during the months of July and August 1992. For most people the situation had become much too insecure, not promising anything good for the future, and I was often told: 'If Kosovo stays in Serbian hands, there is no place for us, and if the Albanians get their republic, we will be even worse off.' Nonetheless, there was sometimes strong disagreement – notably between men and women – about whether to leave immediately or to await further developments. In most cases, women preferred to stay: their lives had always been confined to the home – their primary source of pride and symbol of achievement – and they had rarely set foot outside the village. They dreaded the prospect of leaving their homes to go to a distant land where hardly one of them had ever been.[12] Most men, however, were in favour of leaving: they had always had to face to the wider world, and tended to perceive migration as a chance of new opportunities. The disagreement between men and women

[10] In Kosovo this is jokingly called *Ari i Janjevës* (in Albanian) or *Janjevačko zlato* (in Serbo-Croatian): 'Gold of Janjevo'.

[11] Traditionally, the Croats of Janjevo were also the main providers of priests for the small (Albanian and Croat) Catholic community of Kosovo.

[12] This corresponds with the findings of Peter Loizos, who, in his book on Cypriot war refugees, notes that the loss of a home is particularly painful for women, who experience it almost as a kind of personal amputation (Loizos 1981:176-7).

resulted in fierce discussions, even to the extent of physical confrontations, in which men tried to induce their women – together with the children – to leave for Croatia. Sometimes the attempts to persuade wives did not succeed immediately, and sometimes even not at all. I know of an older couple, of whom the husband finally left his wife behind in their home in Letnica. She wanted to take care of her old and sick parents, who had also decided to stay.

In the end most people chose to leave Kosovo 'before it is too late'. They used the opportunity offered by a Croatian Catholic charity, the Foundation of St Isidorus (*Fond Svetog Izidora*), to be evacuated to Croatia without the requirement of passports or other travel documents. The majority of people were transported by bus from Skopje via Bulgaria, Rumania and Hungary, while some of the ill and the old were airlifted direct to Zagreb.[13] Almost all of them – except the more well-off who could afford a lorry – left behind everything, their houses and almost all of their possessions. Some sold their furniture and cattle to Albanians, at too low prices. Older people who remained were asked to keep an eye on their property, in the event of their return. From May 1992 on, the Catholic priests of Letnica handed out hundreds or even thousands of so-called *krsni listovi* (baptismal certificates) in the presbytery of Letnica. Since the Croatian authorities refused

[13] *Fond Svetog Izidora* had been set up as a charity organisation some years before the outbreak of the war (1986) to help the Croats in Kosovo (in the Catholic church, St Isidorus is the patron saint of peasants and agricultural labourers). Baretić (1993) writes that this foundation organised transports of people completely independently, without any prior agreement with the Catholic church and the Croatian state authorities. The main initiator and organiser of this massive resettlement, Eugen Šooš, also declared in 1993 in an interview that he had not received any co-operation from the state (Majetić 1993:9). To me this seems quite unlikely: how can a charitable organisation transport hundreds or even thousands of refugees (many without travel documents) to Croatia through four other Balkan states, and how can it resettle them in a deserted and strategic area, without the assent and co-operation of some important institutions, such as the Croatian government, the Catholic church, the local authorities in Djulovac and Voćin, and the Red Cross, to mention only the most obvious ones? In 1995 the Croatian minister Adalbert Rebić indeed admitted that his Bureau for Displaced Persons and Refugees had given the green light to the *Fond Svetog Izidora* to resettle the Croats from Kosovo in Djulovac (Kovačić 1995).

Yugoslav citizens entrance into Croatia, proof of Catholic Croat identity was the only ticket of admission to Croatia. In June 1992 the first buses with refugees arrived in Croatia, and half a year later the majority of the population of Letnica had left. Between May 1992 and May 1993 there were about ten organised convoys, transporting more than 2,200 persons.[14]

Resettlement in Western Slavonia

After returning to the Netherlands, I did not hear much from my friends for almost a year, until I decided to go to Croatia to find out what exactly had happened to them. Some had mentioned to me plans to resettle the inhabitants of Letnica in a number of villages in Western Slavonia. I even heard the names of some of those villages, without knowing the situation on the ground. I only knew that some people had visited these villages, feeding the imagination of those who considered leaving Letnica and going to live in a new environment. Nonetheless, I doubt whether people knew all the details of these resettlement plans. During my work in Letnica in the summer of 1992, most people were speculating about the living conditions they would encounter 'abroad': the only things they were sure of was that food and shelter were provided, and that they probably would have to go to school to learn 'Croatian', for their own local dialect, a peculiar mixture of Serbian, Croatian and Macedonian, is anything but standard Croatian.

In December 1993 I went for the first time to visit Western Slavonia where they had been resettled. As the war in Croatia had developed in 1991, I had not followed where fighting had

---

[14] I visited Letnica again in December 1992. By then more than half of the population had left. My last visit took place in August 1994 at the time of the pilgrimage. At that time there were about twenty households left in Letnica itself (similar numbers in other Croat villages nearby), many of them consisting of old married couples not willing to start a new life as refugees. Approximately 15% of the Croat population has stayed (800 people). In August 1997, Nikola Dučkić, former parish priest of Letnica and now diocesan vicar for the Croat parishes in Kosovo, declared in an interview with the Zagreb daily *Večernji list* that in the last two years or so the situation of the remaining Croats in Kosovo had improved '180 degrees' and the attitude of the Serb authorities was much better than before.

been going on or who held exactly which territory. So I was ignorant of the fact that this area (between the towns Pakrac, Virovitica and Podravska Slatina) had been the stage of atrocities and violent confrontations between Croats and Serbs. Before the war started, Western Slavonia had a substantial Serb minority – there were many villages that were predominantly Serb – and therefore, in August 1991, it was taken by Serbian paramilitary forces who incorporated it into the Serbian Krajina.[15] It formed a kind of Serbian wedge in Croatian territory, stretching almost as far as the Hungarian border near Virovitica and Podravska Slatina, and threatening to cut off Eastern Slavonia from the rest of Croatia. In line with Serb nationalist aspirations, this area was supposed to become the new border area of Greater Serbia, which would also include the rest of Slavonia.[16] In November of the same year, however, Croatian forces started an offensive in order to recapture this strategic area, and they managed to reconquer half of it, at the price of a high number of Croatian casualties. When Serbian paramilitary troops were forced to retreat from Western Slavonia, they killed many Croat civilians – who had already been living under Serb terror for almost five months – and they destroyed a great number of houses and churches. Since then, this part of Western Slavonia has been in Croatian hands, initially under the supervision of the United Nations. Western Slavonia was in fact the only United Nations Protected Area in Croatia that was *de facto* partly controlled by the Croats. The rest of the UNPA zones – comprising Krajina and Eastern Slavonia – were in Serb hands.[17] The UN permitted Croatian police forces in the area, but a Croatian military presence was not allowed.

[15] In the historical literature this area is also called the *Pakračko-voćinska krajina* ('the frontier of Pakrac and Voćin') or *Mala Vlaška*. In the sixteenth and seventeenth centuries, when the Turks occupied Slavonia, Orthodox Serbs from Bosnia (together with numerous Muslims) were settled here by the Ottomans to defend the border with the Hapsburg empire. At that time the area was completely deserted by the original Catholic Croat population. The Catholics who stayed converted to Islam (Šuvak 1994:13).

[16] According to the Serbian nationalist designs of people like Šešelj, the borders of Greater Serbia should have been drawn roughly along the line of the towns Virovitica - Karlovac - Karlobag.

[17] In the spring of 1995 the United Nations negotiated a new mandate for the former UNPA zones, and their mission in Croatia was renamed UNCRO.

So in December 1993 I went by train to Virovitica, and from there entered Sector West in an old and shaky wooden train. Next to me in the train sat a small group of Kosovo Croat refugees, an old woman wearing *dimije*, and a young couple with a baby tightly wrapped up, which was being breastfed by its mother. It seemed as if the woman had just given birth to the baby; she looked weak and was unable to sit up properly. They were being stared at by the other passengers, who were clearly displeased by the 'dirty' look and lack of civilisation displayed by these refugees. The train brought us to Djulovac, a village formerly called Miokovićevo, as was still written on my train ticket. Previously, it had been inhabited by a mixed population of Croats and Serbs, and according to the census of 1981 there had also been a considerable number of 'Yugoslavs'. The name of this village changed frequently – from the original Hungarian name Gjulaves into Miokovićevo (1928), into Djulovac (1940) and again into Miokovićevo (1944) – as did the ethnic composition of its population. Before World War II, Croats, Germans and Hungarians and only a few Serbs lived there. After that war, the communists expelled the Germans and the Hungarians and their place was taken by Serbs who had come from Bosnia-Hercegovina and from villages in the nearby Papuk mountain range (Baretić 1993). During the most recent war (1991), all the Serbs left again, and their place was taken by Croats from Kosovo, who presently form the majority in the municipality of Djulovac.[18]

In August 1991 Djulovac (or Miokovićevo at that time), became part of Serb-held Western Slavonia. It was a Chetnik stronghold, and a prison or concentration camp was established in the village. Some Croats were detained here, among them the Catholic priest of the village. During those months of Serb occupation, thirty Croats were killed (Baretić 1993).[19] Finally, at the end of 1991,

---

As a result of this, the UN withdrew a substantial part of its forces in accordance with Croatian demands. In the beginning of May 1995, in a two-day offensive, Croatian government forces took the remaining part of Western Slavonia.

[18] According to Baretić, there are roughly 1,200 native Croats living in the municipality of Djulovac, whereas the number of 'imported' Croats (mostly from Kosovo) is 1,652 (Baretić 1993).

[19] Kostović and Judaš (1992) contains a chapter on Serbian camps in which the Miokovićevo concentration camp is mentioned in testimonies given by

the Croatian army took the village and the Serb inhabitants fled *en masse*, leaving their houses and most of their possessions behind. During the fighting Croat houses were burnt down and many were damaged. As the Croatian forces advanced, the Serbs also blew up the Catholic church. They had requisitioned it as a 'storage place' for weapons and ammunition which was detonated only a day or two later (Kostović and Judaš 1992:248; Baretić 1993). Today, only the clock tower is left standing beside the ruins of the church.

Nonetheless, Djulovac was not as devastated by the war as was for instance Voćin, some twenty kilometres to the east. There, most houses and public buildings were destroyed or heavily damaged, including the monumental Catholic church, which met with the same fate as the church in Djulovac (Kostović and Judaš 1992:68; *Le livre noir* 1993:160). There is not a single stone left of this building which had been a popular Marian pilgrimage centre since the 1880s, dedicated to the Virgin of Lourdes (Lukinović 1986:80-99).[20] Apart from the enormous amount of material destruction, Voćin and two nearby villages had also been the scene of a brutal massacre of forty-three Croat civilians when the Serbs withdrew from the area on 13 December 1991 (Kostović and Judaš 1992:118-21). After that, the invading Croatian forces for their part burnt many houses of former Serb residents.[21]

---

former prisoners (1992:183-93 *passim*).

[20] This was the second time this century that this church had been destroyed: in May 1944, the Germans ravaged Voćin, burning the Catholic and the Orthodox church and devastating the rest of the village (Lukinović 1986:34-7). The Papuk mountain area, of which Voćin is part, was a partisan stronghold. After the war, under the communists, it took about twenty years before parish life in Voćin could start anew: until 1963, Voćin did not have a Catholic priest. The pilgrimage to Voćin also came to a halt, beginning again in the 1960s. The church was rebuilt in the 1970s, and re-consecrated in 1984 (Lukinović 1986:41-7).

[21] The excesses committed by the Croatian forces during their 1991 campaign in Western Slavonia led to protests by the human rights organisation Helsinki Watch. On 13 February 1992 this organisation sent a protest letter to President Franjo Tudjman (*Le livre noir* 1993:75-6, n.2; see also Kostović and Judaš 1992:263). In November and December 1991 more than 20,000 Serb civilians fled the area following the retreat of the Yugoslav People's Army (JNA) and Serbian paramilitary forces. Most of them ended up in Banja Luka (Bosnia), from where they later were resettled in Serb-held Eastern Slavonia (see *Le livre noir* 1993:159-60; Judah 1997: 285-8).

'This is Croatia' – graffiti at railway station, Koreničani, Western Slavonia, December 1993.

Voćin and Djulovac are only two of the five villages where the Croats from Letnica have found shelter. There is also the village of Ćeralije near Voćin, and the villages Koreničani and Bastaji not far from Djulovac.[22] Until 1991 all those settlements had a clear Serb majority, with Djulovac (the former Miokovićevo) as the only exception.[23] For the time being, the Croats from Kosovo found new homes in former Serb houses, those that were not destroyed by the violence of the war. Most of these houses were in poor condition, due to war damage and subsequent

[22] According to the information I received on the spot, the former inhabitants of Vrnez and Vrnavokolo have been mainly resettled in Djulovac and Ćeralije, and those of Letnica in Voćin. The former residents of Šašare have been divided between Bastaji, Voćin and Koreničani.

[23] According to the 1981 census, the ethnic composition of these villages was as follows: Ćeralije had 376 inhabitants, of which 325 were Serbs, forty-one Yugoslavs and eight Croats. Voćin had 1,534 inhabitants, 904 Serbs, 404 Croats and 226 Yugoslavs; Koreničani 409 inhabitants, 304 Serbs, seventy-one Yugoslavs and twenty-nine Croats; Miokovićevo 541 inhabitants, 201 Serbs, 200 Croats and 118 Yugoslavs. And finally, Bastaji had 530 inhabitants, 375 Serbs, ninety-seven Yugoslavs and thirty-three Croats.

negligence. Officially, their stay in these Serb houses was temporary, and they were obliged to leave as soon as the original owner turned up to reclaim it. Although this was not very likely to happen, many people nevertheless believed that it might occur. Therefore, they were usually not motivated to maintain the houses, except for the most urgent and necessary repairs (like putting glass in windows). They did not have the energy or the financial means to fix or improve the houses. At the time of my visits, many houses were without running water, some of them did not even have basic heating, and electricity was often the only luxury.[24]

Though the Croats from Letnica were happy that they did not end up in refugee camps, most of them felt highly embarrassed occupying the dwellings and using the furniture of people who had fled their homes too. For most, the fact that they themselves had abandoned their homes and possessions did not offer much consolation. They felt like intruders in the personal domains of other people whose presence could be felt in every corner of the house, and in the objects and the big gardens that they left behind. A woman told me that, in the beginning, she would often 'hear' voices or knocks on the door in the middle of the night, expecting the previous inhabitants to return (there were many accounts at that time of Serbs crossing the Serbian-Croatian lines at night to find out what had happened to their villages and houses). Above all, to enter somebody else's home was (and is) considered a dishonourable act which will in the end cause misfortune. People often say: '*Tudje nikome nije donijelo sreću*' (Somebody else's property has never brought luck to anybody).[25] Ideally, the Croats from Letnica would prefer to build new houses for themselves. But for the moment this is not feasible, so they have to remain where they are until all private property issues can be solved in a mutual agreement between Croatia and Serbia, or they have to find another solution. Since the Croatian authorities

---

[24] This description refers to the situation during my last visit to the area in the spring of 1995.

[25] Stories about the destiny of the refugees in Croatia also reached the stay-behinds in Letnica. During my last visit to Letnica, in August 1994, some of them condemned the fact that refugees had entered Serb houses. I know of at least two people who refused to go to Croatia because of moral objections of this kind.

are confronted with a growing resistance among the Croat refugees from Kosovo to staying in these Serb houses permanently, there was some debate about building new houses for them in parallel settlements. However, the Croatian government seems never to have taken these plans very seriously, for obvious reasons.[26]

During those few days that I was there, nobody openly admitted regretting the decision to leave Letnica and go to Croatia. Nevertheless, here as well as in Kosovo, I heard concealed criticism of the Catholic church, which is alleged to have encouraged the exodus, or at least not to have done anything to prevent it. The independent Croatian weekly *Feral Tribune* – the *enfant terrible* of the Croatian press – published two very critical texts on the population resettlement issue and its unfavourable results. The first was written by Drago Hedl (1993), the second by Domagoj Horvat (1995). The latter conveys an image of the political manipulation and instrumentalisation of the fate of the Kosovo Croats, and expresses some of the painful truths and disillusion which these refugees have encountered:

The history of the arrival of the Croats from Kosovo is covered with a veil of silence and patriotic hypocrisy: the newcomers tell how already at the end of the 1980s many people [from Croatia] visited them and told them fairy tales about the wonderful life in their original homeland, from where they had fled for fear of the Turks sometime in the Middle Ages. At the beginning of the 1990s, the Serbian war against Croatia and the racist repression of non-Serbs in Kosovo have particularly encouraged this dubious idea of a delayed repatriation. It was not very difficult to induce these poor and frightened Croats to 'go home'. There, they were told, everything was waiting for them: houses, a job, land, and flocks of sheep were already being brought from Australia, only for them ... Three years later, the promises are of course behind them. They live in Serb houses, houses that are not theirs and which are anything but warm homes. With the natives they barely get along or not at all. Jobs they do not have, and if they find a job, they are badly paid. They are convinced that people steal humanitarian aid from them. And they live amidst 3,000 hectares of unfarmed land which they are not allowed to cultivate. In short, there are millions of problems,

---

[26] In October 1995 the Croatian minister for reconstruction and development, Jure Radić, declared that the building of new settlements is out of the question because 'nowadays, Croatia has many more empty houses and apartments than people interested in living in them' (Kovačić 1995).

but they can not articulate them, neither do they know whom to address to get help. While the capital shouts about demographic renewal, the children of Djulovac, who are the most numerous to be born in this state, are coughing painfully under photos of the Pope's healthy face (Horvat 1995).

Hedl (1993) points to the political background of these population exchanges. In the first half of 1992, as Hedl points out, they were agreed upon between the president of Croatia, Franjo Tudjman, and the president of Yugoslavia at that time, Dobrica Ćosić. They had a meeting in Geneva, at which they both agreed to 'humane' exchanges of populations.[27] Since then, the Croatian and the Serbian leadership have been working closely together in what Hedl calls the practice of 'demographic engineering', exchanging and resettling populations in order to achieve their desired version of a homogeneous national state. More recently, Kosovo Croats have once again proved useful in this respect: since March 1997, the Croatian government has resettled Croats from Janjevo in Kistanje, a small town near Knin which was emptied of its Serb population during Operation Storm in August 1995. The plan is to rename Kistanje as Janjevo or Novo (New) Janjevo (Despot 1997). The Croatian government has received the full support of the church for this operation.[28]

Besides repopulating areas that were abandoned by Serbs, the Croatian regime has had one other important motive for bringing Croats from Kosovo to Croatia. In the eyes of conservative nationalists, one of the gravest maladies of modern Croatian society is the so-called 'white plague' (*bijela kuga*) of small and childless families. Croatia has a very low birth-rate, and in most areas

[27] It is widely believed that the partition of Bosnia and the exchange of populations between Serb and Croat territories were already agreed between Franjo Tudjman and Slobodan Milošević before the start of the war, in a meeting in Karadjordjevo in March 1991 (Silber and Little 1996:143-4).

[28] As the journalist Jelena Lovrić writes, church representatives played a significant role in the Croat colonisation of Kistanje. Priests and bishops encouraged Croats from Janjevo to resettle in Kistanje. The church organised special meetings to prepare the *Janjevci* 'spiritually' for their resettlement. On one occasion the Archbishop of Zadar, Ivan Prendja, said to the people from Janjevo that their 'moving to Kistanje was the will of God' (Jelena Lovrić, 'The church in election campaign', internet http://www.aimpress.ch/dyn/trae/achive/data/199704/70 414-003-trae-zag.htm).

demographic growth is even negative. This is regarded as an issue of national importance, which threatens the existence of Croatia and the Croatian nation as much as the war did.[29] As the conservatives within the Catholic church and the government attempt to counter this development, by propagating the so-called 'demographic renewal' of Croatia, it is very likely that they thought that the Croatian nation could benefit from the high birth rate among the Croats from Kosovo, directly as a demographic 'push', and indirectly as a shining example for other Croats as well. Families with five, six or more children are common among Kosovo Croats. That this is more than mere speculation was shown in a statement by a Croatian government minister: in October 1995 the Croatian minister of reconstruction and development Jure Radić claimed that the high birth rate of the Croats from Kosovo was a blessing for Croatia (Kovačić 1995).

Since this is a politically delicate subject, it has been difficult for me to find out what are the details and circumstances of the exodus of Croats from Letnica, and their massive resettlement in Western Slavonia, and who were the main organisers. But it is clear that it was not an entirely 'spontaneous' process caused only by the threat of Serbian terror in Letnica. Serbian designs to cleanse Serbia of Croats and other non-Serbs, and Croatian blueprints to repopulate Western Slavonia and to give Croatia a new demographic 'push' seem to have gone hand in hand. This policy of demographic engineering has led to hideous results, as Hedl writes, especially in the case of the Croats from Kosovo, who seem to be extremely unhappy in this sinister environment of ruins and burnt houses. They have huge problems in adjusting to this hostile environment, in which they are not accepted by the autochthonous Croats. Though they are proud of having upheld a strong Croat and Catholic identity in a much more hostile environment than the Croats ever had in Croatia, they are now called and treated by the latter as *Šiptari* (a pejorative

[29] One of the champions of the 'demographic renewal' of Croatia is the conservative and nationalist Catholic priest Anto Baković, who has been the leader of the Croatian population movement (*Hrvatski populacijski pokret*). This obsession with reproduction and the demographic renewal of the nation is not typical for Croatia alone. For an analysis of nationalist moral majority and pro-life movements in Slovenia, Croatia, and Serbia, see Sofos (1996:77-9).

synonym for Albanians). Native Croats see them as primitive and dirty, as impulsive and unreliable, as 'oriental' Croats who are not and simply never will be part of the civilised world. These are two cultures in collision: the original inhabitants who try to do their best to resume their life as it was before – although it has been changed irreversibly by the traumatic experiences and the huge material damage of the war – and those 'damned newcomers' who did not go through the terrors of war, and yet settled down in great numbers in the middle of the ruins left behind by the war.

The tensions between natives and newcomers have been most serious in the villages where natives still form a considerable group, as in Voćin and Djulovac. There the huge influx of Croat refugees from Kosovo (and from Bosnia-Hercegovina and Eastern Slavonia) has changed the demographic make-up drastically without completely eliminating the native component.[30] This has resulted in serious frictions, for instance in Djulovac where refugees accused local dignitaries of withholding humanitarian aid and other goods (for instance glass for windows, stoves, tractors and other agricultural materials), distributing it among their own people or selling it. Since these accusations were expressed openly and Croats from Kosovo took matters up with the higher authorities, a lot of bad blood developed between natives and newcomers. According to the refugees, local dignitaries – notably the mayor and the Catholic priest – used their ordeals in the war as a justification to rule the roost and claim preferential treatment with regard to humanitarian aid and other benefits. They had difficulties in accepting that the situation in the village had changed, and they were afraid to lose their positions of power. In an interview the mayor of Djulovac made this very clear by complaining that the Croats from Kosovo want to take over power in Djulovac (Horvat 1995). The same tensions have been reported from Voćin, where the numerical preponderance of the Kosovo Croats in comparison with the native Croats is more pronounced than in Djulovac. As a result the native Catholic priest in Voćin was replaced by a Croat from

---

[30] According to Mustapić, Voćin numbers 353 autochthonous Croats and 1,247 newcomers (Mustapić 1995). In the municipality of Djulovac, in 1993, the number of 'imported' Croats was 1,652 (it is certainly higher now), whereas the number of natives was roughly 1,200 (Baretić 1993).

Kosovo (in 1994). In Koreničani, Bastaji and Ćeralije – villages that were almost entirely Serb before the war – these problems have been less serious, because there are hardly any natives left. Here, the people from Kosovo stick to their traditional community life in splendid isolation, almost without adapting to the new situation (Mustapić 1995).

As far as my latest information goes (the last time I visited the area was in April 1995), the situation has improved. For approximately two years after their arrival, the Croats from Letnica were formally refugees, which meant that they could not find or apply for jobs, and they were largely dependent on humanitarian aid. Since this did not satisfy their needs, they started to work small plots of land, at least to provide for a minimum subsistence. Since the beginning of 1995, however, they have received Croatian citizenship (the *domovnica* or the Croatian identity card), which means that most of the formal obstacles to their integration into Croatian society have been taken away. They now can find jobs, get the normal health insurance, and obtain Croatian passports. Despite these clear improvements, for most of them it will be very hard and even impossible to make a living in this devastated part of Croatia – where nothing is functioning normally and where the economy has to be built up almost literally from the ground – without the help of the state.

I will conclude this chapter with a few more general observations, in order to asses the prospects for the future integration of the Croats from Kosovo. I want to refer briefly to the work of the Polish anthropologist Zdzislaw Mach, who in his essay 'Migration, ethnic identity, and the significance of territory' (see Mach 1993) provides us with some very useful ideas based on examples in Poland after World War II. Mach gives a kind of inventory of conditions and factors that determine whether a migration is successful or not. He starts with the idea that territory – the idea of the homeland – is a main component of ethnic identity. Since ethnic and national groups organise their territory culturally (for instance in architecture), the homeland is part of a group's model of the world, and the only proper place for the community to live. Migration undermines the territorial rootedness of identity, and it takes a huge effort for migrants to reconcile their own identity and cultural traditions with the new cultural landscape. Much depends, according to Mach, on whether migration is voluntary or enforced. If it is voluntary, then migrants will be ready to reshape their life in the new land, and all efforts are made to reconstruct the identity in such a way that the new land becomes part of it. If it is enforced, as is the case with most refugees, this will often lead to prolonged passiveness and indifference, and also to the refusal to create a new identity in a new environment. The refugees will not accept the new land as their own, and there is little hope left for their ultimate integration.

According to Mach the prospects for a successful integration of migrants depend on many factors. Dissatisfaction with former conditions of life and the lack of emotional attachment to the land of origin may help successful integration. When migrants can choose their new land, they will be more motivated to integrate since they themselves have made the choice instead of a force above them. The process will also be easier when there are similarities between the new and the old land. This has natural and cultural dimensions: the natural terrain is important as well as the cultural organisation of that natural landscape. If the new territory is inhabited by a community, the willingness of the natives to accept newcomers is crucial, and the cultural differences between the two groups should not be too pronounced in order to enable successful integration. Another contributing factor for successful integration are legal guarantees that the new land is the property of the new settlers, and that this arrangement is stable and permanent. What is also essential is that legal, social and political conditions allow for independent, spontaneous forms of organisation and self-government among the migrants. Last but not least, the existence of funds for investment and other economic opportunities are crucial.

When we look at the situation of the Kosovo Croats in Western Slavonia, some of these elements are present and others absent. From my description it is clear that the cultural rift between the Kosovo Croats and the native Croats, as well as the unwillingness of the latter to accept the former, are inhibiting further integration. On the other hand the fact that the Croat communities in and around Letnica have been transplanted into an area that is very similar to Letnica, leaving those communities more or less intact, will considerably mitigate the difficulties connected to the exodus. Apart from the resemblances in natural landscape – the Papuk area is almost as hilly but not so barren as the Skopska Crna Gora –

there is a clear correspondence in cultural landscape, an important factor which should not be underestimated. As the Croats from Letnica are very religious, viewing the church and Madonna of Letnica as their main source of identity, it is vital that they have found themselves again in a place where Marian devotion is central and alive.

Nevertheless, there are many questions and ambiguities which complicate this case. Are these people refugees or simply migrants who have tried their luck elsewhere? Was the exodus voluntary or forced? What does the concept of homeland Croatia mean to these 'Diaspora Croats' who have now, as it were, 'returned home' after several centuries? Is being in Croatia really being at home or is there a sense of a homeland lost in Kosovo? What can be made of the huge differences in perspective between men and women? And what of the emotional attachment to the land of origin? Does the fact that it is named Serbia make the emotional bond less strong? I do not know the answers to the questions, and I wonder whether anyone among the Croats from Letnica really does either.

3

CHRISTIAN SHRINES AND MUSLIM PILGRIMS
JOINT PILGRIMAGES AND AMBIGUOUS SANCTUARIES

The previous chapter mentioned the 'ecumenical' pilgrimage to the Catholic church of Letnica, which is only one of the many places in this part of the Balkans where the devotion to a particular saint or shrine has been shared by different ethnic and religious groups. In this chapter I will further pursue this subject, focusing primarily on (Serbian) Orthodox shrines, which are much more numerous in the southern parts of the Balkans and have demonstrated a similar propensity to attract pilgrims of various ethnoreligious backgrounds. The main questions to be addressed are the following. How can this kaleidoscopic image of pilgrimage and worship of saints in Kosovo be reconciled with the now dominant image of sharp divisions between quarrelling groups of differing ethno-religious backgrounds, which have turned the province into one of the most dangerous hotbeds of ethnic strife in the region? In the words of Victor Turner, to what extent do these 'shared' places of pilgrimage create real *communitas*, beyond ethnic and religious boundaries? Are ethnic and religious oppositions temporarily 'forgiven and forgotten', or is it a matter of continuous differences and conflicts? We will see that a certain degree of *communitas* is not entirely absent, but it is always a precarious matter and under certain conditions can turn into the opposite. As was pointed out in Chapter 1, because of their mixed and ambiguous character pilgrimages and forms of saint veneration like that in Letnica exhibit an intrinsic tendency towards tension and conflict. A sanctuary may become a bone of contention and, as the case may be, can be Islamicised, Christianised, annexed or destroyed. This is in sharp contrast with Turner's view of pilgrimage as generally harmonious, and confirms the criticism that has been launched against him ever since, notably by Michael Sallnow (1981, 1987), who demonstrated that pilgrimages can be an arena for competition and conflict between and within local communities. We will begin with a description of three recent examples of mixed Christian–Muslim pilgrimages to Orthodox shrines. The first two are mainly described on the basis of my own observations (1986, 1990 and 1991), while the third is based on an analysis of press reports (1988).[1] In the first case, the *sabor* (religious festival) in the monastery of Gračanica, despite some friction, an overall picture of relative harmony between the different groups of pilgrims emerges. In the second case, in Zočište (near Orahovac), increased tensions between Albanians and Serbs almost brought an end to this example of a 'mixed' pilgrimage. And in the third case, the monastery of Ostrog (Montenegro), problems occurred between Muslim pilgrims, especially dervishes and sheikhs, and the Orthodox custodians of this famous shrine. To identify the sources of conflict and conditions for harmony, the three examples will be compared. We will then examine at some length the history of ambiguous sanctuaries in this part of the Balkans, primarily using examples connected with the Bektashi order. The Bektashis, who have been the most important and influential dervish order in Albanian history, have always demonstrated considerable tolerance towards prevailing Christian traditions, especially among Muslim converts.

The Muslim Gypsy pilgrimage to Gračanica

The Serbian Orthodox monastery of Gračanica, a few kilometres south of Prishtina, is one of the largest and best preserved medieval sanctuaries in Kosovo. It was built at the beginning of the fourteenth century by the Serbian king Milutin, and survived Ottoman rule relatively unscathed. The monastery is a reminder of the heyday of the Serbian kingdom and serves as an important national symbol for Serbs in a region now almost entirely inhabited by Albanian Muslims. Since the end of the 1980s the monastery has become an important meeting-place of Serbian nationalists, and in June 1989 a massive Serbian pilgrimage took place there as part of the

---

[1] Apart from the cases analysed in this chapter, there are other examples of Christian shrines which have always attracted Muslim pilgrims, like the Serbian Orthodox monasteries of Devič and Visoki Dečani in Kosovo.

commemoration of the Battle of Kosovo (1389).[2] Several hundred thousand people gathered at the monastery and in Gazimestan, where the battle took place more than six hundred years ago. In the monastery the relics of Prince Lazar, commander of the Serbian armies and martyr on the Kosovo battlefield, were displayed.[3]

Although this 'political' pilgrimage was a one-off event, Gračanica also has an established reputation as a place of pilgrimage in a more traditional sense. Every year on the Feast of the Assumption (*Uspenje Bogorodice* or *Velja Bogorodica*) a large *sabor* takes place there, which I have witnessed several times (1986, 1990, and 1991). It makes a surprising spectacle if we consider the symbolic importance of Gračanica for Serbian nationalists. A great number of Muslim Gypsies from all over Kosovo take possession of the monastery grounds and celebrate this holy day together with the Serb pilgrims. Most arrive the day before and bivouac in the *porta*, the large walled garden around the magnificent monastic church. The Gypsy pilgrims include people who are ill and women who are either barren or pregnant, who usually come with their relatives. They believe that an overnight stay will hasten their recovery or promote a pregnancy or an easy delivery. However, the majority of the sojourners, Gypsies and Serbs alike, are primarily attracted by the prospect of having a good time. The taverns in the vicinity offer live music and ample facilities for dancing. A small field just outside the convent walls is transformed into a fairground and in the *porta* traders sell souvenirs and trinkets.

As far as I could judge in the years when I witnessed the event, Muslim Gypsies do not attend the lengthy church ceremonies on the eve of the holy day or on the day itself. This is mainly a Serbian affair. Nevertheless Gypsies, in particular women and children, enter the church to kiss the altar icons, light candles and leave small gifts, in money or in kind. After vespers barren

[2] In the nineteenth century this battle, in which the Serbs were defeated by the Turks, became the main source of inspiration for the Serbian national movement. In the late 1980s, under conditions of rising ethno-religious tension, the Kosovo myth regained its significance and became once more the main cornerstone of Serbian nationalism (see Chapter 8).

[3] After this event, the monastery of Gračanica has continued to be a centre of nationalist activity. It became the scene of gatherings of Kosovo Serbs and Serbian nationalists, a place where Chetniks – armed Serb irregulars – took oaths of loyalty to the Serbian cause (Thompson 1992:142).

Serbian Orthodox religious procession, Gračanica, August 1990.

Gypsy women circle the church three times with long coloured ribbons, which remain tied round the building overnight. These are taken home and a belt is made of them for a woman and sometimes her husband to wear. This is a widespread practice which happens at many other shrines, like Letnica, and it is believed that within the year the woman will conceive. At daybreak the next morning, many Gypsy families sacrifice a hen or a lamb, which they prepare for a festive family meal on the spot.

One noticeable detail is that the Gypsies perform their rituals individually or within a small circle of close relatives and friends, whereas the ceremonies and festivities of the Serbs are much more communal in character. Led by Orthodox priests, Serbs jointly sing and pray at vespers on the eve of the holiday and at matins on Assumption Day itself, without Gypsy participation. After the morning prayers, Serbs march three times around the church in a procession headed by the clergy, which in this case includes also the *igumanija* (prioress) of the convent. The priests carry processional banners and icons, and they are followed by the choir and congregation displaying Serbian flags. Finally the priests bless the bread and wine and consecrate huge amounts of water. While Serbs line up to be blessed by the priests, Serb and Gypsy women jostle one another before the vessels filled with holy water, which they will take home in bottles. At noon the ceremonies are concluded, and dozens of Serb pilgrims who come from far away and have spent the night in the monastery are regaled with a dinner by the nuns, who usually work day and night to prepare the meals and welcome the guests.

Although Serbs and Muslim Gypsies jointly congregate at Gračanica, they do not seek each other's company or intermingle in the religious or ritual sphere. Each group has more or less its own domain in or around the church. The Gypsies occupy the *porta*, where they spend the night, sacrifice animals, eat, drink and enjoy themselves. The Serbian domain consists of the monastery buildings, including the church in the centre of the *porta* and the taverns just outside the walls. Gypsies frequently enter the church, but Serbs who gather there often seem to perceive this as an infringement of their own religious ceremonies and regard the Gypsies' behaviour as somewhat disrespectful and improper. During the church ceremonies Gypsies bring noisy children and hens inside, and make their round through the church undisturbed by Serbian glances, performing their own private rituals that do not always conform with the prescribed Orthodox ones. Once in a while, the nuns and other attendants posted inside intervene, and meanwhile keep a close watch on the money pilgrims leave on the icons for fear of Gypsy thieves. From time to time, they collect the money and put it safely away in wooden money boxes underneath some of the icons. However, apart from minor irritations and stereotypical suspicion towards Gypsies, there seems to be no serious friction between the two groups. Serb and Gypsy pilgrims meet in relative harmony, though without direct contact.

It seems that the Gypsy pilgrimage to Gračanica is a relatively recent phenomenon. The Serbian ethnographer Tatomir Vukanović writes that in the past it was exclusively a place of pilgrimage for Kosovo Serbs; only since the 1950s has it grown into an object of veneration for Muslim Gypsies as well (Vukanović 1966). Janićije Popović, the village teacher who wrote a short but extremely interesting monograph on Gračanica (1927), does refer to *Velika Gospa* as the church's major festival but does not mention the presence of any Gypsy pilgrims. He writes that the *sabor* was the only one in the whole region, and was visited by Serbs from all over Kosovo (Peć, Djakovica, Prizren and, above all, the region of Morava, i.e. Gnjilane and surrounding areas) (Popović 1927:52-3).[4] As early as Turkish times the Serb congregation gathered here, mistrustfully observed by Turks and Albanians, who looked forward to a better future without it. As Popović writes: 'in front of the wide-open eyes of Turkish police, gendarmerie and unruly and armed *Arnauts*, who made their way bristling through the thick crowd and peered into each corner, people were singing – to be sure, only innocent songs – and dancing to the sounds of

---

[4] At the time of his writing, however, the festival seems to have been on the decline (Popović 1927:54). Popović's monograph is fascinating because of the historical details it offers regarding the conflicts between the caretakers of the monastery, a Serbian family of priests who, between 1759 and 1870, established a kind of independent and hereditary religious regime over the shrine, and the higher church authorities in Priština and Prizren who tried to bring the monastery under their control. The efforts of the latter were only successful in 1870, when the monastery was brought under the control of the Priština municipal church council. However, this state of affairs continued to arouse strong opposition for the next forty years, not only from the priestly family, but also from the local village population.

drums, fiddles, a trumpet, clarinets and flutes; and behind the formers' backs, they secretively whispered of their hope of imminent liberation' (Popović 1927:53).

Even though Muslim Gypsies have started to join Serb festivities in Gračanica relatively recently, I can only guess at the specific reasons for this development. The recent Gypsy veneration of Gračanica might be related to the fact that in Kosovo many Gypsies feel at odds with the Albanian majority, and have therefore started to identify with the Serbian minority (for more on this subject see Chapter 6). As early as 1986, I heard from Gypsies living near the monastery that Gračanica had become a kind of refuge for Muslim Gypsies from nearby Prishtina who accused Albanians of attempts to assimilate them. Nevertheless, despite Serb hospitality the municipality of Gračanica has not been very tolerant toward these Gypsy newcomers, and the Serb authorities have prohibited the building of a small mosque to serve Muslim Gypsies. And in 1991, when I visited the *sabor* in Gračanica for the last time, new signs of growing Serb exclusivism – clearly reflecting wider political developments – were discernible. In particular Gypsy pilgrims were ousted from the *porta* which had been their domain in the years before, and because they were not allowed to camp, sacrifice animals or prepare meals there, they were forced to do so outside the monastery. I heard one Gypsy plead, 'We have been coming to this Serbian monastery for over five centuries', trying to invoke an image of Gypsy fidelity to the Serbs since the Battle of Kosovo, but this did not impress the *igumanija*.

Zočište: the end of a 'mixed' pilgrimage

In July 1991 I went to visit another shrine in Zočište, a small mixed Serb-Albanian village some 4 km. south-east of Orahovac. Just outside the village, on a hilltop, is a medieval Serbian Orthodox monastery (fourteenth-century or earlier), a shrine which has the reputation of being particularly helpful in cases of eye diseases and mental and psychosomatic disorders. The church is called *Sveti Vrači* (the Holy Healers) after its patron saints Kuzman and Damnjan. The church is (like Gračanica) situated in the middle of the *porta*, but (unlike it) consists only of a low and very sober single-aisled building.

I wanted to visit this shrine because, until the late 1980s, many

Muslim Albanians from Zočište as well as from nearby Orahovac would go to the Zočište monastery to join the festivities accompanying the *sabor*, which takes place every year on July 14.[5] The story goes that before the Albanian protests of 1989, which were violently suppressed in Orahovac, Albanian pilgrims were even more numerous here than Serbs, and in a more distant past local Albanians had once joined with the Serb inhabitants of the village in helping the priest defend himself against external Albanian attackers (Kostić 1928:55-6).[6] However, as a result of the tense political situation, Albanians have recently stopped visiting the monastery, and the growing distrust between Albanians and Serbs brought this 'mixed' pilgrimage to an end. As I heard from a local Albanian, only a handful of old and very sick Albanians would make the effort to go to Zočište, along with perhaps some Muslim Gypsies, Slav Muslims and Turks from Prizren. In the village itself relations seemed to have deteriorated, partly because the Albanians with their higher birth-rate, had started to outnumber the Serbian inhabitants. Local Serbs told me that they felt they

[5] Most Albanian Muslims in Orahovac are not strictly orthodox (Sunni) Muslims, but belong to one of the several dervish orders which are very active in this part of Kosovo (Krasnići 1957:94). See also Chapter 5.

[6] In a number of other important Serbian Orthodox monasteries in Kosovo (Visoko Dečani, Devič, and the patriarchate of Peć) protection was formalised in the institution of the so-called *manastirske vojvode* (Serbian) or *vojvodat e kishës* (Albanian), i.e. monastery 'dukes' or guards. They were provided by powerful Muslim Albanian clans who posted one of their members in the monastery to guard it against outside attacks, and in return they received payments or certain privileges. This has probably saved these sanctuaries from destruction, especially in times of war and upheaval. Sometimes these guards also provided pilgrims who travelled to the shrine with protection against bandits. The main study of this phenomenon was done by the Kosovo Albanian ethnologist Mark Krasniqi (Krasnići 1958). In a recent publication Milutin Djuričić (a Kosovo Serb lawyer and specialist in Albanian customary law) criticises Krasniqi for presenting too 'romantic' a picture of these monastery guards (Djuričić 1994: 675-93). Their main motive, Djuričić says, was not the solemn oath (*besa*) to protect monasteries (required by Albanian customary law), or the prestige connected to this position, or even respect and awe for these sanctuaries, but rather material gain and exploitation. Djuričić claims that the monasteries were forced to accept protection by powerful Albanian clans which would otherwise cause trouble. In the patriarchate of Peć relations with the monastery *vojvoda* were broken off in the beginning of the 1980s, whereas in Visoki Dečani this institution continued to exist until 1991, when the Albanian guard resigned for political reasons (Djuričić 1994:690-1).

were being pressured into leaving the village, especially by the strong Albanian clans of the village. The small town of Orahovac, where ethnic relations had been quite harmonious before, was now ethnically segregated. Because since 1990 most Albanians had been sacked from their jobs, there was bad blood between Serbs and Albanians, who started to boycott the Serbian *sabor* in Zočište *en masse*.[7]

During the *sabor* the Zočište monastery, though much smaller than Gračanica, offers a very similar spectacle: near the entrance towards the monastery's *porta* there are booths mainly manned by Gypsies selling snacks and all kinds of toys and trinkets, whereas within the confines of the *porta* there is an outdoor café run by Serbian youths from the village. Gypsies run simple and improvised fairground attractions to earn some money. During my visit in 1991 a Serb trader was selling posters and badges within the *porta*, with the images of leading Serbian nationalists like Vuk Drašković, Slobodan Milošević, and Vojislav Šešelj, and small Serbian flags and Chetnik paraphernalia. From the café I could hear old Chetnik songs, and down in the village I saw later that afternoon an Albanian café with Albanian music pouring out of the speakers opposite a Serb marquee with even more deafening Serbian songs.

Pilgrims enter the church and crawl under a small altar where

---

[7] Orahovac is a fascinating place with regard to Albanian-Serb relations, because of mutual assimilation and absorption. One of the most interesting features is that most Albanian *starosedeoci* (the old urban families) are Slavophone, i.e. they do not speak Albanian but a Slavic dialect ('naš govor' - our tongue) at home. During the 1921 census, the great majority of Muslim Albanians in Orahovac was therefore registered under the category 'Serbs or Croats' (Krasnići 1957:121-22 and 125). During my own research, some of them told me that their tongue is similar to Macedonian rather than Serbian (it is clear they want to dissociate themselves from everything Serbian). It is likely that they are the last remnants of what is known in Serbian sources as *Arnautaši*, Islamicised and half-way Albanianised Slavs. At the end of the nineteenth century Branislav Nušić wrote that many (Serbian speaking) *poturice* (converts to Islam) in Orahovac begin to talk Albanian, because they started to marry Albanian women (Nušić 1902:25). Hadži-Vasiljević confirms this, while he also claims that during his visit to Orahovac (in World War I) he was unable to distinguish Orthodox from Islamicised and Albanianised Serbs. They spoke the same language and wore the same costumes, some claiming that they were Serbs, and others that they were Albanians or Turks (1939:123,141). Another interesting aspect of the local Serb-Albanian symbiosis is that Serbian families consider themselves to be part of one or another Albanian tribe or clan (Krasnići 1957:123).

they expect to be most susceptible to the graces of the two saints. Especially older people and women with sick children lie down, sometimes covering their heads with the red table cloth that hangs from the altar. Some mentally retarded children – their faces showing ignorance, surprise or amusement – are kept in check by their mothers who try to push them down under the altar. This ritual is generally considered most effective at night, even more so if priests and nuns are singing, and therefore the church's altar is surrounded and occupied by pilgrims throughout the night. In addition, some pilgrims carry small metal plates on their heads, sometimes wrapped in scarves, which are meant to heal headaches and diseases thought to be located in the head. Other pilgrims keep such plates on other parts of their bodies (legs, arms, around the heart, or on the mouth) for similar purposes. In return pilgrims bring pieces of cloth and towels, and chickens, sheep and lambs with them as gifts to the monastery. The animals are carried twice round the church before being brought to the collection point.

While in 1991 Albanians boycotted the pilgrimage, Gypsies were present in substantial numbers. These are mostly Orthodox or 'Serbian' Gypsies (*Srpski cigani*) from Suva Reka and Orahovac who seem quite well assimilated into the Serbian community.[8] Unlike the Gračanica *sabor*, which attracts many more people and is therefore much more crowded and anonymous, Serbs and Gypsies intermingle in Zočište apparently knowing each other quite well. While I was present, there was also a smaller but quite conspicuous presence of Muslim Gypsy women, wearing the characteristic wide baggy trousers and speaking Albanian, who hardly joined in with Serbs and Orthodox Gypsies; obviously they were not part of the Orthodox *communitas* developing within the monastery walls. Although this was meant to be a feast, the atmosphere was quite tense during my visit: the war had just started and as a Dutchman I sensed a great deal of suspicion – this was the time when the Dutch Foreign Minister, Hans van den Broek, was heading the European Community's efforts to stop the war in former Yugoslavia. At dawn shots were fired, probably by some drunken Serbs, and later that morning army jets flew over – a reminder to everyone that the situation was far from normal.

[8] In Orahovac, Gypsies living in the 'Gypsy' *mahala* (called Stolići) are regarded as 'Serbs' (Krasnići 1957: 99).

However, suspicion was not only directed at foreigners: I witnessed a Serb pilgrim from Prizren accusing a local peasant of being an Albanian 'spy' because of his local dialect, which sounded to him like an Albanian speaking Serbian. After the poor peasant showed his ID to his fellow Serb from Prizren he was told jokingly, but not without serious overtones, 'You had better change your language if you want us to become friends.'

Deep distrust is a characteristic of the Kosovo Serbs. After many years of political unrest and ethnic tension, they have developed a strong suspicion or even outright paranoia towards anybody who appears not to be 'one of us'. During my visit to Zočište I hardly met any ordinary Serbian pilgrims who were willing to speak to me, except for a deeply religious woman from Prizren, daughter of a prominent Serb partisan fighter and post-war communist, and herself an admirer of both Tito and Milošević. She explained to me that many Serbs in Kosovo lock themselves up in their houses. Her elder brother, for whom she went on pilgrimage to Zočište,was suffering from paranoia and schizophrenia: he constantly heard voices and did not dare to join her (something of which he had dire need in her eyes) because police and army would try to prevent him at all cost, at least that is what he thought. He slept on the kitchen floor, locking himself in at night. She herself thought Albanians to be non-believers – Islam was not a religion – and to embody the devil himself. Since 1981, a year after Tito's death, she said, they have tried to realise their evil plans to destroy Yugoslavia, and they have managed to infect Croats and Slovenes as well.

The highpoint of the *sabor* in Zočište is the *litija*, a procession three times around the church on the morning of 14 July, headed by priests and flagbearers who carry Serbian flags and a banner with an image of the two patron saints. Most Gypsies remain at the side, which again shows that the major religious ceremonies on occasions like these are usually not 'mixed'. After the procession priests bless the table with *kolače* (holy bread), *žito* (wheat), candles and wine, and women start to serve pilgrims with wheat and *bonboni* (sweets), as well as glasses of *rakija* (brandy), congratulating those present on the feast day of the church. In front of the church, pilgrims queue to be blessed by the priests and to receive part of the holy bread, whereas at the other side of the *porta* people push each other aside to get a bottle of holy water.

During my visit to Zočište it was clear that this pilgrimage, in this particular location and point in time, was primarily to be interpreted as a demonstration of Serb presence in Kosovo amidst a 'sea' of Albanians. Since the start of the 1990s, the Serbian Orthodox church (especially the head of the Raška-Prizren diocese, Bishop Artemije)' has been trying to revive ecclesiastical life in Kosovo, particularly monasticism: in Zočište, some new guest rooms have been added, and in 1991 the monastery, which until then was manned by only one monk (at present the abbot), was rejuvenated with three young monks. These local activities have been part of a much wider 'offensive' by the Serbian Orthodox church to strengthen its presence in Kosovo, among other things by erecting new religious buildings, the most prestigious of these being a huge cathedral in Prishtina. The recent war, however, has deeply affected the Serbian Orthodox church in Kosovo: on 21 July 1998 the monastery of Zočište was taken by the Kosovo Liberation Army, the first Albanian attack on a Serbian monastery. According to Serbian sources, the Albanians are said to have claimed the monastery as belonging originally to the Albanian Orthodox church. Seven monks and a nun, as well as a few dozen Serb citizens who had taken shelter there, were taken hostage. Although they were later released, the monastery remained under Albanian control for several weeks until it was retaken by Serbian forces.[9]

Unrest in the Ostrog monastery

The Ostrog Monastery (Manastir Ostrog), not far from the Montenegrin town of Nikšić, has been visited by Muslims from time immemorial. Here one finds the relics of Sveti Vasili Ostroški, who is worshipped by people throughout the southern parts of former Yugoslavia. Before the war in Yugoslavia started, the monastery was visited on important holidays by pilgrims from Serbia, Montenegro, Bosnia and Kosovo, and in a more distant past, even Muslim pilgrims from Albania travelled there. The famous Balkan traveller Edith Durham, who witnessed a pilgrimage

---

[9] This information is taken from the internet, July 1998: http://www.decani. yunet.com/zociste.html and http://www.serbia-info.com/news/1998-07/23/ 3447.html.

on Pentecost in the 1900s, wrote that thousands of Christians, as well as Bosnian and Albanian Muslims, gathered here in perfect concord (Durham 1904:40-1).

However, in 1988 Muslim pilgrims from Kosovo seem to have caused problems in Ostrog, at least according to some press reports published at that time in Belgrade.[10] These reports were published at the height of a strong Serbian propaganda campaign against Albanians and need to be treated with caution, but they are nevertheless worth looking at. They allege that the main culprits for the unrest in Ostrog were dervishes, members of Muslim brotherhoods which enjoy wide popularity among Albanians (on this subject see Chapter 5). They were accused of rowdyism, especially on non-holy days: the Orthodox monks who guard the shrine said that dervishes had thrown stones and even threatened them with guns. Contrary to the monastic rules, the monks said, they sacrificed animals and performed Islamic ceremonies in the monastery grounds.

In *Ekspres Politika* (26 June 1988), the *iguman* (prior) Georgije Mirković, the custodian of the relics of Saint Vasili, was reported as stating that dervishes regularly came to Ostrog in groups of twenty to thirty to perform their ceremonies, and that with their immodest and unruly behaviour they disturbed the peace of the place and scared other visitors. In an article published two weeks later in *Intervju* (8 July 1988) the story of dervishes attacking Ostrog was further embroidered with claims that they threatened the *iguman* with a gun and sung a *mevlud*,[11] all of which was allegedly aimed at expelling the monks and Islamicising the Ostrog monastery. To make matters even worse, the priest said, some dervishes had deposited their excrement on the clean bed linen in the guest rooms, and spilled a liquid at the entrance of the monastery which gave off a terrible stench.

In these articles it was claimed that these were Albanian dervishes from Kosovo: the monks of the Ostrog monastery accused Albanian sheikhs of intending to turn the monastery into a *tekija* (lodge of a dervish order, *teqe* in Albanian) or a mosque and to expel

[10] See the press reports in *Novosti*, 29 May 1988; *Politika*, 12 June 1988; *Ekspres Politika*, 26 June 1988; and *Intervju*, 8 July 1988.

[11] A *mevlud* is a song in praise of the Prophet Mohammed's birthday, in the above-mentioned article wrongly spelled *melvut*.

the monks. The intended Islamicisation of Ostrog was said to coincide with territorial aims of Albanian nationalists. Yet information on the incidents in Ostrog was inconsistent, as the statements of the monks in question and their superiors contradicted each other. In the Belgrade-based newspaper *Politika* (12 June 1988), the Serbian journalist Dragomir Bečirović put the accusations in a different perspective. The higher-ranking clergy, in particular the abbot of the Ostrog monastery who resides in Donji Manastir, some 3 km. away, and the *metropolit* (bishop) of Cetinje unmistakably played the problems down. The purport of this article was that the monks had exaggerated their complaints in order to arouse concern about serious personnel problems in the monastery.[12] Furthermore, the text indicates that these 'dervishes' were probably not Albanians but Gypsies. In any case, the organisation of sheikhs in Kosovo flatly denied any responsibility for the conflict at Ostrog; indeed the charges brought against them seem to have been largely unfounded (see also Chapter 5).

It seems clear that the monks of the Ostrog monastery worded their complaints in this way to achieve the maximum effect at a time of anti-Albanian frenzy. Still, it cannot be excluded that they felt genuinely intimidated by Muslim pilgrims. Under circumstances of structural understaffing, the unannounced presence of large groups of Muslims and the display of 'non-Orthodox' (Muslim or whatever) ritual can give rise to tensions, especially if the custodians feel that they are losing control over their shrine to Muslims (all the more so if these Muslims are believed to be headed by their own religious leaders). At Gračanica things have been different, as far as my observations go: there were no Muslim leaders present and the Gypsies refrained from ostentatious ritual behaviour *en masse*. It is especially these elements which are felt to pose a threat to the position and authority of those in control of a devotional regime and to the religious 'signature' of the shrine.

---

[12] The problems were closely linked with the drastic decline in the number of active monks and priests within the Serbian Orthodox church at large, which has affected Montenegro most. The Orthodox diocese of Cetinje (Montenegro) has had huge problems with recruiting personnel. In the 1980s it had by far the lowest proportion of priests of all dioceses of the Serbian Orthodox church.

Ambiguous sanctuaries and dervish orders

Although the 'Islamicisation' of Ostrog seems to be largely an invention, the usurpation of Christian sanctuaries by dervish orders was not an uncommon practice in this part of the Balkans. In the past, dervish orders, one of the driving forces behind Islamicisation in the region, annexed and Islamicised numerous local Christian sanctuaries, often without provoking any serious conflict. In the course of this process, they transformed and incorporated Christian popular devotions. In addition, they created new saints' cults, based on Muslim saints. However, Islamicised shrines often acquired an ambiguous aspect because they continued to attract Christian pilgrims who went on worshipping the old Christian saints there. Some Christian sanctuaries, in particular the larger ones administered by Christian priests, were more resistant to Islamicisation, but they too became ambiguous as a result of the increasing influx of Muslim pilgrims, who carried on the traditions of their Christian ancestors.

The ordinary believers, Christians and Muslims alike, did not care whether the saints they worshipped were in fact Muslim or Christian; they simply had a reputation as wonder-workers able to work miraculous healing or fulfil other wishes. Christians even called upon authentic dervish saints for help, and put aside all their religious prejudices in the event of dire need. As Hasluck remarked, the animosity that exists in theory between Christians and Muslims was hardly relevant to the case of popular devotion. In his monumental work *Christianity and Islam under the Sultans* (1929), published after his death, he characterised the almost symbiotic relationship between the different confessional groups (Muslims, Orthodox Christians and Roman Catholics) in the Ottoman Empire as follows: 'Practically any of the religions of Turkey may share the use of a sanctuary administered by another, if this sanctuary has a sufficient reputation for beneficent miracles, among which miracles of healing play a dominant part' (Hasluck 1929:68-9).

For instance, sanctuaries administered by Christian priests which had a reputation as places of healing could count on considerable interest from Muslims. This meant that after a while they could become susceptible to claims from sheikhs or other Muslim leaders, which in turn led to conflicts in which the control over the sanctuaries was at stake. Hasluck:

It is [...] important to remark that [...] frequentation of Christian sanctuaries by Moslems does not seem to imply any desire on the part of the Moslem population to usurp the administration of the sanctuary in question. Participation is in normal circumstances sufficient for them, and they are perfectly content to leave Christian saints in the hands of Christian priests. Usurpation comes from the organised priesthood or the dervish orders, who, in the event of successful aggression, stand to gain both in prestige and materially (Hasluck 1929:69).

The instigators were thus not ordinary pilgrims but religious leaders who wanted to gain control over the sanctuaries as sources of power and income. Whether they were successful depended on the political circumstances, which tend to favour one religious regime over another. In Albania and the southern parts of the former Yugoslavia, the dervish orders benefited from Ottoman political hegemony, and many sanctuaries fell into their hands. Afterwards, during the Balkan wars, when the geopolitical situation in the Balkans changed dramatically, a number of Muslim sanctuaries were (re-)Christianised or dismantled. These processes of Islamicisation and subsequent Christianisation of ambiguous shrines as a result of political changes can best be illustrated by the history of the Bektashi order in Albania, Macedonia and Kosovo.

The Bektashi order and Sari Saltuk

At the end of the eighteenth century the Bektashi order became the most influential and popular dervish order in Albania.[13] With the help of autonomous Albanian pashas the order grew and gained a strong hold on the population, particularly in southern Albania and western Macedonia. In the last quarter of the nineteenth century the order developed into a virtually independent religious community and became one of the cornerstones of the Albanian national movement (see also Chapter 7). It called on the Albanians to put aside their confessional differences, presenting itself as a

---

[13] For general information on the Bektashi order, see: Birge (1937). Hasluck (1929) is an important source with respect to the history of this order in Albania (see also Norris 1993:123-37). Recently Nathalie Clayer published a book on the dervish orders of Albania, which is largely devoted to the Bektashi order (Clayer 1990). She succeeded in constructing a detailed historical overview out of a large number of dispersed and incomplete sources. It is by far the best study available on this subject.

force of national unity, bridging the gap between Muslims and Christians. This national propaganda enabled the order to increase its following and extend its influence into northern Albania and Kosovo. According to Hasluck, the Albanian Bektashis even hoped to establish a state of their own (1929:438). One of the order's means of achieving religious supremacy was to gain control over Christian sanctuaries and manipulate the veneration of saints.

The order tried to take over Christian sanctuaries by identifying popular Christian saints with Muslim ones, who were then superimposed. The Muslim saint usually shared external and hagiographic characteristics with the Christian counterpart, and was thus presented as a superior reincarnation of the Christian predecessor. Sometimes the identification was based on superficial similarities, such as a resemblance in name (Kissling 1962:56-7). The most important Bektashi saint to serve this function was undoubtedly Sari Saltuk. This legendary saint is said to have spread Islam in the Balkans as far back as the thirteenth century, long before the arrival of the Ottomans. During his wanderings, he wrapped himself in the Christian habit of St Nicholas who was very popular with Balkan Christians. Sari Saltuk was also identified with dragon legends, which can be traced back to the legend of St George. Among Albanians, Gypsies and the Slavic population of these regions St George is a celebrated saint: his feast day, known as *Djurdjevdan*, is a major religious holiday, celebrated by Christians and Muslims alike.

Almost all *tyrbes* (mausoleums) of Sari Saltuk were connected with the Bektashi order.[14] These sanctuaries had a markedly ambiguous character and were visited by both Christians and Muslims. In some cases the Bektashi order seems to have succeeded in completely transforming a Christian saint's cult into a Sari Saltuk cult. A mountain near Kruja (Albania), where one of the *tyrbes* of Sari Saltuk was located, was probably once a Christian place of pilgrimage, dedicated to St Spiridion (Kaleshi 1971:821). In other cases, the transformation was incomplete or had been brought to a halt. These *tyrbes* remained under Christian administration.

---

[14] Judging from the older ethnographic literature, there were at least ten *tyrbes* of Sari Saltuk in Albania and Kosovo. The original number was undoubtedly much higher. For instance in the vicinity of Gjakova (Djakovica in Serbian) alone, four *tyrbes* of this saint can still be found.

Sveti Naum, for instance, a small Christian Orthodox monastery at Lake Ohrid, was claimed by Albanian Bektashis to be one of the tombs of Sari Saltuk.[15] Every year massive Bektashi pilgrimages took place there. The Greek Orthodox church of St Spiridion, on the island of Corfu off the Albanian coast, is a similar example. The tomb of the Christian saint Spiridion, patron saint of Corfu, was regarded by the Albanian Bektashis as a major tomb of Sari Saltuk. It was similarly a destination for annual pilgrimages by Albanian Bektashi dervishes and sheikhs (Hasluck 1929:583-4). There is no information available on the extent to which the order used these pilgrimages as an opportunity to campaign for the annexation of these sanctuaries, but it is almost certain that religious propaganda by the order encouraged Muslim pilgrimage (Hasluck 1929:70). It also seems likely that this provoked conflicts with the Christian clergy stationed in these shrines.[16]

In its efforts to gain control over Christian sanctuaries, the Bektashi order was supported by Albanian pashas. The most illustrious among them was Ali Pasha (1790-1822), who exploited the organisation and religious doctrine of the Bektashis to win popular support for his government, widen his political influence and underline his independence *vis-à-vis* the central Ottoman authorities. The majority of Muslims in his territory was loyal to the Bektashi order and it was held in high esteem by Christians as well. Under the political patronage of Ali Pasha the order enlarged its following considerably. One of the ways it did so was by Islamicising Christians. In turn that helped Ali Pasha increase his power and occupy new territories. According to Hasluck, the Bektashi pilgrimage to Corfu and the identification of Sari Saltuk with St Spiridion, patron saint of the island, were probably related to Ali Pasha's territorial ambitions to get hold of the Ionian islands (1929:439).

Although the order tried to gain control of Christian sanctuaries,

---

[15] Sveti Naum is still a place of Muslim pilgrimage (Smith 1982:223-4).

[16] Sometimes conflicts of a more violent nature arose, for instance at Shkodra (northern Albania) where the ruins of an old church served as a place of pilgrimage for both Christians and Muslims. Muslim fanatics claimed that the ruins were a former dervish lodge and this resulted in a fierce reaction from the Catholic population, with the result that the local Ottoman authorities hesitated to comply with the demands of the Muslims (Degrand 1901: 80).

it never intended to bar Christian pilgrims. On the contrary, the Bektashis encouraged Christian pilgrimages to Bektashi sanctuaries and tolerated the worship of Christian saints. Hasluck even claims that authentic Bektashi saints were deliberately made ambiguous by identifying them with popular Christian saints; they were thus made fit for Christian 'consumption'. There are numerous examples of this. In the huge Bektashi lodge at Tetova (Macedonia), Christians worshipped St Elias (Hasluck 1929:582). The renowned Bektashi sanctuary on the summary of Mount Tomor (Albania) was the destination of a Marian pilgrimage (Bartl 1968:107). At Kanatlarci (Macedonia) Christians visited the Bektashi lodge to worship St Nicholas (Djordjevic 1984, III:398), and in the Bektashi lodge of Aleksandrovo (Macedonia) Christians celebrated *Djurdjevdan*, the feast of St George (Evans 1901:202).

The Bektashis' motive for allowing and even encouraging Christian pilgrimages to their shrines was undoubtedly their wish to gain religious supremacy in Albania and western Macedonia. Being an important pillar of the national movement, the order aspired to religious leadership over Albanian Muslims and Christians, and its ultimate aim was to become the national Albanian church. Bektashi lodges were generally known to be centres of Albanian national activity, and many ambiguous shrines under the control of the order became breeding grounds of national unity. However, the religious ambiguity of these sanctuaries carried with it the danger that under changing political circumstances the sanctuaries might again be claimed by Christians, which was exactly what happened. After the First Balkan War, when the Ottoman empire was almost entirely swept from European soil, several Bektashi sanctuaries were burnt down, dismantled or Christianised (cf. Elsie 1995:200-8). For instance at Martaneshi (Albania) a lodge was burnt down by the Serbian armies. As Hasluck states, 'they added insult to injury by shaving the abbot's beard' (1929:551). The Bektashi lodge at Prizren was confiscated and transformed into a Serbian orphanage (Hasluck 1929:525). The large Bektashi lodge at Tetova was temporarily occupied by Serbian army units, which expelled or killed the dervishes (Choublier 1927:441). Under Serbian rule a number of Bektashi sanctuaries were 're-Christianised', like those in Aleksandrovo (Hasluck 1929:92) and Kišova (Hasluck 1929:524). During these years the Bektashi order was given the final blow in what later became the Kingdom of Serbs, Croats and Slovenes (still later Yugoslavia). In Albania proper, the order recovered only partly from the devastation of war and occupation (especially by the Greeks in the south of Albania), but continued to play an important role after Albania became independent. However, in 1967, two decades after the communist rise to power, Enver Hoxha's Stalinist regime prohibited all forms of religious activity, and the Bektashi order completely disappeared in Albania.

Thus pilgrimages in the Balkans (Kosovo, Albania, Macedonia and Montenegro) have often been characterised by a blurring of formal religious boundaries. Muslims and Christians of different ethno-religious backgrounds have visited each other's shrines, shared the veneration of certain saints and often disregarded their priests' objections to the crossing of religious boundaries. In this borderland of two major religions, Christian and Muslim forms of pilgrimage and veneration of saints have amalgamated, in spite of the fact that different ethno-religious groups have been continuously engaged in bitter conflicts. The case of Gračanica demonstrates that religious gatherings of different ethno-religious groups need not end in conflict, as long as neither the administration and religious signature nor the cultural dominance of one group over the other becomes an issue. Serbian control over this shrine is not threatened by the presence of Muslim Gypsies, since they accept their ritually inferior position within this system of 'hierarchised pluralism' (Roux 1992). Other historical examples similarly suggest that ethno-religious differences need not be an impediment to a certain degree of *communitas* during pilgrimages. In the past, in Ostrog and many other places, notably Bektashi sanctuaries, Muslims and Christians of different ethnic backgrounds gathered peacefully and, as far as we know, without any serious conflict. The various groups of pilgrims found each other, literally and figuratively, in the holy space of a sanctuary and shared their awe for the supernatural powers of certain saints, regardless of the religious complexion of the saint in question. Their motives as pilgrims were the same and are probably universal: health, well-being and happiness for their close relatives and themselves.

As was illustrated by the history of shrines connected with the Bektashi order, this 'spontaneous' *communitas* can acquire a political and ideological function and can be manipulated by worldly and religious authorities alike. As a matter of fact, the role of these elites always makes *communitas* across ethnic and religious boundaries

an extremely precarious matter. Because of their mixed and ambiguous nature, these pilgrimages exhibit an intrinsic tendency
towards tension and conflict, especially over the religious signature
of and actual control over the shrine in question. These conflicts
are provoked primarily by religious and political elites, for whom
sanctuaries are also a source of power and income.[17] So, although
these pilgrimages may help to bridge ethnic and religious differences
and create a certain degree of 'shared' communal identity, they
can easily become arenas for competition and conflict between
and within local communities. Just as it is in the nature of rituals
and symbols to conceal a diversity of beliefs and reconcile opposing
interests and loyalties, so periods of increased tension may cause
these contradictions to rise to the surface rapidly. General political
conditions and important shifts in these are of the utmost importance: they are the background of these conflicts and determine
their final outcome.

---

[17] It is hardly surprising that conflicts over 'shared' or 'ambiguous' sanctuaries
have resurfaced during the wars in the former Yugoslavia. One example is a
small church near Sutomore (Montenegro), which contained an Orthodox as
well as a Catholic altarpiece, which was destroyed and removed from the church
in 1996 (Internet Newsgroup g.exyugoslav - Podgorica 5 May 1996, Press
TWRA, 'Altarpiece in the common church in Montenegro destroyed'). One
can probably find other examples in Croatia and Bosnia-Hercegovina as well.

4

THE MARTYRS OF STUBLLA
ALBANIAN CRYPTO-CATHOLICS AND
THE FRANCISCAN MISSION

During the winter of 1845-6, almost a century and a half before the mass exodus of Croats, the parish of Letnica was the scene of another exodus, this time caused by processes of religious rather than ethnic fermentation. At the instigation of the local Ottoman pasha, twenty-five Albanian families from the neighbouring village of Stublla and some other Albanian hamlets – about 160 people – were deported to Anatolia after they publicly renounced Islam and declared themselves Catholics. They claimed to be crypto-Catholics who wanted to return to their 'original' and 'authentic' Catholic faith. Their conversion was rejected by conservative Muslim circles which feared that recognition might lead to new waves of collective apostasy. The deportation of crypto-Catholics seems to have been primarily aimed at deterring others from openly becoming Catholics. Eventually the survivors were allowed to return home after foreign diplomatic intervention, in particular from France. Nearly 100 crypto-Catholics died during the three years of their exile and have become known as 'Martyrs of Stublla'.

This case is illustrative of conditions in Kosovo during the late Ottoman period, when religious divisions were still more important than ethnic ones. Religion was the dominant marker of identity, in this case dividing Albanians into Muslims and Christians, or into those conservative circles determined to defend Muslim hegemony against those who were or intended to become Catholics. Yet this case also marks the beginning of a new period of Ottoman reforms, which led to attempts by the Roman Catholic church, notably the Franciscan order, to gain back some of the souls lost to Islam during the long period of Ottoman rule. The development of Marian devotion in Letnica, as well as the policy of offering the sacraments on to non-Catholics, were the main devices used to

86

accomplish this, i.e. to re-Catholicise part of the population in the Karadag mountains. The concept of crypto-Christianity was instrumental in the policy of the Catholic church. Instead of taking crypto-Catholicism simply for granted, I would suggest that at this stage (i.e. in the first decades of the nineteenth century) it was primarily a church *category* which initially did not correspond with the 'lived realities' of those who received this label.[1] It was designed to redefine the identity of people who had a vague or ambivalent sense of religious belonging, and to explicate and justify a church policy of Catholic recovery and expansion into Ottoman territory. Through the workings of the devotional and missionary regime in the parish of Letnica, however, the category became increasingly real for those involved.

In this chapter I view Letnica's Marian shrine and pilgrimage as a laboratory of identity, a place where identities change and are made contingent upon wider political developments. I therefore concentrate on the role which religious regimes, particularly the Roman Catholic church and the Franciscan mission, have played in defining and (trans)forming local identities. Before turning to the main events surrounding the martyrs of Stublla, a short history of the parish of Letnica is in order so that events can be seen in a wider historical context.

A historical survey of the parish of Letnica

We do not know when the parish of Letnica, also called the parish of *Cernagora* or *Montenegro di Scopia*, was established. But there is no doubt that it has a long history, probably going back to the time of the Serbian kingdom (fourteenth century) or the initial period of Ottoman rule (fifteenth century).[2] At the height

---

[1] I do not dispute that at an earlier stage, at the time when Albanian Catholics were converting to Islam (during the seventeenth and eighteenth centuries), crypto-Catholicism was indeed a 'lived reality'. There is ample documentary evidence for that (see for instance Malcolm 1998: 173-5). I want to question, however, the common assumption that there was a clear continuity of crypto-Catholicism up to the nineteenth century. I believe that the awareness of belonging to two different and radically opposed religious traditions was gradually lost among ordinary converts (after two or three generations).

[2] The main sources I used for my description of Letnica's history are: Urošević (1933 and 1993), Türk (1973), and Gjini (1986).

of their power, the Serbian kings allowed mining and trading colonies to be established by Dalmatian (Ragusan) traders and Saxon miners (Jireček 1990-I:269-71). This happened particularly in Kosovo, which was not only the heartland of the Serbian empire, but also was – and still is – an area rich in minerals. To exploit and market this natural wealth, of vital importance for the finances of the empire, the Serbian kings engaged specialists from abroad. Although elsewhere in Serbia Catholicism was suppressed, trading and mining centres such as Janjevo, Trepča, Prizren, Priština and Novo Brdo possessed flourishing Catholic parishes (Gjini 1986:79- 85).

Letnica is not mentioned in medieval Serbian sources: probably it was of secondary importance, inferior to other mining centres in both the quality and quantity of its mineral resources. Yet the name of the nearby village of Šašare (the largest settlement in the parish of Letnica) points to a former Saxon presence, and in addition the name Vrnavokolo is reminiscent of mining activities: *Kolo* or '[mill] wheel' was a common designation for water-mills processing the ore. When mining in Letnica collapsed, many colonists probably left the area, leaving the poorest among them behind. It is likely that the latter changed in due time to subsistence agriculture and animal husbandry. We know that Letnica possessed a church at the start of the sixteenth century though not when it was built. During the seventeenth century Letnica is mentioned in the visitation reports of Catholic ecclesiastics who investigated Catholic church life in the areas that were now under Ottoman control. At that time the parish possessed two churches, which were probably destroyed after the Austrian invasion of the Ottoman empire in 1690 failed and hostility and suspicion towards Christians increased considerably (Turk 1973:17; Urošević 1933: 163; Malcolm 1998:163-6). There was no church for more than a century and a half (until 1866), and according to local tradition masses were held in the open air, under an oak tree where the Black Madonna of Letnica was placed. The Croats from Letnica claim that the statue was crucial in helping to preserve the Catholic and Croat identity of their forefathers.

Although a locally-based Marian cult may have existed before, the massive pilgrimage on Assumption Day probably developed only in the course of the nineteenth century, when an officially endorsed popular resurgence in Marian devotion emerged in the

Catholic world at large (Pope 1985).[3] In Western Europe this phenomenon was part of a conservative Catholic reaction against the emergence of industrial society and modern political ideologies. In Ottoman territories the situation was different; here the revival of Marian devotion was meant to recover some of the church's influence after a long period of Ottoman domination. It is not clear when the pilgrimage to Letnica started to gain larger dimensions, but we know that on Assumption Day 1872 the shrine was already attracting numerous pilgrims (Turk 1973:24, 28). And in 1889 the Madonna of Letnica was crowned by the archbishop of Skopje with the approval of the Holy See (Urošević 1933:11). It is very likely, therefore, that the pilgrimage – as an organised religious event – started around 1866, when a new church was built and the statue of the Madonna was moved inside (Turk 1973:26). A popular devotion of only local dimensions would thus have been appropriated by an increasingly powerful clerical regime which slowly transformed it into a regional shrine. The Madonna has since then attracted a growing numbers of pilgrims: Catholic and Muslim as well as Orthodox; Croats and Albanians, as well as Gypsies and Serbs.

The Martyrs of Stublla, 1846-48

Letnica is one of the few predominantly Slav parishes in the diocese of Skopje, where most Catholics are Albanian. Nevertheless, up to the beginning of the twentieth century the parish included several Catholic Albanian (and geographically also Muslim Albanian) settlements, among which Stublla and Binçë were the main ones. It was in and around these villages, and especially in Stublla's hinterland (the Karadag area), that people could be found who were not really Catholics and not really Muslims, but a combination of both: the so-called *laramans*.[4] During the nineteenth

---

[3] From the 1840s there were many Marian apparitions in France (La Salette 1846, Lourdes 1858) and elsewhere in Europe. Popes Pius IX (1846-78) and Leo XIII (1878-1903) were both personally committed to the cult of the Virgin Mary and approved coronations of Madonna statues. They also granted special indulgences for mass pilgrimages (Pope 1985:183).

[4] The term *laraman* is derived from the Albanian adjective *i larmë* which means variegated, motley, two-faced.

Black Madonna of Letnica and a local Croat, August 1992.

century they became the object of missionary activity by the Catholic (Franciscan) priests in Letnica. This is the main subject of this chapter.

It is important to keep in mind that in the mid-nineteenth century, the period of our main concern here, the Muslim Albanians in villages adjacent to Letnica had undergone Islamicisation quite recently, i.e. since the beginning of the eighteenth century, after they had moved from the northern Albanian highlands to Kosovo.[5] The first Albanians came to the Gornja Morava district as Catholics but soon converted to Islam to secure their newly-acquired properties and position of supremacy *vis-à-vis* the Serbian population (Urošević 1933:166-7). Yet they were only superficially Islamicised, and many of them continued to observe Catholic customs. According to present-day Albanian Catholic priests and church historians (cf. Gjini 1986; Gjergji-Gashi 1988), their conversion to Islam was only nominal, i.e. they adopted a Muslim name to escape Ottoman repression or avoid having to pay the Christian poll tax; usually only the men converted since it was they who had to pay taxes, while the women and children remained Catholics (Gjini 1986: 141).

Most historians assume that the religious life of these Muslim converts continued to be essentially dualistic, split between two separate and radically opposed traditions, of which one (Islam) was 'fake' and only fostered to present to the outside world, while the other (Catholicism) was 'genuine' but secret. Gjergji-Gashi, an Albanian priest from Kosovo, who wrote a pseudo-historical and hagiographic account of the Martyrs of Stublla, thus tends to see crypto-Catholicism as a continuous phenomenon: these converts only took Muslim names, and for the rest they continued to celebrate important Christian feasts; they baptised their children, invited Catholic priests to their homes, attended church and did not go to the mosque (see for instance Gjergji-Gashi 1988:26). This image of an uninterrupted continuity of crypto-Catholic communities, which were simulating Muslim identity

---

[5] For Gornja Morava, the area in which Letnica and Stublla are located, this process has been described in great detail by the Serbian ethnographer Atanasije Urošević in his book *Gornja Morava i Izmornik* (Urošević 1993; originally published in 1935). Urošević also describes the Islamicisation and gradual Albanianisation of Serbs (and others) in the area.

while retaining a largely uncorrupted but secret Catholic identity at home, has been produced and reproduced in church documents, and to some extent in scholarly texts as well (see for instance Skendi 1967; Bartl 1967; Malcolm 1997; Malcolm 1998:131-3). It is, however, questionable whether this image is accurate.

Gjergji-Gashi does not position his statements historically, yet it seems likely that some (or perhaps most?) of these 'crypto-Catholic' practices were emerging only in the last decades of the nineteenth century, when the Catholic church had established a more stable presence in the area. These practices had largely disappeared at an earlier stage. Until 1866, to mention only one element, attending church was practically impossible because there was no church in Letnica. Also, at the beginning of the nineteenth century there were hardly any priests in Kosovo to administer the sacraments. It is therefore more likely that crypto-Catholicism had become obsolete for most converts, a situation which only changed when the church started to 'reinvent' it and 'retrieve' it from memory. It was during the nineteenth century that, under the auspices of the church, the *laraman* population of the Karadag (re)emerged, with crypto-Catholics wishing to 're-convert' to Catholicism. In short, it would seem that crypto-Catholicism as a lived reality was historically and politically determined, much more so than is reflected in church historiography.

The first conversion attempt of crypto-Catholics in the parish of Letnica occurred in 1837, but was violently suppressed by the local Ottoman governor who put the *laramans* in jail,[6] where they were tortured and circumcised, as the bishop of Prizren later reported to the Congregation for the Propagation of the Faith (Propaganda Fide) in Rome. After retracting their conversion they were released and sent back home in the company of Turkish policemen and Muslim clergy (Gjini 1986:181; Gjergji-Gashi 1988:35-6). In 1845 prospects for conversion seemed more promising after

[6] It is possible that this event is linked to the establishment of Austria's protectorate over the Albanian Catholics in the Ottoman empire in the same year. Although the foundations for the Austrian *Kultusprotektorat* over parts of the Catholic population in the Ottoman empire were laid earlier (from the beginning of the seventeenth century), real Austrian influence on the position of the Catholics developed only during the nineteenth century; Austria started to send financial aid for the building of new churches and the maintenance or reconstruction of old churches, the building and maintenance of Catholic schools, etc. (Ippen 1902).

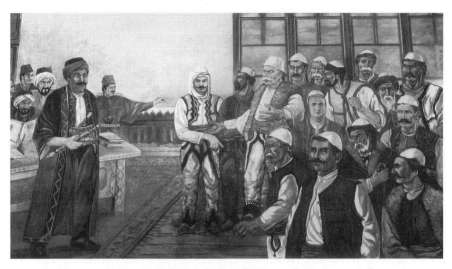

Wall painting in Catholic church of Bincë, depicting confrontation between *laramans* and Turkish officials.

laramans in other parts of Kosovo had been officially recognised as Roman Catholics (Malcolm 1998:186-7).[7] In February that year, the heads of twenty-five *laraman* families from the parish of Letnica went to Gjilan (Gnjilane in Serbian), the district capital, in order to persuade the *kajmakam* (Ottoman governor) and *kadija* (judge of the Sharia court) to grant them recognition as Catholics. The Ottoman governor refused and attempted to persuade them to abandon the idea. According to Gjergji-Gashi's romanticised narrative, he pointed to the advantages of being a Muslim, in particular the prerogatives Islam offers to men: polygamy and the possibility of separating from wives at any time. When they insisted they were Catholics they were sent to jail in Skopje and Constantinople. After a few months they came back with an Ottoman *ferman* granting them recognition as Catholics, but on their return they were imprisoned again. The conservative Muslim elite in Kosovo feared that their shift to Catholicism would lead to conversion on a much wider scale, and in order to deter others they deported these twenty-five men and their families to Anatolia

---

[7] This happened for instance in Prizren, Peja (Peć) and Gjakova (Djakovica). The Ottoman Grand Vizir granted them official recognition as Catholics (Gjini 1986:145-6; Gjergji-Gashi 1988:35).

during the winter and spring of 1845-6. Many of them died during their exile.[8] Finally, in November 1848, after diplomatic intervention by the Great Powers, the survivors were brought home by the Turkish government (Gjergji-Gashi 1988:34-48).[9]

Gjergji-Gashi has made these crypto-Catholics into martyrs, who sacrificed their lives for the Catholic faith and the Albanian nation at the same time. But another contemporary account of the events, that of the nineteenth-century German historian Georg Rosen, is probably more accurate in stressing motives that are much more down-to-earth. According to his version, the attempted conversion needs to be seen in the light of strong Albanian resistance to the Tanzimat reforms, in particular to the introduction of the system of conscription into the Ottoman army. He makes clear that the deportation was instigated by conservative Muslim circles, who tried to obstruct these reforms and resented newly-introduced religious freedoms. Rosen also notes that British, French and German diplomats provided help to the deportees, and tried to put pressure on the Ottoman government to stop its harsh treatment (Rosen 1866, II:93-8).

---

[8] Gjergji-Gashi takes great pains to establish the exact number of deportees. He arrives at a total number of 166 persons, and when babies born during the period of exile are included, the total number is 176. Not more than 79 persons returned. This means that almost 100 died during their exile (Gjergi-Gashi 1988:51-2). Half of the twenty-five deported families were from Stublla, seven from Binçë, three from Vrnavokolo and two from Terzija (Karadag). To give some indication of the relative importance of these numbers: in 1882 the priest of Letnica, Nikola Mazarek, estimated that the total number of *laraman* families in the Karadag area was 400 at the time of these events (Gjergji-Gashi 1988:144). This means roughly 2,500 persons. The size of the Catholic population was considerably smaller: in 1846, the parish of Letnica counted only 766 Catholics divided over nine villages, *laramans* not included (Gjergji 1972:8).

[9] Gjergji-Gashi's account is based on a great number of original archival documents. He also uses manuscripts and letters written by priests and missionaries. Important sources are two chronicles, one written in 1882 by the local priest (Nikola Mazarek), who based his description on stories told by survivors, and the other by archbishop Dario Bucciarelli. Both have been reprinted in Gjergji-Gashi's book in a Croatian translation. Gjergji-Gashi himself held interviews with old people in Stublla who had known the survivors personally (1988:5).

The Tanzimat reforms and the Franciscan offensive

These events indeed appear closely connected to the new conditions created by the Ottoman reforms commonly referred to as the *Tanzimat* or 'reordering' (1839-76). The primary goal of these reforms was to save and revitalise the Ottoman empire by introducing European standards of organisation and administration. The empire was seriously threatened by administrative chaos, military weakness and the rise of national movements, particularly in the Balkan provinces. The reforms started with the imperial rescript of *Gülhane* (Rose Garden), a declaration of intent from the part of the Ottoman government establishing security of life, honour, and property, introducing a fair and effective system of taxation; a regular army based on conscription; and the equality of all subjects irrespective of religious affiliation (Zürcher 1993:53). The introduction of equal rights for the Christian population was meant to bring to a halt the rise of nationalism, especially in the Balkans. In 1840, a revised penal code was introduced which recognised legal equality for Muslims and non-Muslims, and in 1844 the Porte abolished the death penalty for apostasy from Islam, a measure which applied particularly to recent Muslim converts who wished to return to their original (Christian) faith (Davison 1973:45). This did not bring an end to sanctions against apostasy – a *murtat* ('one who turns back') could be imprisoned or deported instead (Heffening 1993) – but it undoubtedly made conversion of much less consequence.

Yet in practice, many of the reforms were half measures or total failures. They were undermined by many factors, one of which was the conservative opposition of the *ulema* and the majority of Ottoman officials. Also many ordinary Muslim believers resented the doctrine of equality between Muslims and non-Muslims, seeing it as against the natural order of things (Davison 1973:43). This eventually led to fanatical outbursts by Muslims against Christians, especially in towns. The greatest problem was the lack of trained and reliable personnel who could carry through these radical reforms. They often had to be carried out by those very people whose abuses they were intended to stop. The reforms were particularly sabotaged in the provinces, such as Kosovo, where they were still not being fully implemented even decades after they had been introduced. Local notables refused to comply with measures that would inevitably have brought to an end their almost absolute power and introduced a high degree of state intervention from the Ottoman centre.

In the 1830s and 1840s there were numerous Albanian revolts against the reforms. It was especially the conscription system (*nizam*) which met with enormous resistance, as Albanians had been largely exempted from service in the Ottoman army. In Kosovo conscription was introduced in 1843, followed by large-scale uprisings when the Ottomans indeed started recruiting people (Malcolm 1998:185-6). Even though Christians were also required to serve in the army, they were soon offered the alternative of paying a special exemption tax which they usually preferred (Zürcher 1993:59).[10] It is safe to assume, as Rosen (1866) did, that the conversion of *laramans* in Stublla was a local reaction against the introduction of the system of conscription; the same is certainly true for the groups of 'crypto-Catholics' in areas around Gjakova and Peja who converted to Catholicism in 1845 (Gjini 1986: 145; Malcolm 1998:186-7).

In 1856 the Tanzimat went into its second phase of reforms with a new imperial edict, the *Hatt-i-Hümayun*. This edict was proclaimed under major western pressure (especially from France and Britain which had supported the Ottoman empire against Russia during the Crimean War) and laid particular stress on the equality of all peoples of the empire, specifying a number of ways in which this could be guaranteed (Davison 1973:3). The abolition of the death sentence for apostasy was reconfirmed (Davison 1973: 55). As a result of this new edict, the situation for *laramans* (and Catholics) in Kosovo improved notably. After 1856, there were no further reports of serious abuses (Gjini 1986:184; Urošević 1933:168-9).

As the situation for Catholics improved, the Catholic church saw new opportunities to do something about the enormous loss of influence it had suffered in the past. During the seventeenth and eighteenth centuries, many Albanian Catholics had converted to Islam despite attempts by the church leaders and lower clergy to halt this process in one way or another. The response of the church had been quite ambivalent and contradictory: the higher

---

[10] The exemption tax replaced the much resented poll tax for Christians (*cizye*) which had been abolished in accordance with the new Ottoman policy of religious equality.

clergy was usually much stricter than ordinary priests in its condemnation of individual converts. This became clear in 1703 when the first *Concilium Albanicum* (a meeting of Albanian bishops) strictly condemned conversion, especially if done for opportunistic reasons (e.g. to avoid the poll tax). It urged Christians not to adopt signs of Islamic identity (such as Muslim names) or in any other way to pretend to be 'Turks', and not to conceal their Catholic faith before Ottoman officials even in perilous situations (Stadtmüller 1956:73-4). It also explicitly regretted the fact that many Muslim converts still received sacraments from Catholic priests, and it put the blame on the clergy's ignorance. As for baptism, the Council made clear that baptising children of 'Turks' was prohibited under all circumstances.[11]

While higher ecclesiastics favoured a principled approach, local priests and missionaries were much more pragmatic, trying to keep converts within the orbit of the church and tolerating practices that were explicitly forbidden by their church leaders. In particular the Franciscans, who established missionary outposts in Ottoman territories, built up a reputation for tolerating popular customs that did not always correspond with the Church's prescriptions.[12] They continued to administer sacraments like baptism and matrimony to new converts in spite of the church's ban. During the eighteenth and nineteenth century, the Holy See and the Congregation for the Propagation of the Faith (Propaganda Fide) were repeatedly forced to issue strict instructions to their priests how to proceed with these 'crypto-Catholics', and they usually did not allow the administering of sacraments to new converts.[13] In addition, the church hierarchy tried to keep some control over the local priesthood by sending off regular visitation commissions (Radonić 1950).

[11] The baptising of Muslims was quite a common practice among the Orthodox as well as the Roman Catholic priesthood, in Kosovo as well as Bosnia (Filipović 1951).

[12] For the role of the Franciscans in Bosnia, and the traditional rivalry between them and the more recently established diocesan church structures, see Bax (1995).

[13] Similar directives were issued in 1744 by Pope Benedict XIV. According to Gjini's account, further instructions were issued in 1762, 1768, 1840 and 1882 (1986:143-4).

None of these measures, however, was able to bring the process of Islamicisation to a halt. At the start of the nineteenth century, the Catholic church in the Ottoman empire was in a deplorable state. In Kosovo, where the process of Islamicisation was in full swing, the Catholic population was left almost without care of the church, and the bishop of Skopje sent pleas to the Congregation for the Propagation of the Faith to do something about this situation (Gjergji-Gashi 1988:35). There were only six active parishes left in Kosovo (Prizren, Gjakova, Peja, Zym, Janjevo and Letnica) and the total number of Catholic believers was reduced to only 6,000.[14]

In 1835, Propaganda Fide in Rome started to take measures to 'rescue' the *laramans* in the Skopje area,[15] and Letnica was chosen as the centre of Franciscan missionary activity under its direct supervision. In 1838, a year before the start of the Tanzimat reforms, the parish was assigned to Anton Maroević, a Franciscan who as an Austrian citizen – he was born on the Dalmatian island of Hvar – enjoyed some degree of immunity and protection. Taking advantage of the Tanzimat reforms, he tried to encourage the *laramans* to become Catholics. He not only had the support of his superiors, but he also enlisted the help of European diplomats in Constantinople: the case of the *laramans* had thus been 'internationalised' in order to make successful conversion possible (Gjini 1986:181).[16]

Although events around the case of the Stublla martyrs showed that there were still some serious difficulties for (would-be) Catholics to overcome, the church strengthened its influence, especially through the Franciscan mission.[17] The Franciscans in-

[14] Approximately one-sixth were Slavs (in Letnica and Janjevo), the rest Albanians. See the statistics on the last (unnumbered) page of Gjergji-Gashi's book (1988).

[15] This is the purport of a document Gjergji-Gashi found in the Archives of the Congregation for the Propagation of the Faith in Rome (Gjergji-Gashi 1988:81, Document 117; see also p. 26).

[16] Urošević claims that in 1843 Maroević wrote a letter to the French ambassador in Constantinople to ask for his support in case the *laramans* in his parish were to convert to Catholicism (1933:167). In 1842 the Apostolic visitor and administrator Ivan Topić called upon the Congregation for the Propagation of the Faith to 'find a consular protector, whom you could send in these areas. [...] All Albanian crypto-Catholics would publicly and openly confess their national and religious affiliation, and their union with the faith of Christ' (Gjergji-Gashi 1988:28).

[17] The Franciscan order came to Albania in the thirteenth century. During the

tensified their attempts to win the souls of hundreds of *laramans* living in many small and remote villages in Stublla's hinterland.

Here I attempt to reconstruct church policy towards the *laramans* in the period beginning from the 1840s, mainly on the basis of research in the local church archives of the parish of Letnica, where the baptisms of *laramans* were registered meticulously by most of the Catholic priests active in Letnica and Stublla during the nineteenth and the first half of the twentieth centuries. There were several baptismal registers in which *laraman* baptisms were recorded, and I listed all baptisms of *laraman* new-borns (and some adults), usually identifiable from the added qualifications '*(ex) occultis*', '*(ex) parentibus occultis*', or '*(ex) occultis conjugibus*' (the popular expression '*laraman*' is rarely ever used in the church registers). In addition, from these registers it was also possible to gather data on where these *laramans* were living and who the priests were who baptised them. First, I will summarise my main findings, and then try to draw some more general conclusions from them.

Initially priests included *laraman* baptisms in the regular baptismal registers, but afterwards, during a period of almost fifty years (1893-1940), they kept separate books for *laramans*.[18] Between 1842 and 1940, the total number of baptised *laramans* (almost exclusively the new-born) was between 1,700 and 1,800, the bulk of which (almost 95%) occurred in the years between 1872 and 1924. Before and after, the number of baptised *laramans* is

Ottoman empire the order is said to have saved Catholicism in these parts from total extinction, especially during the seventeenth and eighteenth centuries (Skendi 1967:8). In the nineteenth century, the Franciscan mission in Albania gained momentum again under Austrian protection (Malaj 1990). The prominent role of the order in the attempts to revive Catholicism in these Ottoman areas is evident from the fact that in the crucial period between 1845 and 1888 the Franciscans provided as many as three archbishops in the archdiocese of Skopje.

[18] I found three registers which contain only baptismal records of *laramans*: one without a title, concerning the years 1893-1924 (including a few baptisms in 1940), *Liber Baptizatorum Occultorum br. 1* (for 1906-15) and *Liber Baptizatorum Occultorum br.2* (1920-36). The first belonged to the parish of Letnica, and the second and third to the parish of Stublla, which was established as a separate parish in 1906. For the period before 1893, when baptisms of *laramans* were not registered separately, I found two registers in which baptisms of *laramans* were recorded: *Libro dei Battezzati della Parrocchia di Zarnagora dall'Anno d'84-due* (for 1842-64) and *Matična knjiga rodjenih od 1866 do 1889 god. – Letnica* (1866-89).

small. It is remarkable that for the years of Anton Maroević's presence in Letnica as parish priest (1842-56) I could find not one case of a *laraman* baptism, at least not in the register I saw. For the years between 1857 and 1865 I counted seven cases of baptism of crypto-Catholics, which indicates that the phenomenon of baptising *laramans* started gradually after the introduction of the Ottoman reforms of 1856.[19] The year 1866 was truly exceptional with more than twenty-five baptisms in one year, which can be explained by the fact that in that year the church of Letnica was built. Another element that is likely to have played a part in this process is the fact that in 1865 the Ottoman government made an end to the tyrannical rule of the Gjinolli family in the districts of Gjilan and Prishtina (Maletić 1973:146, 676). After 1872, the baptising of *laramans* became a normal phenomenon: the average number of *laraman* baptisms was over thirty per year, with numbers increasing in later years. In 1925, the number dropped again drastically to only six (from forty-seven cases in 1924), and in the following years, there were only a few cases.

Most priests also noted the matrimonial status of the parents of the baptised child. Roughly half of the baptised children between 1842 and 1940 were born in marriages not consecrated by the church ('*ex illegitimis conjugibus*'), with a preponderance of 'illegitimate' cases until the 1880s and 1890s. The villages mentioned most frequently in the records are (in order of importance) Dunav, Selište, Stublla, Sefer, Kureć, Stančić and Terzija. One Catholic priest was particularly active in baptising crypto-Catholics: Don Michael Tarabulusi, who between 1893 and 1992 baptised almost 500 *laramans*, registering them separately (in a special register for them alone). In 1897, he became *administrator parochialis* of Stublla and later, when the parish of Stublla was founded (1906), was appointed its first parish priest. Also, one archbishop contributed his mite when visiting the area: between 1880 and 1882 Fulgentius Carev (a Franciscan from Dalmatia) baptised a number of adults during a mass in Letnica in the presence of other Muslims. Apart

---

[19] We should bear in mind that at this stage the usual parochial tasks of parish priests, such as the administering of baptism and matrimony, were probably not the Franciscans' main priority. They were much more engaged in trying to prepare the ground for that, i.e. to map the (crypto-)Catholic population of the area, to create an infrastructure, to build a church, etc.

from that, the archbishops of Skopje regularly inspected the baptismal registers and approved them with their signature. One of the most interesting elements of these registers is that priests often recorded two names for a baptised child of *laraman* background. Apart from the Catholic name, they also wrote down the Muslim name given by the parents, which would be the one used in public. So boys might have such pairs of names as Mark-Muharem, Simon-Osman, David-Tefik, Mark-Ali, Simon-Serifi, Zefi-Mehmeti. Often they were phonetically similar. The majority of girls were baptised Mary, whereas their Muslim names varied: e.g. Amide, Baftia, Arifia, Kadisha, Zaide, Tahibe, Fata, Raba, Hajria. The church probably used the widespread veneration for Mary by *laraman* (and Muslim) women as its main leverage to incorporate these groups into the church, i.e. as one of the devices to (re-) Catholicise part of the Islamicised population in the Karadag mountains.

The attempts to bring 'crypto-Catholics' within the church's orbit continued well into the twentieth century, especially after the Ottomans were swept from the region in the First Balkan War. Kosovo became part of Serbia (1912), and was later incorporated in the Kingdom of Serbs, Croats and Slovenes (1918). After World War I, the main role regarding the *laramans* was reserved for Ivan Franjo Gnidovec, a Lazarist from Slovenia who was bishop of Skopje from 1924 to 1939. He put most of his energies into restoring the church after five centuries of Turkish rule, *inter alia* by building new churches in places that did not have a church before (Osvald 1989). He attempted to bring Catholics and *laramans* in isolated and remote places more into contact with organised church life, and Letnica became the main pilgrimage shrine in the diocese (Turk 1973:18). Between 1928 and 1934 he built a new church in Letnica. In the 1930s, he also built the church of St Anne in the small and remote village of Dunav, one of the main crypto-Catholic centres in the Karadag, in spite of opposition by local Muslim Albanians and the Serbian authorities in Gnjilane (Sopi 1989:184). By creating a devotion to St Anne, the church probably hoped to reach the local *laraman* families through their mothers and grandmothers.[20]

---

[20] St Anne is believed to be the mother of the Virgin Mary and grandmother of Jesus. As she gave birth to Mary at an advanced age, after God answered

Gnidovec also seems to have been behind the drastic fall in
laraman baptisms after 1924 observable in the baptismal records.
This development coincides with his appointment as bishop of
Skopje in November 1924, and it was possibly the result of a
change in church policy introduced or implemented by him. I
suggest that a possible explanation for this fall in *laraman* baptisms
is not a mass conversion to Catholicism but rather the unwillingness
of the bishop to tolerate these baptisms any further. After the
end of Ottoman rule there was no need for *laramans* to conceal
their Catholic identity, as he and other Catholic ecclesiastics might
have thought. By taking a tougher line, they could probably be
forced to abandon Islam and become Catholics once and for all.
Indeed, only a few years later (in 1929), some *laraman* families
converted to Catholicism, in Stublla, Terzija and some other villages
in the Karadag (Sopi 1989:185; Turk 1992:149). These collective
conversions continued into the 1930s. However, a considerable
group of crypto-Catholics did not convert because of traditional
marital ties with Muslim clans and out of fear of their Muslim-
dominated environment. I heard that in Stublla in these years
Catholics organised negotiations with *laramans* in order to facilitate
their conversion to Catholicism. Since these *laramans* feared repercussions from Muslim clans and deplored the loss of the bride-price
for their daughters, they demanded compensation. The inhabitants
of Stublla are said to have collected money to pay it, although
this did not bring the desired result.[21] In addition it seems that
the Yugoslav authorities were obstructing the bishop's attempts
to bring about these conversions of *laramans* to Catholicism (Sopi
1989: 182-3).

The failure to reconvert a large number of crypto-Catholics

---

her prayers to become pregnant, St Anne is often invoked by women who
want children. As the grandmother of Jesus, she has been an example for grandmothers, especially in rural societies, where extended families are still dominant.
Grandmothers usually manage household life and help their kin in their life
crises. The main domains of St Anne are thus procreation, matrimony and the
household. She is the patroness of mothers, pregnant women and widows. In
the second half of the nineteenth century there was a revival of devotion to
her, parallel to the Marian revival (Brandenberg *et al.* 1992).

[21] In his article on the parish of Letnica, Urošević mentions that there were
still *laramans* in most villages of the Karadag, although it was impossible for
him to establish their exact numbers (1933:167).

shows that their identity was perhaps less 'Catholic' than the church hoped. As stated in the introduction to this chapter, their sense of identity was probably ambiguous and fragmented. Their memories of Catholic belonging were diffuse, and knowledge about religious prescriptions and obligations shallow. Therefore, it is important to be cautious in assuming that these people were consciously aware of the fact that they were 'combining' two distinct faiths. Many ordinary believers probably did not perceive their religious life in terms of a split between two separate traditions, of which one was 'false' and for outside consumption while the other was secret and 'genuine'. As Malcolm has noted, 'With so many practices either shared or replicated between the faiths, these people probably did not notice such a dramatic difference in kind between all forms of Christianity on the one hand and Islam on the other' (Malcolm 1998:131).[22]

With this in mind, the notion of crypto-Catholicism should be treated with caution, at least where the early nineteenth century is concerned. It seems likely that when the church first re-established its presence in the area, crypto-Catholicism was more an idea propagated by the church than a genuinely popular phenomenon.[23] Yet the fact that the church started to develop policies on the basis of its categorisations produced self-fulfilling prophesies: in the end, crypto-Catholicism became increasingly real in the minds of the people involved. As Malcolm has noted, the complicity of the priests was of crucial importance for the existence of cryp-to-Catholicism: 'without the co-operation of the priests, crypto-

[22] There is some ethnographic evidence to show that there was a great deal of overlap in Muslim and Catholic customs. Baptism was not only demanded by crypto-Catholics; real 'Turks' (Muslim Albanians) also quite commonly asked for it, particularly for male children (Filipović 1951:121). It is unclear whether Catholic priests drew a clear boundary between these two categories in accepting or refusing such a demand. The adoption of double names was also not typical only of crypto-Catholics. Nopcsa notes that Muslim names were very popular among Catholics in northern Albania, for instance among the Mirdites (Nopcsa 1907:29). Also Filipović mentions that it was common for Catholic Albanians to adopt Muslim names as a protective measure against 'evil' (1951:125). See also Malcolm (1998:132).

[23] See Peyfuss (1992), who follows a similar argument. He stresses 'the traditionally very low level of education (including religious education) of the rural population of the Balkans, including the clergy' (1992:132), as the main reason for widespread ignorance of religious doctrine and ritual practice.

Christianity could not function properly at all' (Malcolm 1997:11).[24] This case shows, more generally, that it is not easy to disentangle the legacies of religious 'mixing', and that it is difficult to establish religious orthodoxy in peripheral and/or frontier situations (as it is already in homogeneous situations), especially if no solid ecclesiastic organisation is present. The belief systems of ordinary people at the intersections of different states and religious formations are often based on unconscious and unreflective fusion and borrowing. The centres of religious power have tried to overcome this situation, attempting to eradicate these elements of mixture and multiple religious 'orientations', and pressing for clear-cut single identities, by various means and mostly with limited success.

Catholic priests told me that at the time when I was doing my fieldwork, there were still *laramans* in the Karadag, in some remote places like the villages around Dunav. After half a century of almost complete silence, crypto-Catholicism became visible again, attracting renewed attention in Kosovo and beyond (see for instance Sabalić 1991). This interest, shared by Catholic and Muslim Albanians alike, had a clear political background related to questions of Albanian national identity: 'Who are the Albanians?' and 'Where do we belong: in the East or in the West?'. When Kosovo's autonomy was abolished (in 1989) and the Albanians started to organise their resistance, these questions were most acute, but the answer was formulated almost immediately: Albanians need to look to the West instead of the East for help and political support. Shkëlzen Maliqi, a leading intellectual from Kosovo, wrote that at that time many Albanians were considering renouncing Islam to become Catholics, which they saw as the direction to take if Western sympathy was to be obtained: 'During 1990, when the situation in Kosovo deteriorated day by day, Muslim Albanians were openly reflecting on the idea of a collective con-

---

[24] Urošević provides us with one further interesting detail: on some post-World War I Yugoslav maps the Karadag area is designated as 'Laraman', although the toponym is never used there. According to Urošević, it has been copied from older Austrian maps (Urošević 1933:167). The ethnographic as well as geographic label apparently developed in conjunction; church policy and Austrian imperial policy coincided.

version to Roman Catholicism. They asked themselves and friends around – some of this I heard myself – whether it was possible to return to the "faith of our ancestors' " (1997:119). Muslims even started to go *en masse* to Catholic services, especially during Christmas and other important festivals.

Again crypto-Catholicism became a useful concept to think with and to do politics with, as it helped the Albanians to present themselves as an originally 'Christian' and 'European' nation in spite of their present-day Muslim appearance. Instead of causing religious troubles – as it had done in the middle of the nineteenth century – crypto-Catholicism now became a concept that united the Kosovo Albanians, making Islam and Christianity both part of their common identity.

5

ALBANIAN DERVISHES *VERSUS* BOSNIAN ULEMA
THE REVIVAL OF POPULAR SUFISM IN KOSOVO

In the West many people tend to regard the Muslim world as an undiversified and monolithic entity, and this image has been replicated for Islam in the Balkans as well. Although there is a vague notion of Bosnian Muslims being more 'European' than those in Turkey and the Middle East, the Western view is still dominated by a general fear of Islam as a religion which threatens European and Christian civilisation. This fear is not exclusive to Western Europe, but has been strong in the Balkans as well, particularly in Serbia but also (to a lesser extent) in Croatia, where the image of the oriental 'other' has also been projected on to the 'Byzantine' Serbs (Bakić-Hayden and Hayden 1992). In this system of 'nesting orientalisms' the Serbian version has been most outspokenly Islamophobic and primarily directed against immediate neighbours: the Albanians in Kosovo and the Muslims in Bosnia. Open animosity towards these Muslims surfaced several years before the outbreak of the war, particularly after Milošević's rise to power in 1987. At that time the Serbian nationalist mass media started to depict them as fundamentalists who were embarking on a *jihad* against the Orthodox Serbs.

This chapter is intended to show that Balkan Islam is not a monolith and, as in most other parts of the Muslim world, encompasses a broad variety of forms and expressions, which have given rise to internal conflicts and divisions (Poulton and Taji-Farouki 1997:2). The focus of this chapter is on the division between dominant and orthodox (Sunni) Islam and popular Sufism in Yugoslavia during the 1970s and '80s, which to some extent coincides with the ethnic and geographic divide between Albanians in Kosovo and Slavic Muslims in Bosnia. In the middle of the 1980s Alexandre Popovic wrote a short introduction on dervish orders in Yugoslavia

(1985), in which he notes that although they have almost completely disappeared in the rest of south-eastern Europe, Yugoslavia forms a marked exception: 'The Muslim mystic orders of this country have not only continued to exist, but moreover seem to be characterised by a renewal that is very curious and at the very least unexpected. This is all the more so as these orders, after a difficult survival at the end of the nineteenth and the first half of the present century, tend to disappear from 1945 onwards' (1985:240).

Popovic observes the revival of popular Sufism in Kosovo, but does not provide an explanation, which is attempted in this chapter. It shows that the phenomenon is not particularly linked to the rise of tension between Serbs and Albanians, a view echoed in the Serbian nationalist press, but that another divide proves much more salient: namely, that between the dervish orders in Kosovo, which recruit their membership primarily from the Albanian rural masses, and the Bosnian-dominated official Islamic Community (based in Sarajevo). In the first place, the conflict between dervish leaders and the Islamic Community, as manifested in Yugoslavia in the 1970s and '80s, is an example of the classic antagonism existing between orthodox Islam and heterodox Sufi orders. This is all the more obvious since the conflict has been couched mainly in religious terms. Nevertheless, the antagonism appears to have had an ethnic dimension as well: the revival of popular Sufism was largely confined to the Albanian-inhabited areas of Yugoslavia (particularly Kosovo), and although at the beginning a small number of Bosnian sheikhs joined the Albanian sheikhs in their opposition to the Bosnian Muslim establishment, they soon pulled out, returning to the ranks of the Islamic Community. The vigorous polemics that developed between Albanian sheikhs and the representatives of the Muslim establishment can be seen in the light of the asymmetric relations which existed between Albanians and Bosnian Muslims, within the Islamic Community and in society as a whole. It is those segments of the rural Albanian population that are socially and politically most deprived, in those areas of Kosovo that are most underdeveloped and peripheral, which have comprised the backbone of the dervish movement.

Although I will describe in some detail the way Serbian nationalist journalists and scientists have dealt with this subject, presenting dervish orders as the vanguard of Islamic fundamentalism and Albanian nationalism, I will concentrate on how came to view it in the course of my fieldwork – not so much as an expression of 'Albanian' fundamentalism and anti-Serbianness, but rather as an example of a religious protest movement carried almost exclusively by Albanian Muslims, rebelling against the Islamic establishment. By using religious ecstasy, one of the most powerful 'weapons of the weak' (Scott 1990:140-2), Albanian sheikhs and dervishes have tried to overcome their position as second-rank believers within the Islamic Community. Although the renewal of dervish orders in Kosovo has other (social) causes as well (as is shown later), the growing ethnic division within the Islamic Community in Yugoslavia, between Bosnian Muslims and Muslim Albanians, seems to be one of its major components.

Dervishes under attack from Serbian nationalists

We start here with a description of the 'Sultani-Nevrus'[1] ritual of the Rufai dervishes in Prizren. This ritual, the trademark of the Rufia dervishes in Prizren, is a relatively violent one in which dervishes, in a state of trance, pierce their cheeks and throats with needles and swords. It is a highly theatrical performance, a demonstration of the 'true' faith, which takes place in the presence of a huge and excited audience. As an old dervish told me, 'Through this ritual we show that our faith is strong and authentic. By piercing ourselves we repeat the miracles [*keramet*] that Hazreti Ali [Mohammed's cousin and son-in-law] once performed, proving that God is on our side. While we pierce, we do not bleed and we feel no pain because He is protecting us.'

The impact of this performance, in which about eighty dervishes participate, is overwhelming. The monotonous sound and entrancing rhythm of the songs, which last for several hours, is also very much a physical experience for the audience. The dervishes, by moving their bodies to and fro on the accelerating pulse of the music, by singing and shouting loudly and breathing deeply to the rhythm of the music, slowly fall into a deep trance. After the sheikh perforates the cheeks of young and inexperienced dervishes, the climax of the ritual draws near when the sheikh and

---

[1] The term *Sultani-Nevruz* or *Nevruzi-Sultan* is of Persian origin. It means 'New Day', i.e. the first day of spring (21 March). The following description is based on my visit on 22 March 1989.

some older dervishes start to produce a deafening noise with cymbals and drums. Now it is the turn of a small number of religious virtuosi, four aged dervishes who 'dance' with long needles, throw their bodies on to the sharp ends and finally pierce their throats and cheeks. They are surrounded by the other dervishes who watch this scene, moving their bodies and holding needles – pierced through their cheeks – between their teeth. Finally the sheikh takes a sword, passes it slowly between his lips and puts it with its edge on the bare stomach of an older dervish who is lying on the floor. After the sheikh mounts the sword, he repeats the same procedure with another dervish, but now the sword is placed on the dervish's throat. A small child is put on top of it, with its feet on the edge of the sword, and is paraded around. Finally, the sheikh stabs his own cheek with a long sword.

In the second half of the 1980s, the seeming irrationality and violence of this ritual (which has always attracted attention in the media) reinforced the stereotypical image of Islam and fuelled growing anti-Muslim sentiment in Serbia. Occasionally these sentiments were directly targeted at dervishes, especially in the Serbian nationalist press where they were portrayed as Muslim fanatics, fundamentalists and, at the same time, Albanian nationalist extremists. The best example is the writing of the political scientist Miroljub Jevtić, the most outspoken recent protagonist of Serbian Islamophobia. From the late 1980s he popularised his ideas about Islam – in particular about the Muslim Albanians in Kosovo and the Slavic Muslims in Bosnia – through numerous articles and interviews in newspapers like *Politika, Intervju* and *Svet*. In his first book *Savremeni džihad kao rat* (Contemporary Jihad as War), published in 1989, he accused sheikhs and dervishes of condoning the continuous emigration of Serbs from Kosovo.

It is logical that many excesses and attacks on the Slavs would not have taken place if sheikhs and Muslim priests had protested against them. [...] In this sense, one can ask what sheikhs have done to stop the sale of Serbian property, in Djakovica where they are very strong and also elsewhere. All this becomes clearer when one knows that during the war [World War II] almost all the members of Muslim dervish brotherhoods in Yugoslavia collaborated with the Albanian separatist movement (Jevtić 1989:314).[2]

---

[2] Jevtić published a second book, dealing with the war in Bosnia, *Od islamske*

Similar views were expressed in a book called *Tajne albanske mafije* (Secrets of the Albanian Mafia) – best characterised as nationalist pulp – written by the journalist Dejan Lučić (1988). In one chapter the author provides a short anthology of quotes about dervishes in Kosovo which supposedly reveal their political role us the main stormtroops of Muslim fundamentalism in Yugoslavia, acting with the tacit support of Islamic Community officials in Sarajevo. Jevtić, who is represented as a specialist on the subject, is quoted extensively: among other things he claims that dervishes not only want a Greater Albania but want to create a Balkan *Islamistan* uniting Albania and Bosnia-Hercegovina.

Apart from these two publications, the Serbian press produced an image of dervishes as bloodthirsty fanatics, who kill in fits of insanity and blindly follow the orders of their sheikhs. In one article a monk described a gruesome spectacle in the yard of the Ostrog monastery in which dervishes killed a big ram, tied up to a big tree by its legs and hanging head down:

> The unlucky animal bleated helplessly. As if they were getting drunk on rancour, they started a crazy 'game' with the knives which were glimmering in their hands. They moved away from the suffering animal and started to aim at it from a distance. The blades went bluntly into the warm body which curled up and quivered with pain. The blood was running down the womb and the head of the increasingly exhausted animal. The bleating became less and less powerful until it faded away above a big puddle of blood (Lučić 1988:94).[3]

Leading sheikhs from Kosovo denied any involvement in these happenings and sent official complaints to the newspaper and the authorities for religious affairs in Serbia, Montenegro and Kosovo, but nothing was done.[4] Apart from this case, Albanian dervishes were also mentioned in connection with another affair, magnified

---

deklaracije do verskog rata u BiH (From the Islamic declaration to religious war in Bosnia-Hercegovina), in 1993, and a compilation of his articles on Albanians, *Šiptari i Islam* (Albanians and Islam) in 1995. See also Mufaku (1993).

[3] This passage is reprinted in Lučić's book, with the following comment: 'The massacring of animals in which a lot of blood flows is meant TO FRIGHTEN THE MONTENEGRIN PEOPLE (*sic*), who have not yet had as much experience with Albanian expansionism as the people in Kosovo and Macedonia' (Lučić 1988:94)

[4] See *Derviš* (Prizren), October 1988, pp.23-7.

in the familiar nationalist propagandist fashion of the time: the so-called Prizren trial (Bulatović 1988). This political trial, at which a number of Albanians were sentenced for espionage on behalf of Albania's *Sigurimi*, took place in the 1950s. One of the most influential sheikhs in Kosovo, Sheikh Muhjedin (from the Halveti lodge in Rahovec), was a key witness at this trial after he had been sentenced for similar offences in the so-called 'sheikhs' trial'. Both affairs cast an unfavourable light on the activities of the Albanian dervish orders in Kosovo. Apart from being branded as nationalists and as key figures in the political machinations there during the 1940s and '50s, dervishes were portrayed as religious fanatics, and sheikhs as small potentates with enormous power over their followers, reinforcing an image of Islam as irrational and totalitarian. The Serbian journalist Liljana Bulatović wrote of the sheikhs: 'They are like small gods, and everybody will defend their authority at any cost' (Bulatović 1988:41).[5]

Dervish orders in Kosovo: a survey

After the communists took over power in Yugoslavia in 1945, it seemed inevitably that dervish orders would slowly disappear, as they have done in most other parts of the Balkans. At the end of World War II, the communists launched a rigorous anti-religious campaign: freedom of religion was curtailed, the power of the churches was restricted, and religious leaders were appointed who were loyal to the regime. Priests opposing the new socialist order were sidelined and in some cases even physically liquidated (Ramet 1998). Most of the dervish orders were pushed underground: more than other religious communities, they tend to resist outside control because their religious leadership is family-based, i.e. based on the principle of inherited spiritual power.

Eventually, in the 1960s, Yugoslav policy towards the religious communities became much more liberal, yet under a regime that remained essentially totalitarian in character; freedom of religion was still conditional. The churches were expected to pledge full

---

[5] In July 1998 Sheikh Muhjedin was murdered in his lodge, probably by the Serbian police (Amnesty International, *A Human Rights Crisis in Kosovo Province. Document Series B: Tragic events continue, #3 Orahovac, July-August 1998, AI Index: EUR 70/58/98*, pp.4-6).

loyalty to the communist authorities, who supervised their activities through the special Commissions for Religious Matters, which were represented at all levels of the administration. The official Islamic Community, in particular, was co-opted by the Communist system, more than the Catholic and Serbian Orthodox churches: its close symbiosis with the regime was facilitated by Tito's benevolent attitude towards the Muslim world as one of the leaders of the Conference of Non-aligned States. It was sometimes compared with a melon: green (the colour of Islam) outside but thoroughly red inside.

In 1952 the Islamic Community officially prohibited the work of dervish orders in Bosnia-Hercegovina (Hadžibajrić 1979:273; see also *Glasnik Vrhovnog Islamskog Starješinstva* 1952:199). As Sorabji has noted, 'When the *Zajednica* [the Islamic Community] realised that in such a [socialist] state there was only so much religious authority to go round, they were anxious to have as much of it as possible [...] and to quell any potential competitors' (Sorabji 1989:163). The impact of this ban was severe. Most dervish lodges were closed down and handed over to the Islamic Community, as a result of which some continued their activities in private homes or in mosques. Even though the prohibition formally did not apply to Kosovo and Macedonia, the number of lodges there also declined rapidly, probably as a side-effect of the persecution and discrimination Albanians suffered in the 1950s. In those years most lodges led a semi-clandestine existence. In 1962 the Islamic officials in Sarajevo tried to extend their ban on dervish orders to Kosovo and Macedonia, labelling them as reactionary and 'an obstacle to the development of a proper religious life in these areas' (*Glasnik Vrhovnog Islamskog Starješinstva* 1962:186). However, this ban seems never to have been carried out presumably because the state authorities disapproved of such a measure. The regime thrived best on a policy of divide and rule, playing religious and ethnic communities off against one another.

During this period, many observers expected that dervish orders would cease to exist, as happened in most other Balkan states. However this was contradicted by an unexpected revival of the phenomenon in the 1970s. In 1974 Albanian sheikhs from Kosovo founded an association of dervish orders which has been headed since then by a Rufai sheikh from Prizren (Sheikh Xhemali

Albanian sheikh standing beside tombs, Prizren, autumn 1986.

Shehu).[6] Three years later this Association of Dervish Orders was recognised as an independent religious community, despite major objections by the Islamic leaders in Sarajevo, who protested vehemently at the creation of a second Muslim religious community in Yugoslavia and at the publication of the dervish bulletin *Hu*. In spite of such opposition, this new Community of Dervish Orders recruited many fresh members, i.e. sheikhs as well as lower clergy and other religious functionaries.[7] Within ten years (between 1974 and 1984), its membership grew from thirty-two

[6] The association was called *Lidhja e Rradhëve Dervishe Islame Alijje*, three years later renamed as *Bashkësia e Rradhëve Dervishe Islame Alijje* (henceforth 'the Community of Dervish Orders'). In Serbo-Croat the organisation was first called *Savez Islamskih Derviških Redova Alijje* and accordingly renamed *Zajednica Islamskih Derviških Redova Alijje*. The first initiatives to create this association were taken in 1971.

[7] Not only sheikhs were invited to become members, but also *veqils* (deputies of a sheikh) and other functionaries of dervish lodges, like *rehbers* (guides), *tyrbedars* (who take care of the graves) and *kafexhi*-s (who receive the guests and serve coffee and tea) (*Buletin HU* 1978/(2):3).

members (representing a corresponding number of lodges) to 126 members in 1984. The increase was highest in 1980 when the association enrolled no less than forty-two new members (*Buletin HU* 1984:12). In the early 1980s the Community claimed to represent more than 50,000 dervishes, mainly concentrated in Kosovo (*Bilten HU* 1982/2:2).[8] The Priština sociologist Sladjana Djurić mentions that they now claim to have 100,000 followers in Kosovo alone (1998:107).

The Community recognises twelve 'authentic' orders of which nine were active before the start of the war in the former Yugoslavia (in Kosovo, Bosnia and Macedonia): the Rufai, Kaderi, Halveti, Sadi, Bektashi, Nakshibendi, Sinani, Mevlevi and Shazili (*Buletin Hu* 1978(2):6). In 1986 most of these orders were not significant in terms of numbers of lodges and members. However, some orders (notably the Halveti, the Sadi, the Kaderi and the Rufai) had a large membership, with thousands of followers and a widely ramified network of lodges. The bulk of lodges are located in small towns and a number of villages, whereas in Prishtina there is only one (Kaderi) lodge. In Prizren and especially in Gjakova the concentration of lodges is much higher. At the time of my research, the total number of lodges in Kosovo was approximately sixty (*Bilten Hu* 1982/2:2-3). This situation had probably not changed substantially at the time of writing.[9]

In Kosovo the phenomenon is geographically not evenly divided.

---

[8] With the help of Alexandre Popovic I have been able to collect an almost complete set of issues of the dervish bulletin *Hu* for the 1970s and 1980s, which was published both in Albanian and Serbo-Croat. *Buletin Hu* refers to the issue in Albanian, *Bilten Hu* to the one in Serbo-Croat.

[9] On the basis of my research in 1986 I have compiled the following list: *Halveti* lodges can be found in Prizren, Rahovec (Orahovac), Gjakova (Djakovica), Peja (Peć), Mitrovica, and the villages of Junik (near Gjakova), Damnjan (in the Has area at the border with Albania between Prizren and Gjakova), Lukinaj (Has), Rogovo (near Gjakova), and Hoça e Vogel (near Rahovec). *Kaderi*: Prizren, Gjakova, Rahovec, Peja, Prishtina, and the village of Lubizhda (Has). *Rufai*: Prizren, Gjakova, Rahovec, Mitrovica, Peja, and Gjilan (Gnjilane). *Sadi*: Gjakova, Prizren, Gjilan, and the villages of Bec, Doblibar, Crmjane, Duzhne (all near Gjakova). *Shazili*: Gjakova. *Nakshibendi*: Gjakova, and the village of Planeja (Has). *Bektashi*: Gjakova. *Melami*: Prizren and Rahovec. *Sinani*: Prizren. I visited some lodges myself (in 1986). For a very similar list, see Djurić (1998:108). Other lodges are located in Montenegro (Ulcinj, Podgorica) and western Macedonia (Skopje, Ohrid, Tetovo and some other towns).

The density of lodges is much higher in the south-west, in the region bordering Albania (which is best known under the Serbian name Metohija). This area is fertile but underdeveloped and densely populated, and includes the towns of Prizren, Rahovec (Orahovac), Peja (Peć) and Gjakova (Djakovica). It comprises one-third of the province, but contains up to three-quarters of all the lodges. Here the vast majority of the rural population either belong to or sympathise with one of the numerous lodges. Most of them recruit their followers among the poor and uneducated peasantry in the rural areas, although some of the most active lodges also attract young male students of rural background. Popovic seems to be right in suggesting that the centre of gravity of the phenomenon has been gradually shifting to the countryside (Popovic 1985:247).[10] In some rural areas like Has (a mountainous area bordering Albania) the influence of sheikhs has unmistakably grown at the expense of orthodox (Sunni) *imams*.[11]

Among the traditional urban population of Kosovo – at least in Prizren – their following has been almost negligible. Many townsmen qualify the whole phenomenon as an anachronism which is typical of the backward and patriarchal way of life of Albanian peasants. It was a common urban opinion that peasants were most receptive to the superstitious beliefs of these 'sects' and the strict discipline imposed by the sheikhs. However, in Gjakova and Rahovec, two small agricultural towns west of Prizren, the situation is quite different: most of their inhabitants are members of a dervish lodge. Here religious (and social) life is completely tied up with these orders, and religious authority is pre-eminently vested in the sheikhs. It is important to note that the phenomenon is ethnically exclusive, i.e. confined to Albanians: Turks and Slavic Muslims do almost not participate. Only among Gypsies do dervish orders seem to flourish: numerous lodges seem to have been springing up in the poor and overpopulated Gypsy ghettos of the towns (Popovic 1985:245-6). Though the similarly poor social-

[10] See also Kasumi, who states that the Rufai order recruits its followers predominantly from the poor layers of society (1988:66).

[11] In 1979 the dean of the *medresa* (Muslim religious seminary) in Prishtina expressed his concern about the developments in Has, where inhabitants had stopped inviting *imams* during Ramadan. Instead they now 'see all their spiritual happiness as being in the hands of the sheikh' (Ahmeti 1979:284).

economic status of both Albanian peasants and urban Gypsies may account for this, it is essentially a parallel development which has been neatly divided along ethnic lines. The Gypsy lodges are not part of the dervish movement, and the Community of Dervish Orders represents the Albanian orders alone.[12]

In Bosnia, the heartland of Islam in former Yugoslavia, this renewal of popular Islamic mysticism has largely been absent. Although Bosnian Sufi orders have a long and rich history, in recent decades there remained only a handful of active lodges.[13] Their position improved in 1977 after the Islamic Community agreed on a conditional re-opening of lodges, although the 1952 ban on dervish orders was never formally lifted (Hadžibajrić 1990). It is clear that these orders have lacked the widespread allegiance and popularity of their Kosovo counterparts, because of their orthodox and Sunni character (Norris 1993:100-1). During the Ottoman period both the Bosnian *ulema* and the authorities tried to pursue a policy of protection and support for the orthodox orders in order to prevent the spread of more unorthodox *tarikats* like the Bektashi. As Norris points out, Bosnian Sufism has been elitist, somewhat quietist, sober and subdued, contrasting markedly with the ecstatic and violent forms of popular Sufism in Kosovo and Macedonia (1993:114). When all Bosnian lodges were closed in 1952, Bosnian sheikhs and dervishes never set up any organisation in defiance of the official Islamic Community; the aim was to win back the right to exist through negotiation with the Community (Sorabji 1989:163).

In the 1970s the Bosnian lodges continued to follow a very prudent and non-confrontational policy towards the Islamic authorities in Sarajevo, even though they were now able to function more openly. They continued to recognise the authority of the

[12] In 1986 I visited two Gypsy lodges in the Terzi *mahala*, a Gypsy quarter in Prizren, not far from the Rufai lodge of Sheikh Xhemali Shehu. It seems that originally both were offshoots of the 'Albanian' lodge of which Sheikh Xhemali is now the leader. They were founded some decades ago by former Gypsy dervishes of this lodge. At present there are no formal ties, which indicates a breach along ethnic lines. Popovic observes a similar division between 'Albanian' and 'Gypsy' lodges for the Sinani (1991:109).

[13] Sorabji mentions five: one Kaderi and four Nakshibendi (Sorabji 1989:165). For a detailed account of dervish orders in Bosnia see Ćehajić (1986). See also Popovic (1994).

Gypsy dervish piercing himself in Rufai lodge, Terzi *mahala*, Prizren, autumn 1986.

Islamic Community as legitimate and tried to accommodate themselves to its rulings (Sorabji 1989:158). The Bosnian dervish orders also differ in other ways from those in Kosovo. The Bosnian sheikhs' authority does not extend beyond religious matters, which is quite different from the situation in Kosovo (Sorabji 1989:166). Furthermore, as Sorabji states, 'Unlike their Albanian counterparts, contemporary Bosnian dervishes do not appear to indulge in practices such as standing on sabres and piercing the cheek with needles (although certain evidence suggests that the practice continues in great secrecy and with low frequency in the countryside)' (Sorabji 1989:167-8).[14]

---

[14] There is, however, a recent current of Sufism which Sorabji labels New Mysticism. It is scripturalist and intellectual in character and has been popular among young educated Bosnian Muslims since the 1980s. These New Mystics do not constitute a religious movement in the usual sense – they have no recognisable organisation – but are instead grouped around a number of charismatic leaders, 'men who call themselves Sufis and who are deemed by their followers to be sheikhs'. Contrary to traditional mysticism, many of the sympathisers are female. Although the number of practising New Mystics is probably not very high, they are much esteemed and respected among the Muslim population (Sorabji 1989:172-3).

Polemics between Kosovar sheikhs and the Islamic Community

The conformism of the Bosnian dervish orders has contrasted sharply with the recalcitrant stand of the Kosovo sheikhs, who have engaged in open conflict with representatives of the Islamic Community. These differences came to light soon after the establishment of the Association (later Community) of Dervish Orders, especially when Muslim religious officials put strong pressure on the Bosnian sheikhs to abandon the movement, which they did.[15] In return for their loyalty, the Islamic Community allowed Bosnian lodges to function more or less normally again. The establishment of the *Tarikat Centar* in Sarajevo in 1977 almost completely ended the work of the Community of Dervish Orders where the Bosnian lodges were concerned (Hadžibajrić 1979:276; Hadžibajrić 1990:22-3; *Bilten Hu* 1979(1):3-4). Except for one Rufai lodge in Sarajevo, which served Kosovo Albanians working and living in Sarajevo, all other Bosnian sheikhs (most of them belonging to the Nakshibendi order) enrolled in the *Tarikat Centar*. Leading sheikhs in Kosovo regarded this as a serious attempt to weaken the position of their Community (*Bilten Hu* 1978:13-14).

Here we will concentrate on the polemics that evolved between Albanian sheikhs and Bosnian spokesmen of the Islamic Community, in which neither side took much trouble to mince words. For the Sarajevan Islamic authorities the founding of the Association of Dervish Orders in 1974 was an act almost of blasphemy. They also protested against the publication of the bulletin *Hu*, and considered taking legal measures to make the work of the Community of Dervish Orders impossible (*Glasnik Vrhovnog Islamskog Starješinstva* 1975:296). They launched fierce attacks in the Islamic

---

[15] Details on the establishment and subsequent development of the Association (later Community) of Dervish Orders can be found in Hadžibajrić (1979 and 1990), as well as in some articles and (anonymous) editorials in *Bilten/Buletin Hu* (1978(2):4-5, 1978(3):8-11, 1978(4):12-16, 1981(3-4):34-6 and in particular 1984/(2) which contains the proceedings of a meeting on the occasion of the 10th anniversary of the association). See also the inaugural speech of Sheikh Xhemali Shehu after he was elected president of the Association of Dervish Orders (*Bilten Hu* 1975). Initially Sheikh Xhemali Shehu claims to have aimed at a dervish association within the Islamic Community, but the Islamic authorities refused (*Bilten Hu* 1978(2):3). In 1973, *Reis-ul-ulema* (the religious leader of the Islamic Community) Sulejman Kemura sent a short and formal letter to Sheikh Xhemali Shehu disapproving of such an organisation (*Buletin Hu* 1979(3):10).

religious press (in the journals *Glasnik Vrhovnog Islamskog Starješinstva* and *Preporod*) on what they called the 'disgraceful primitivism and illiteracy' of the sheikhs and their attempts 'to disrupt the unity of the Islamic Community'.[16] An anonymous *imam* from a small town in Kosovo accused dervishes of drinking alcohol and smoking in public during Ramadan, to demonstrate their non-compliance with Islamic norms:

As soon as you become a dervish, you are exempted from all basic Islamic obligations, such as praying, fasting, the *zakat* [alms tax], etc. The sheikh takes care of your life, here on earth as well as in the hereafter, because he is 'omnipotent'. During Ramadan, you can see dervishes walking around in broad daylight where we live with cigarettes in their mouths, to show everybody that they do not fast. As if that was not sufficient, they mock believers who do fast, calling them *Yazids*. As far as fasting is concerned, up to this very day I have seen not one dervish in our mosques, at either the daily prayers or the Friday prayer (S.R. 1979).

In March 1979, the Islamic Community organised a meeting to address the problem of dervish orders in Kosovo.[17] Although its tone was mild, the message was still unequivocal: most of the dervish orders in Yugoslavia had drifted away from the original Sufi ideals, and the Islamic Community should do all in its power to bring them back on the right track. One contributor mentioned the major drawbacks of these orders, *inter alia* their separatist tendencies (reminiscent of the accusations against Albanians in general), the personality cult surrounding the sheikhs, their use of magical practices and superstitious beliefs, and the antagonism directed against the *ulema*. The director of the *medresa* (Muslim theological seminary) in Prishtina attacked the dervish orders more directly, voicing much the same criticism as the anonymous *imam* quoted above. In his eyes the main responsibility for these religious transgressions lay with the sheikhs, who he said were unskilled because most were appointed on the basis of heredity without the necessary professional qualifications. They tended to abuse

---

[16] See for instance Neimarlija (1978).

[17] For an account of this meeting see *Glasnik Vrhovnog Islamskog Starješinstva* (1979:198-200). Most of the contributions presented during this meeting were reprinted in *Glasnik Vrhovnog Islamskog Starješinstva*, 1979, no.3 (May-June).

their privileged position for personal gain (Ahmeti 1979:285).[18]

The leaders of the Community of Dervish Orders reacted vigorously to these attacks. In the bulletin *Hu* they commented scathingly on the *Preporod* publications, blaming the authors for their arrogance and lack of self-control (*Bilten Hu* 1978(3):1-4, 1978(4):12-16). The ban on dervish orders was called a crime of 'genocidal' proportions (*Bilten Hu* 1978(2):5). Sheikh Xhemali Shehu justified the existence of the official dervish community by using the communist rhetoric of Brotherhood and Unity, referring to the rights of *ethnic* (as opposed to *religious*) communities under Yugoslav socialism:

Thanks to the society in which we live, we share freedom and equal rights with all nations and nationalities in Socialist Yugoslavia. Islam cannot be monopolised by thugs, it lives in the hearts of the true believers, where it smoulders, flares up and breaks out, saying 'This is enough!', as we are doing. We will not tolerate terror or oppression any more (*Bilten Hu*, 1978(3):3).

In 1979 the polemics calmed down, probably after the intervention of the state authorities (see *Buletin Hu* 1979(4):3), and for five years no open criticism against the Islamic Community was heard again. In December 1984, at the tenth anniversary of the Community of Dervish Orders, Sheikh Xhemali Shehu recalled the numerous problems with the Islamic Community, repeating: 'In Tito's Yugoslavia second-class citizens do not exist, and we will not tolerate being treated that way' (*Buletin Hu* 1984(2):7).

Shi'ite tendencies

Although the open polemics subsided, Albanian sheikhs continued to wage an implicit ideological war against the Muslim establishment. In defining their position *vis-à-vis* the Islamic Community, they claimed the esoteric (*batini*) knowledge of Sufi mysticism to be superior to the 'cold' and 'formalist' (*zahiri*) sciences of the

---

[18] As positive exceptions he mentioned the Kaderi lodges in Prishtina and Mitrovica, as well as the Melami lodge in Rahovec. To this list of 'orthodox' lodges one can add the Melami lodge in Prizren. The Melami order, which has strong urban and intellectual characteristics, is not represented in the Community of Dervish Orders.

ulema. One sheikh compared Islam to 'an endless sea, an ocean. The representatives of the *tarikat* are in the true sense of the word divers who enter the depths of that ocean and know how to pull out precious stones.' Most other Muslims remained only on the surface of this religious ocean (*Bilten Hu* 1978(4):10–11). The contrasts between Sufism and orthodox Islam are also spelled out at the level of Muslim ritual. For the sheikhs and dervishes the ordinary *namaz* (the daily Muslim prayer) has lost its original religious value, and has become a formality which lulls Muslims into an indolent sleep and makes them forget the *jihad* (*Bilten Hu*, 1978(4):5). The original prayer of Mohammed and the first adherents of Islam is not the *namaz* but the *zikr*, to which Muslims should give priority in order to achieve the highest degree of piety (*Bilten Hu* 1979(2):8).

Apart from pointing at the assets of Sufism, sheikhs and dervishes in Kosovo have made extensive use of ideas and symbols from the Shi'ite tradition within Islam. These Shi'ite tendencies have been noted earlier by several authors, although the way most of them have done this is unspecific and superficial.[19] Norris, in his book *Islam in the Balkans* (1993), makes a more sophisticated distinction between Shi'ite and non-Shi'ite Sufi orders. In his eyes the Bektashi order is essentially Shi'ite, whereas other orders (the Mevlevi, Kaderi, Nakshibendi, Melami, Rufai and Tidjani) are not (Norris 1993:82–137). In my view it is difficult to draw a clear line between Shi'ite and non-Shi'ite orders, although some (notably the Bektashi order) are traditionally more Shi'ite than others. Most leading sheikhs in Kosovo (who adhere to different orders) have made use of Shi'ite doctrine and symbolism to express the idea (and felt reality) of a 'suffering community of believers' (Gilsenan 1982:55), although they deny being openly Shi'ite (*Bilten Hu* 1979(1):9).

To clarify this point, it is necessary to elaborate the connections between Sufism and Shi'a Islam in more general terms. Although Sufism is not intrinsically linked to the Shi'a tradition in Islam,

---

[19] In a book dealing with the religious communities in Kosovo, the author bluntly states that 'Shi'ites are known under the term dervishes' (Kasumi 1988:65). In a report of the Arab journalist Fahmi Huwaydi, who visited the province in 1981 and drew most of his information from officials of the Islamic Community, dervishes are also portrayed without exception as Shi'ites (Norris 1990:47).

Gypsy dervish in Rufai lodge, Terzi *mahala*, Prizren, autumn 1986, with above his head the image of Ali (Mohammed's cousin and son-in-law).

there are important similarities. A main point of correspondence is the special devotion to Mohammed's cousin and son-in-law Ali and his son Husayn, who is the paramount martyr of Shi'ite Islam.[20] Ali has always occupied almost as important a position in Sufism as in Shi'a Islam, which has caused several Sufi orders to evolve from Sunnism to Shi'ism (Momen 1985:96). Yet Sufi orders

---

[20] In the eyes of the Shi'ites, Ali was the rightful successor to Mohammed, predestined to lead the Muslim community. However, after the Prophet's death the Umayyads (the clan from which Mohammed's wife Aisha originated) successfully claimed the caliphate and blocked Ali's accession to this position. They provided the first caliphs of Islam (leaders of the Muslim community of believers). In spite of Umayyad opposition, Ali was elected the fourth caliph, but soon afterwards he was removed and assassinated. Umayyad rule culminated in the reign of Yazid, who – in the eyes of the Shi'ites – symbolises the evil forces that corrupted Islam. Ali's son Husayn started a revolt against Yazid's rule in which Husayn and his followers were surrounded in the desert of Kerbela. Since Husayn refused to surrender, the troops of Yazid killed him and his followers (on the 10th of Muharrem, 10 October 680). Husayn's martyrdom at Kerbela became the founding legend of Shi'ism. Recollections of the legend of the Kerbela battle can be found in Momen (1985:28-31), Fischer (1980:13-27), and Ayoub (1978:93-139).

have flourished most in areas dominated by Sunnites, where they have often been vehicles for pro-Shi'ite sentiments.

This history of revolt against Sunni tyranny has furnished Shi'i Islam with a powerful and emotional theme of resistance and martyrdom, which has been used repeatedly to frame discontent and opposition, as during the Islamic Revolution in Iran. Michael Fischer has called this the 'Kerbela paradigm', viewing the legend primarily as an ideological and rhetorical device which provides moral and political guidelines *vis-à-vis* Sunni understandings of Islam (Fischer 1980:21).[21] We should not forget, however, that Shi'ite Islam has been quietist for most of its history. In almost all parts of the Muslim world Shi'ites have formed minorities, occasionally persecuted and at best tolerated. 'For most of the first millennium of Islam, Shi'ism was the faith not of rebels and rulers, but of cautious minorities seeking ways to reconcile religious ideals with practical realities. [...] The strategies of accommodation developed by these Shi'is were far reaching, and even included the deliberate concealment of their true beliefs' (Kramer 1987:2). When political circumstances allowed, Shi'is often rebelled, but not necessarily. Shi'ite Islam has an extraordinary ambivalence, oscillating between extreme submission (and religious dissimulation, *taqiyah*) on the one hand and revolt on the other. 'Those who wish to lead the Shi'i masses can, if the opposition seems overwhelmingly superior or it is expedient to do so, enjoin upon the Shi'is the patient endurance [...] of the Imams. And yet when the opportunity seems right, the Shi'i masses can be whipped up to the frenzy of revolution by appeal to the spirit of uprising [...] of Husayn' (Momen 1985:236). Fischer calls this use of the Kerbela myth to trigger revolutionary (political) action 'Kerbela in the Active Mood', illustrating this for the Islamic Revolution in Iran (1980:213).

Also, Shi'ites outside Iran have applied the Kerbela myth to express opposition to orthodox Sunni Islam – the rise of the Al-

---

[21] In Fischer's view the Kerbela paradigm entails '(a) a story expandable to be all-inclusive of history, cosmology, and life's problems; (b) a background contrast against which the story is given heightened perceptual value; in this case, primarily Sunni conceptions, but other religions at times serve the same function; and (c) ritual or physical drama to embody the story and maintain high levels of emotional investment' (1980:27).

banian dervish movement in Kosovo, in whose religious writings the battle of Kerbela is a dominant theme provides a good example of this. Most of the texts in the bulletin *Hu* are devoted to the Shi'ite heroes Ali and Husayn.[22] The Kerbela theme is also integrated into the ceremonial calendar: *Matem*, instead of Ramadan, is observed during the first ten days of the month of Muharrem. Then, secluded in their lodges, sheikhs and dervishes fast and meditate as they commemorate Husayn's martyrdom and the thirst he suffered in the desert of Kerbela by drinking no pure water but only tea, coffee and other unsweetened drinks. In addition, they eat no meat or any other food that contains animal fat (*Bilten Hu*, 1978(4):8). *Sultani-Nevrus* (the 'New Day'), the seasonal feast described at the beginning of this chapter has been interspersed with Shi'ite meanings as well: sheikhs and dervishes in Kosovo consider the day to be both Ali's birthday and the day when he became caliph.

What is most important for our discussion is that the Kerbela theme has been put to use to disqualify the representatives of the Islamic Community in Sarajevo as well as those in Kosovo. They are put on a par with the adversaries of Ali and the murderers of Husayn, and in the jargon of the bulletin *Hu*, are branded the *Yazids* of today (see footnote 20). According to Sheikh Xhemali Shehu, the Muslims and *ulema* who now mock sheikhs and dervishes in Kosovo, do not differ very much from those who once organised the conspiracy against Husayn (*Buletin Hu* 1978(4):5-7).

The revival and its background

This description of particular events and religious controversies concludes with an attempt to explain the revival of these dervish orders in Kosovo. First, this phenomenon does not stand on its own: in Turkey and other parts of the Muslim world, Sufism

[22] In the period under consideration the bulletin *Hu* published at least two regular features about Ali: (1) Three hundred and three words spoken by Hazreti Ali ('Treqint e tri fjalë të thëna nga Hazreti Ali'), aphorisms allegedly written by Ali, and (2) what the Koran tells us about Hazreti Ali ('Çka na thotë Kurani mbi Hazreti Aliun'). Husayn and the battle of Kerbela were the main topic of two other regular features: (1) 'Xhylzari Hasenejn', a detailed narrative of Husayn's revolt against Yazid, culminating in the battle of Kerbela; and (2) 'Mersije', an elegy lamenting Husayn's death.

has also demonstrated a remarkable resilience, defying earlier ex-
pectations that Sufi orders – often seen as strongholds of conser-
vatism and traditionalism – would disappear. The failure to
acknowledge that 'traditional' forms of religion and ritual may
retain their vitality under modern and secularised conditions has
been more general (Boissevain 1992:1).[23] However, it is clear
that both in the Muslim world and the West one sees a widespread
reappraisal of tradition, ritual and religion. As Hutchinson has
noted, in the United States and in Europe it has been intertwined
with ethnic revivals and the rise of nationalism. According to
Hutchinson, 'Common to all these movements is a moral critique
of the anomie of secular modernity, which has resulted in rising
levels of divorce, crime, alcoholism, drug abuse, nervous disorders,
social conflict and levels of inequality, and a demand for a revival
of essential religious principles as a basis of individual morality
and social organisation' (1994:65). It is not surprising to find this
sort of motive in the statute of the Community of Dervish Orders:
in article 4 it notes that, apart from the spiritual elevation and
moral education of Muslims and the teaching of love, brotherhood
and religious tolerance, one of its basic tasks is 'the constant fight
against alcoholism, murder, revenge, plunder, prostitution, theft,
laziness and other vices' (*Bilten Hu* 1975). The moral corruption
among the *ulema* is also considered one of the main modern vices
against which sheikhs and dervishes need to fight: they are criticised
for collaborating too closely with an infidel (socialist) regime.
This is a common theme among Muslim revivalists (Hutchinson
1994:83).

There is one particular social factor which may partly account
for the renewed importance of dervish orders in Kosovo: the
demographic boom and rural overpopulation, which have ag-
gravated the conditions of rural poverty and existential and political
insecurity.[24] This provides a fertile breeding-ground for ecstatic

[23] Most surprising is, according to Boissevain, Victor Turner's apparent failure to
note this trend despite his lifelong interest in ritual manifestations (Boissevain 1992:1).

[24] In 1984 the growth rate of Kosovo's population was still 25.2 per 1,000
inhabitants per year. Compared to Yugoslav and European standards, this figure
is extremely high. Since 1948 the total number of Albanians in Yugoslavia has
almost tripled, and more than half of the Albanian population in Kosovo is
under the age of twenty (*Komunat e KSA të Kosovës më 1983 – Të dhëna statistikore,*

cults, especially where there is no possibility of voicing protest in a more overt way (Lewis 1971). Since Kosovo still has a predominantly agrarian economy, there is a huge pressure on the scarce agricultural land. Land prices have increased steadily to a level that has been considerably higher than in the rest of former Yugoslavia.[25] The judicial means of regulating property and land sales have been ineffective, and thus conflicts over land have been endemic, resulting in a rising number of blood feuds: 'Among the Albanians in Yugoslavia, the number of crimes committed in vendettas is not only not on the decline but is even rising. Between 1964 and 1970, for instance, the circuit court in Prishtinë tried 320 cases involving blood feuds. There are such feuds in almost every one of the communes of the province of Kosovë, most of them in the remote villages' (Marmullaku 1975:88).

As Karan has noted, most cases of homicide in Kosovo are the result of unresolved conflicts over land (1985:86). Cases of threats, forced selling of land and even violent annexation are no exception, while local administration has been unable to escape the influence of powerful clans. Sometimes, such conflicts have had an ethnic dimension, when rich and influential Albanian clans put pressure on Serbian peasants to sell their land, usually offering exorbitantly high prices.[26]

Under such conditions of perpetual communal strife and internal dissension sheikhs have played a crucial role in settling disputes and pacifying and integrating rural society.[27] This is confirmed by Popovic, who speaks of 'the decisive role that may be played by

---

Prishtinë, 1984:32). Although Kosovo's population density was just under the Yugoslav average at the beginning of this century, the area is now the most densely populated in the former Yugoslavia (Roux 1992:149).

[25] Kosovo is the only area in the former Yugoslavia which has seen a rise in the absolute number of people employed in agriculture (Roux 1992:322).

[26] In Serbia it is widely claimed that the exodus of Serbs and Montenegrins from Kosovo in the 1970s and '80s has been the result of these pressures – which is often seen as part of a more encompassing Albanian 'master plan' to cleanse Kosovo of Serbs. In my view, this problem has been taken out of its context and 'ethnicised' by Serbian nationalists. It is not at all a problem existing only between Serbs and Albanians: among Albanians themselves conflicts over land have been more numerous and at least as vigorous.

[27] This is very similar to the role Bax has described for the Franciscans in Bosnia (Bax 1995).

the sheikh of Kosovo in the settlement of a vendetta' (1985:247).
Djurić also notes that sheikhs have taken up a leading role in
solving these kind of conflicts, whereas Sunnite *hoxhas* and Catholic
priests rarely mediate.[28] If dervishes of two different orders are
involved in a conflict, both sheikhs work together to solve it
(Djurić 1998:109 and 249). Historically it is especially the south-
western part of the province – in the areas around the towns of
Prizren, Gjakova (Djakovica) and Peja (Peć) where most lodges
are concentrated – which been especially noted for feuding (Baerlein 1922:55-6). The state authorities have never been capable
of handling these conflicts effectively, and have left them to be
solved by sheikhs who, acting with the knowledge and tacit support
of the authorities, seem generally to have been quite successful
(*Bilten Hu* 1978(4):12). In the 1980s and '90s the political relevance
of these activities has increased: in overcoming internal conflicts,
and bringing about reconciliation between feuding clans, they
have helped to to create unity *vis-à-vis* the common enemy, the
Serbs.[29]

Apart from these social-economic and demographic factors,
the ethno-political dimensions of the dervish revival, which play
a role in the background, should be highlighted. Sheikhs in Kosovo
have tried to revive and institutionalise a version of Islam which
was seen as less corrupted by communism and at the same time
as more traditionally 'Albanian' than the established Islam of the
Muslims in Bosnia and their collaborators in Kosovo. Through
applying Shi'ite ideas and symbolism as well as stressing the communist ideals of the equality of nations and ethnic groups, Albanian
sheikhs have evoked the image of an oppressed religious community
of true believers who, because of their profound 'otherness' – i.e.
because they are implicitly stereotyped as 'primitive' and illiterate
Albanians – have suffered extra humiliation and discrimination.
Now they have entered on a struggle against the official and
corrupted Islamic establishment in an attempt to overcome their
position as second-rank believers within the Islamic Community.

---

[28] In the past, however, Catholic priests played an important mediating role
in the northern Albanian highlands (Black-Michaud 1980:91-103).

[29] I do not know whether sheikhs played a role in the series of mass reconciliations
in the early 1990s. It seems that the initiative came primarily from the urban
intelligentsia.

This can be understood against the background of the traditional cultural gap between those 'westernised' and relatively urbanised Muslim Slavs of Bosnia and the backward, predominantly rural and 'oriental' Muslim Albanians in Kosovo and Macedonia. In the past, even after Yugoslavia was created, Albanians and Bosnian Muslims stood somewhat apart from one another, divided by tradition, language and ethnic consciousness. The difference was increased by geographical distance: Bosnia and Kosovo were quite separate regions only connected through the Sandžak, a Muslim-dominated stretch of land on the border of Serbia and Montenegro. Like most other Balkan nations, Bosnian Muslims have looked down on Albanians and their archaic and tribal way of life, and in the twentieth century this gap has widened, although they have been living in the same state. Contrary to the Albanians, who as non-Slavs in a South Slav state were treated as second-class citizens, most Bosnian Muslims adopted a lifestyle not very different from that of Roman Catholic Croats or Orthodox Serbs. It is one of the ironies of former Yugoslavia that before the start of the war Bosnian Muslims preferred a spouse of Serbian or Croatian background to an Albanian co-religionist from Kosovo (Canapa 1986:102-3, 123). Among ordinary Bosnian Muslims anti-Albanian feeling has been widespread, as is seen in the common accusation 'that their Kosovan co-religionists [are] lazy, ungrateful, undisciplined and therefore somehow not properly Muslim' (Sorabji 1993:34).

On the religio-political level, relations between Albanian and Bosnian Muslims have clearly been asymmetrical: the Islamic Community was always dominated by Slavic Muslims from Bosnia, not only because of the higher educational level of the Bosnian *ulema* (which ensured that Bosnia, unlike Kosovo, developed a class of Muslim intellectuals with a serious interest in Islam). It is indicative that until the mid-1980s Albanians did not have a translation of the Koran in Albanian. It is also revealing that the highest position within the Islamic Community in Yugoslavia, that of the *Reis-ul-ulema*, was never held by an Albanian, although Albanians comprised half of all Muslim believers in the state.[30]

---

[30] Only the last Yugoslav *Reis-ul-ulema*, Jakub Selimoski, was not a Bosnian, but a (Slav) Macedonian who had taken the trouble to learn Albanian. He was evicted from his post after the declaration of Bosnian independence (Noel Malcolm,

In 1987 most representatives within the Islamic Community refused to accept Albanian candidates for this position because of the alleged attempts made by Muslim Albanian *hoxhas* or clerics to Albanianise the small minority of Muslim Slavs in Macedonia (*Intervju*, 6 November 1987, p.22). These anti-Albanian sentiments within the Islamic Community grew in strength after the demonstrations in Kosovo in 1981, when Muslim officials openly dissociated themselves from the Albanian demands for a republic. This contributed to the estrangement of many Albanian Muslim believers: the Islamic Community in Kosovo, even though its officials were Albanians, seemed to enjoy little prestige among the population, and the influence of the *medresa* in Prishtina on intellectual life in the province was minimal (Meier 1984). Most Muslim Albanians, especially in the towns, are not great believers anyhow.[31]

In the 1970s the divide between Bosnians and Albanian Muslims came to be further reinforced due to the fact that the Islamic (religious) authorities in Sarajevo claimed for themselves a leading role in the new *nation* of (Slavic) Muslims. In 1967 the nation of Bosnian Muslims was officially recognised by the state; the term 'Muslim' now referred not only to a religious category (written with a small 'm': *muslimani*), but also to an ethnic category (written with a capital 'M': *Muslimani*) which included practising Muslims as well as atheists of Muslim origin. Nevertheless, because it was difficult to divide the two, the Islamic Community adopted more

---

personal communication).

[31] This somehow puts the local antagonism between Kosovo sheikhs and Albanian representatives of the Islamic Community in Kosovo (see for instance *Bilten Hu* 1988-89:7-25), between 'orthodox' Islam and 'heterodox' Sufi orders, into a different perspective. The social prestige of a sheikh in rural areas, at least in some large parts of Kosovo (particularly Metohija), is much higher than that of the local *hoxha* (Muslim cleric). Even more, the influence of sheikhs has been on the increase (see footnote 11). Their social position and role seems to be not unlike that of the Franciscans in Bosnia: as they are much more rooted in traditional rural society, they are also much more receptive to popular and ethnic sentiment, which has made them also more 'Albanian' and probably more nationalist than the official and 'orthodox' church structures. Only since 1989 has the Islamic Community in Kosovo adopted a more patriotic stance, and it is interesting to note that after that it made attempts at conciliation with the Community of Dervish Orders (*Bilten Hu* 1988-9: 12-15).

and more the role of the supreme guardian of this Muslim nation (leading to a religious revival as well). This meant that the interests of Albanian Muslims were bound to be neglected (see for instance Mojzes 1995:128).

Furthermore, the decentralising measures of the 1974 Yugoslav Constitution created new ethnic and religious divisions and facilitated their institutionalisation and formalisation: it strengthened not only the position of the Islamic Community but also that of the smaller nations and religious communities. With better opportunities for the Islamic Community to organise itself from the late 1960s and early '70s, this also triggered similar reactions among other (rival) religious formations such as the dervish orders in Kosovo, which started to organise themselves on a regional basis. There are clear parallels here with the structural antagonism and intra-confessional dynamics between the diocesan ecclesiastic structures of the Roman Catholic church and the Catholic monastic orders (Bax 1987, 1995), and between official Judaism and the Hasidic sects (Meijers 1989).

What is specific in the case of Kosovo dervishes is that these internal religious antagonisms have an ethnic dimension. Since the 1970s, when the Kosovo Albanians received political autonomy, there have been tendencies to emphasise 'Albanianism' in religion. The dervish revival and official recognition of the Community of Dervish Orders is only one expression of this: in 1969 Albanian Catholics also obtained a form of autonomy within the diocese of Skopje, with the appointment of an Albanian suffragan bishop in Ferizaj (Uroševac). The rising number of Albanian priests ended the traditional predominance of (Kosovo) Croat priests. Here too one sees that ethnic divisions have grown more important, although it remains to be investigated what forms these antagonisms took within the Catholic community in Kosovo.

In 1990, after the violent abolition of Kosovo's autonomy, the Islamic Community gave up its reserved and condescending attitude towards the Albanians in Kosovo. As Sorabji writes: 'After Serbia's increasing self-assertion, particularly over Kosovo, Muslim understanding began to change. Where the Albanians were concerned, images of nobility under oppression began to replace those of idle ingratitude, as Kosovo came to stand less for a threat to Yugoslav unity, than a Serbian threat which might soon redirect itself towards Bosnia' (1993:34). Scenting the great dangers that were about to threaten its own existence and that of the whole Muslim community in Bosnia, it openly sided with the Albanian opposition to Milošević. The process of the violent disintegration of Yugoslavia had started.

6

THE MAKING OF EGYPTIANS IN KOSOVO AND MACEDONIA

'I argue that identity, considered ethnographically, must always be mixed, relational, and inventive. [...] Identity is conjunctural, not essential' (Clifford 1988:10-11).

In the spring of 1991, when Yugoslavia was on the brink of war, some surprising articles appeared in the Yugoslav press on a new ethnic group. In Kosovo and Macedonia thousands of 'Egyptians' were reported to exist, who declared themselves to have settled there centuries ago. It was the first time I had heard of them; I knew of Albanians, Serbs and Macedonians and a number of other ethnic groups such as Turks, Slavic Muslims, Vlachs and Circassians, but these (Muslim) Egyptians were almost completely new to me – 'almost' because in August 1990 I met a few 'proto'- Egyptians at the Serbian monastery of Gračanica without really giving their claim serious attention. It was a warm day in August during the Feast of the Assumption, when the famous medieval sanctuary is visited by numerous pilgrims (see Chapter 3). As in every previous year, countless Muslim Gypsies were visiting the shrine but some of them, with whom I was able to talk, denied they were *Cigani*. 'Our origins are unknown, although there are indications that we are either Greeks or Egyptians', they explained. At that moment I did not take these claims seriously, and when I visited the Egyptian embassy in Belgrade a year later, the cultural attaché told me that his reaction had been similar. He and his colleagues had been astonished and amused, not knowing whether or not this phenomenon should be treated as a practical joke. In spite of seriously doubting the authenticity of the claims of the Yugoslav Egyptians, the ambassador invited them twice, in 1990 and 1991, on 23 July, Egypt's national day.

Since their entry into the Yugoslav ethnic pandemonium, the Egyptians have regularly attracted attention in the press. In their endeavours to become visible as a group they have used strategies that are common among ethnic movements: they published a book of their own folktales, legends and customs, which put flesh on their identity claims and provided the cultural substance needed to make these claims more credible. In the spring of 1991 they offered the book to the Egyptian ambassador in Belgrade.[1] In December 1991 they issued an official statement after Boutros Boutros-Ghali's election as United Nations Secretary-General. Since he is a Copt from Egypt, they congratulated him and asked him to do his utmost to solve the Yugoslav crisis peacefully. Interest was also aroused in Egypt itself, where a television documentary was made on this burgeoning Egyptian community on the other side of the Mediterranean.[2] In June 1992 the Macedonian Egyptians were demanding their own radio and television programmes.

Let us turn to the inevitable questions raised by the unexpected appearance of these Egyptians. How can we explain the emergence of this apparently new national minority? What is its background? Which are the people involved and why do they claim to be Egyptian? What evidence and arguments do they put forward to claim Egyptian origin? Are the Egyptians in Kosovo and Macedonia really new – and is our astonishment warranted – or has their ex-

---

[1] The book was actually written by Stojan Risteski, a Macedonian from Ohrid, one of the main defenders of their cause (Risteski 1991).

[2] The information presented here is primarily based on press reports (Chuck Sudetic, 'Pharaohs in Their Past? So the Yugoslavs Say', *New York Times*, 21 November 1990, A4; *Der Spiegel*, 15 October 1990; *Dnevnik*, 28 October 1990; *Novosti*, 28 October 1990; *Borba*, 18 September 1991, 3 December 1991, 6 December 1991 and 8 June 1992). I have also used data provided by Poulton (1991:91). Barany mentions the Egyptians in a recent article about the position of the Gypsies in Macedonia (1995:517-18), but he provides no new information. The last news I heard was during the peace negotiations at Rambouillet in February 1999, where Čerim Abazi, an Egyptian representative from Prishtina, was a member of the Serbian delegation (*Vreme*, 13 February 1999, p.11). Because my work as an anthropologist has been largely confined to Kosovo, my analysis is mainly based on knowledge of the situation there. I am primarily acquainted with the Serbian point of view (using mostly Serbian sources) and have not had access to the Macedonian press on this topic. Thus I may be ignorant of some details of this phenomenon in Macedonia. Nevertheless, I believe that the parameters of this phenomenon in both areas are largely the same, at least for the period which is most central to my analysis (1990-2).

istence a concealed previous history of which we have not been aware? Were they perhaps a 'silenced' group which has now become vocal and visible? In the analysis which follows, the intention is to show that the Egyptians in the former Yugoslavia did not appear out of the blue: there is a long history of 'Egyptian' presence in the Balkans, which has survived in locally and regionally defined identities.

What is relatively new (since the beginning of the 1980s) is that these local groups of so-called Egyptians have started to develop a national consciousness transcending narrow local confines, an 'imagined community' which goes beyond the level of face-to-face contacts (Anderson 1991). The basis for this process of 'national awakening' was laid in Macedonia (notably in Ohrid), where Egyptians existed as distinct local groups before. Only when they called for recognition as an ethnic category in the last Yugoslav census of 1991 did their claims attract wide attention. For the first time, their demands were taken seriously, also by the state authorities. We are able to show that this development had an important ethno-political background, which incited other groups to become Egyptians too, although they had previously lacked the consciousness of being 'Egyptian'. This latter development has been more characteristic for the Egyptians in Kosovo.

The ethnonym 'Egyptian'

When analysed more closely, the phenomenon of the Egyptians in the Balkans is not as unusual as it may seem at first sight. From the end of the fourteenth century, ethnonyms derived from 'Egyptian' have been widely used for Gypsies, who since then have spread all over Europe. The English term 'Gypsy' is etymologically derived from this, as are its equivalents in many other languages such as Spanish *Gitano*, French *Gitan* and Turkish *Kipti*. In the Balkans too the ethnonym 'Egyptian' has been preserved, although it is not dominant everywhere. In Albania, Gypsies are called '*Evgjitë*' or '*Magjypë*', both derived from 'Egyptian'.[3] In former Yugoslavia, apart from the official label *Romi* and the more popular but potentially pejorative term *Cigani*, a number of local and

---

[3] For Albanian, as well as for Serbo-Croat, the terms are given in the plural.

regional expressions exist, all referring to Egypt: *Egipćani, Edjup(c)i, Adjupci, Gopti, Gipteri, Kipti, Faraoni* and *Firauni* (Vukanović 1983: 137-48). These designations can be translated with respectively 'Egyptians', 'Copts' and 'People of the Pharaoh'.[4]

It is not clear why Gypsies were called by such names, although there has been plenty of speculation. From some historical documents we know that Gypsy chiefs arriving at the city gates of fifteenth-century European towns presented themselves as 'Dukes of Egypt' or 'Dukes of Little Egypt'. Accordingly, until the nineteenth century many believed that they came from Egypt, although these claims were soon doubted. At the end of the eighteenth century, tsiganologists formulated (on the basis of linguistic findings) the now widely accepted theory of an Indian origin for the Gypsies, which necessitated an alternative explanation for the ethnonym. One of the most popular theories was that they borrowed their name from a region in Greece called 'Little Egypt' (cf. 'Asia Minor'). According to this view, they first settled there before spreading over the rest of Europe (Liégeois 1986:28-9), but this theory is itself not much more convincing, as Winstedt pointed out as early as the beginning of the twentieth century: it is almost without doubt, he says, that the name 'Little Egypt' applied to the huge Gypsy colony at Modon in Greece (present-day Methoni). As a geographical designation, it almost certainly came into being only after Gypsies had settled there (1909-10:61). In Byzantium and Greece the practice of calling Gypsies 'Egyptians' was already well established at that time (Soulis 1961:150).

In the fourteenth century Gypsies settled primarily in Venetian colonies, because of the relative stability and security these territories enjoyed (Fraser 1992:50). Modon, a seaport on the south-west coast of the Peloponnese with probably the most important Gypsy settlement of that time was one of them. Furthermore, it was an important staging point for pilgrims travelling to the Holy Land. According to Fraser, this probably explains why Gypsies presented themselves as pilgrims as soon as they arrived in Western Europe. Fraser suggests that they adopted this guise 'when they needed

---

[4] The first two terms originate etymologically from the ancient Greek *Aigyptos*. In the seventh century, the Arab conquerors of Egypt made this into *Kibt*, refering to the Christian inhabitants of Egypt. From this Arabic name the term Copt originates (Atiya 1986).

a cover-story to facilitate their arrival' (1992:53). In places like Modon they gained familiarity with the Christian world and discovered that pilgrims were privileged travellers: 'By claiming to be penitents and pilgrims, the Gypsies could ensure that they were received with a warmer welcome than they had enjoyed hitherto' (1992:63). In addition, Gypsies were able in this way to obtain letters of recommendation (from the Holy Roman Emperor Sigismund and, allegedly, from the Pope) with which they could cross frontiers more easily and were permitted to stay and obtain some basic support.

In Fraser's eyes the pilgrim's guise with its concomitant 'cover-story' was the greatest trick ever employed by Gypsies, in their long history of survival through strategies of superficial assimilation and outright deception: 'It was as if some unsung genius, stimulated perhaps by all the pressures in the Balkans, had realised the potential advantages to be drawn from the religious environment of the time and had devised a strategy for exploiting it and enhancing the prospects of survival' (1992:62). However, he does not really provide an explanation for the fact that Gypsy leaders called themselves 'Dukes of Egypt'. Why Dukes and why Egypt in particular? It is safe to assume that these Gypsy leaders invented their 'titles' as part of their general strategy to gain acceptance among the Christian host-populations and political leaders. Probably they took upon themselves an aristocratic title because they sought favourable treatment from, among others, monarchs and nobles. As for Egypt, their appearance forced them to think of an exotic homeland which would also be meaningful in medieval Christian eyes. In the Europe of that time Egypt was probably one of the few exotic places that were known to most people. Moreover, it had a certain magic, as is pointed out by Clébert: well before the arrival of the Gypsies in Europe 'all mountebanks and travelling showmen found themselves dubbed "Egyptians"' (1967:27). Egypt was the classical homeland of magicians and, as Fraser too suggests, 'Egypt's arcane associations with occultism and divination' may have helped create this legend of Egyptian origin (1992:48). It is most likely Egypt earned its reputation from its prominent role in the Old Testament books of Genesis and Exodus. It was the place where God's chosen people were enslaved and finally threatened with extinction; it formed the central stage for the battle between Moses and the Pharaoh, who forcibly prevented the people of Israel from leaving his realm. With the help of God, Moses succeeded, but not before winning a lengthy trial of strength with the wisest men and magicians of Egypt, resulting in the ten successive plagues of Egypt. Here Egypt symbolised above all pride, ignorance and even blasphemy – qualities repeatedly put to shame by Moses who thereby upheld and glorified the true faith. In medieval eyes (ancient) Egypt was probably an obvious symbolic and ideological adversary of Christianity.

It would seem that the Gypsies referred to this well-known biblical toponym, constructing a plausible and acceptable identity for that time. Early sources attest that they presented themselves as pagans, coming from Egypt, who had dared to challenge or even abandon the Christian faith and were now doing penance for this by a seven years' pilgrimage. They were cursed, but by creating an image of infidels who had adopted the hair-shirt they actually paid homage to Christianity. In this way they created maximum room for manoeuvre, not only in the literal (spatial) sense: as Egyptians, they were expected not to comply too strictly with the Christian rules and prohibitions. Although regarded with suspicion and disapproval, it is likely that they were initially given the benefit of the doubt. Only later were Gypsies increasingly stereotyped as spies in the service of the Turks (Fraser 1992:151).

Nonetheless, up until the present day many Gypsy myths of origin have been cast in biblical terms, alluding to such key events as the Exodus and the Crucifixion. Probably one of the most widespread is the myth that the Gypsies are the descendants of a young man and woman who were part of Pharaoh's troops who followed Moses through the Red Sea; while the rest of Pharaoh's army was drowned, they miraculously survived and became the Adam and Eve of the Gypsies. Between the two World Wars the Serbian ethnographer Tihomir Djordjević gathered versions of the same myth in Yugoslavia; here the biblical story of Moses and Pharaoh is reflected in the various legends about an ancient Gypsy empire headed by the mighty czar Firaun. After challenging God he was severely punished and drowned at sea together with his army, of which the few survivors were the ancestors of the present-day Gypsies (Djordjević 1984b).[5]

---

[5] This myth has a long tradition in the Balkans, as is shown in a fragment of the *Seyahat-name* (Book of Travels) of the famous seventeenth-century Turkish

Whether the Gypsies really designed their ambiguous Egyptian identity as rationally as this suggests remains unanswered. It was probably a process of trial and error, in which the several basic elements of their 'cover-story' were tested and combined before eventually crystallising in the versions we know. Among scholars the Egyptian myth was discarded by the end of the eighteenth century, when linguists discovered many resemblances between Romani and other Indic languages, which strongly suggested Indian origins for the Gypsies. Today this view is almost universally accepted among scholars as well as among Gypsies all over the world, including in former Yugoslavia (see for instance Djurić 1987:13-31, Poulton 1993:44). Nevertheless, general claims based on this Indian 'myth' should be approached with some scepticism, as Judith Okely (1983) and more recently the Dutch historians Leo Lucassen (1990) and Wim Willems (1995) have argued. All express doubts about the Gypsies' alleged single Indian origin, and argue that the term 'Gypsy' has been primarily an outsider's label, used indiscriminately for people more or less permanently wandering. Some might also have adopted the Gypsy identity voluntarily for 'professional' reasons, e.g. to earn money as exotic fortune-tellers (Okely 1983:3-4). In short, they argue that the Gypsies have incorporated disparate individuals and groups of various, often non-Indian and autochthonous origins. Although Fraser does not go so far as to dismiss the Indian thesis, he acknowledges that Gypsies form a 'rich mosaic of ethnic fragments' (1992:9). Especially in the Balkans, there is a situation of an extreme complexity, in which various criteria like language, religion and occupation have generated numerous subdivisions and ramifications among Gypsies (1992: 292-3).[6] These groups, designated by outsiders as 'Gypsies', often define themselves in quite other terms. The 'Egyptians' in former Yugoslavia might be seen as a very recent and at the same time special example.

---

traveller Evliya Çelebi (see Friedman and Dankoff 1991:4-5).

[6] See also Lockwood (1985), who gives a clear picture of these complex ethnic subdivisions, especially for Yugoslavia.

The Egyptians in Yugoslavia

The Egyptians[7] in Kosovo and Macedonia deny categorically that they are Gypsies, and indeed claim antique Egyptian origins. In 1990 they founded their own associations, first in Ohrid (Macedonia) – where the Egyptians have a longer history – and later in Prishtina (Kosovo), where they have emerged unexpectedly, to the surprise even of the Egyptian leaders in Ohrid (Ljubisavljević 1990:35). Their primary stated goal was to halt the process of Albanianisation taking place in western Macedonia and Kosovo. The total number of Egyptians who have since joined these associations is about 10,000, almost equally divided over Kosovo and Macedonia. At the founding assembly of the Kosovo branch held in October 1990, one leading member declared with unlimited optimism that their total number would probably turn out to be more than 100,000 (Djordjević 1990; see also Poulton 1991:91 and Fraser 1992:298). According to the Egyptian leaders in Ohrid, they established a similar association shortly before the 1981 Yugoslav census with the aim of gaining official recognition as a nationality (*narodnost*) to be included in the census questionnaires as a separate ethnic category.[8] Although their demands had not been granted by the government of Macedonia, at least 200 of them declared themselves Egyptians, thus ending up in the category 'unknown' (Friedman 1985:53; Ljubisavljević 1990:34).

In 1990 the federal authorities announced the next census, which took place in April 1991 (the last census held in former Yugoslavia). The Egyptians used the opportunity to express their

---

[7] Although it is questionable whether these Yugoslav 'Egyptians' are indeed of Egyptian origin, I will call them that, without repeated use of quotation marks. It should be clear that we are dealing with controversial and disputable claims.

[8] In federal Yugoslavia an official distinction was made between *narodi* ('state' nations) and *narodnosti* (nationalities). Apart from this distinction, some republican constitutions (like the Serbian and Macedonian) used a third category, *etničke grupe* (ethnic groups), reserved for minor ethnic groups, Gypsies being by far the largest. Each category had specific political rights: *narodi* (like the Croats and the Serbs) had their own republics, *narodnosti* (like Albanians and Hungarians) did not because they possessed their 'own' national states outside Yugoslavia. Nevertheless, in the 1960s the main nationalities obtained substantial autonomy. The third category remained an extremely vague constitutional concept, without specific rights.

demands anew, *inter alia* by offering petitions to the federal assembly, as well as to the Serbian and Macedonian national assemblies. One of the results was that their struggle for recognition did not pass unnoticed; they attracted attention in the press and furthermore their demands were partly granted by the Serbian and Macedonian authorities: during the next census, the officials promised, the Egyptians could officially register as such. Actually, this concession did not mean much, because the Yugoslav census system always provided the possibility of registering according to personal preferences, e.g. as an inhabitant of a certain region or town (or as '*Homo sapiens*', as some did). However, as these idiosyncratic categories were denied recognition by the state, they were usually grouped as 'others', 'regional' or 'unknown' in the census results, and they lacked political significance. In the case of the Egyptians, however, the authorities made one small step in the direction of recognition, by allowing the category of *Egipćani* to be used in the census codex, thereby enabling the exact assessment of their number and the separate processing of other data related to them (Risteski 1991:7-10). On the other hand, the authorities also made clear that this concession still did not imply special minority rights. It appears that only Macedonia published the census figures for Egyptians: the 1991 figures list 3,307 Egyptians in Macedonia.[9] For Serbia (present-day 'Yugoslavia'), only the preliminary results of the census have been published, without any mention of the Egyptians. Whether the Serbian figures for Egyptians will ever be published is questionable. In Kosovo the census in any case largely failed because of the massive boycott by the Albanians.

Although many consider them to be Gypsies, Egyptians resist this label with some determination. They forward a number of arguments which they say 'prove' their non-Gypsy identity. In the first place, they live in the historic centres of towns such as Ohrid and Bitola, whereas most Gypsies have settled in separate and often very poor Gypsy quarters or suburban ghettos. Secondly, they claim to have a relatively high standard of living and do not suffer much from unemployment – something the average Gypsy can only dream of. Thirdly, they say they have always formed a

[9] The (preliminary) results of the 1994 Macedonian census list 3,169 Egyptians. I thank Victor Friedman for providing me with these data (see also Barany 1995:517-18).

specific group of specialised craftsmen; traditionally they worked as blacksmiths, but are now turning towards more sophisticated professions requiring a more advanced education.[10] Nowadays many young Egyptians have become doctors or engineers. Finally, though they are Muslims, they are (in their own words) more 'developed' and 'modern', by comparison not only with Gypsies but also with Albanians. They have abolished the 'medieval norms' of Islam, especially those pertaining to women. It is clear that all these arguments can be regarded as symbolic attempts to shake off the stigma that is attached to Gypsy identity.

Apart from these arguments (quoted in Lazović and Nikolić Pisarev 1990), Egyptians point to the oral traditions which their old people seem to have maintained, according to which Egyptians were among the earliest inhabitants of the Balkans. During the reign of Alexander the Great (fourth century BC) they immigrated to the Balkans, where they founded 'Little Egypt'. From there they spread to other parts of the Balkans and eventually arrived by the shores of Lake Ohrid. In the following centuries other Egyptians followed their example, moving along Roman roads like the Via Ignatia. The Ohrid Egyptians claim to be among the founders of this small, beautiful and historically important town. They also claim that in other Balkan towns, as well as in Sicily, one can still find Egyptians, who are recognisable by their dark skin. All are alleged to be the descendants of groups of Old Egyptians who created a 'ring' of Egyptian settlements along the main trade roads between the Ionian and Adriatic seas.[11] Unfortuna-

---

[10] It should be noted that the blacksmith's craft has always been a typical Gypsy occupation. The Serbian ethnographer Tihomir Djordjević once argued that it is precisely this craft that has set the Gypsies apart, preserving them as a distinct ethnic group. Non-Gypsies never engaged in it, at least in Serbia and Montenegro. For our case here, Djordjević's remarks about Gypsy blacksmiths in Ulcinj (Montenegro) are of special interest. Like the Egyptians in Kosovo and Macedonia, they were Albanophone and refused to be labelled as Gypsies. Since it was clear they were neither Albanians nor Serbs, they called themselves *kovači* (blacksmiths) (Djordjević 1984a:11). It should be remembered that Gypsies in the Balkans often use occupational labels instead of ethnic labels to denote their identity.

[11] I know of only one author mentioning Egyptians in Balkan towns before the Slavic invasions: Fine (1983:12). As I did not attempt to find additional evidence, more data can probably be found in the historical literature. In April 1991 Tanjug (the Belgrade-based official Yugoslav press agency) issued a press

tely, they have forgotten their own language and adopted the languages of the indigenous populations. For that reason, the Ohrid Egyptians, who are predominantly Albanophone, do not consider Albanian their mother-tongue but merely as what they call their *kućni jezik* (home language) (Damnjanović 1990).

Serbian and Macedonian support

From the moment of their appearance the Egyptians won sympathy and support, especially among Macedonians and Serbs. In March 1991 Stojan Risteski, a scholar from Ohrid, published a book entitled *Narodni prikazni, predanija i obichai kaj Egipkjanite / Egjupcite vo Makedonija* (Folk stories, legends and customs among the Egyptians in Macedonia), which attempts to buttress their claims with ethnographic data. A number of Serbian journalists and scholars spoke in favour of them in the months preceding the 1991 census. According to the German weekly *Der Spiegel* (15 October 1990), Serbia's president Slobodan Milošević too supported their demands, claiming that more than half of Kosovo's Albanians are actually Egyptians, who were forced to renounce their identity under Albanian pressure. An example of the warm Serbian support for the Egyptian cause, is an article by the two Serbian journalists, Lazović and Nikolić Pisarev:

The life Egyptians lead is – under the present conditions in Yugoslavia – quite exceptional: they are always very helpful towards others and are receptive to all good influences of other nations. They live in colonies where they dedicate themselves without complaint to crafts that are, on close inspection, not very profitable. They abstain from any form of political activity and concentrate exclusively on their work. They are an unusual people contrasting positively with all other nations of Yugoslavia. Characteristic for them is that they are a rare example of a nation whose members consciously adapt and assimilate and always try to prevent any conflict with society. They are extremely gentle, reliable and diligent (Lazović and Nikolić Pisarev 1990:57).

---

release in connection with the Egyptians, mentioning Vatican documents which were said to state that many Egyptians were brought to Macedonia in the fourth century AD as foot soldiers and horsemen (*BBC Summary of World Broadcasts* EE/1043 B/17, 11 April 1991).

Some Serbian scholars also supported the claims of the Egyptians in statements to the press, especially Rade Božović, a prominent Arabist at Belgrade University, and Miodrag Hadži-Ristić, an ethnologist working at the University of Skopje (Macedonia). Hadži-Ristić claimed he was able to interest important political and scientific institutions in Macedonia and Serbia (the Socialist Alliance of Macedonia, the Serbian Academy of Sciences and Arts, the Ethnographic Institute and the Etnographic Museum in Belgrade) in research into the origins and ethnogenesis of the Egyptians. He talked to two biochemists who claimed that by blood tests it was possible to establish whether the Egyptians differ from Gypsies or not.[12] Hadži-Ristić also stated in an interview that he had found archaeological traces of Egyptian or (to be more precise) Coptic presence in Macedonia. These consisted of unique earthen icons, which he claims were only ever produced by Copts (Lazović 1990).

In interviews, Rade Božović suggested that many beliefs, rituals and magical practices among the Macedonian Egyptians show close similarities with those of the Copts. In addition, though nominally Muslims, they celebrate Christian feasts like those of St Naum and St Athanas.[13] The latter saint was bishop of Alexandria (Egypt) in the fourth century. Furthermore, Božović has stated that the Egyptians show a pronounced preference for uneven numbers in their ritual practices, especially the number three, which they share with the ancient Egyptians.

Other so-called proof is provided by the 'Egyptian' graves that have been found on the Stogovo mountains (western Macedonia), in the vicinity of a former manganese mine where, according to

[12] Although this type of anthropogenetic research seemed to me reminiscent of former Nazi methods, I discovered that it still has respectability among tsiganologists. The blood group distribution among Gypsies is stated to be markedly different from that of (other) Europeans (Fraser 1992:24-5).

[13] Stojan Risteski too mentions the Egyptians' devotion to St Naum, giving some details of their pilgrimage to the shrine of Sveti Naum at Lake Ohrid (1991:165). He also tells of a rich Egyptian from Resen (Macedonia), who donated a belfry to the church of St Naum just after World War II (1991:167-8). In addition he gives a short description of the religious customs of the Egyptians: *Tanasovden* (St Athanas Day) is celebrated at home (1991:192), while *Gjurgjovden* (St George's Day) is celebrated at Muslim shrines (1991:190). Thanks to Gordana Netkovska who translated these stories for me.

oral tradition, Egyptians worked as slaves. In an unpublished paper on the Egyptians, Božović seems more cautious in assuming continuity, although he again sees many parallels in the ritual practices of the Egyptians in Macedonia and Kosovo and those of the ancient Egyptians. In his view this may indeed be the consequence of cultural continuity since cultural-religious forms, especially birth, marriage and death rituals, are durable and stand the test of time the longest (Božović n.d.).

In short, these two Serbian scholars are willing to consider the Egyptian thesis seriously: for them it is not inconceivable that Alexander the Great had already brought Egyptians to the Balkans, in which case it is also possible that they settled in Greece, founded 'Little Egypt', and from there spread to other Balkan towns. It was only in later centuries that the first Gypsies arrived in Little Egypt, from where they continued their migration to the north. As a result the Egyptians were erroneously identified with them (Damnjanović 1990).

Former Albanianisation of the Egyptians

Because the Egyptians were not officially recognised as an ethnic minority, most of them registered as Albanians during previous Yugoslav censuses (Ljubisavljević 1990:34).[14] The reasons for this identification are clear. In the first place, their mother-tongue is in most cases Albanian.[15] In addition, the Egyptians are Muslims and hence share numerous customs with the Albanians. The Albanians, however, consider them to be 'Albanian' or Albanianised Gypsies because of their Gypsy-like (physical) characteristics (Damnjanović 1990:37). The head of the federal commission that organised the 1991 census also thinks that the Egyptians are Albanianised Gypsies (*Der Spiegel*, 15 October 1990).

[14] Obviously, they did not take recourse to other possibilities, for instance registering as *Jugosloven* (Yugoslav) or as *etničko neopredeljen* (ethnically indefinite).

[15] The proto-Egyptians whom I met in Gračanica also spoke Albanian among themselves. Nonetheless, not all Egyptians seem to be Albanophone. According to Rajko Djurić, there are also Turkish-speaking Egyptians in Ohrid (personal communication). Lazović and Nikolić Pisarev (1990) write that some Egyptians speak Macedonian or Serbian. According to Victor Friedman, the Egyptians (*Gjupci*) of Bitola speak Macedonian (personal communication).

For Kosovo, all data indicate that the Egyptians recruit their members mainly from the *Ashkali* (Albanian; *Aškalije* in Serbian), a term that most of these 'Albanian' Gypsies use for themselves. The designation 'Egyptians' is new among them.[16] When this process of Albanianisation took place is unclear: it might be of a quite recent date (see Barjaktarović 1970:746), but according to most of this writer's informants the *Ashkali* became Albanianised during the late Ottoman period, working as peasants on the large estates (*chiftliks*) of Albanian landowners. In general the position of these peasants was worse than that of others and little better than that of agricultural labourers (Jelavich 1983:60).[17] During this period these Gypsies adopted the Albanian language, converted to Islam and adapted themselves to the strong patriarchal way of life of most Albanians. In Kosovo this process was most profound in the south-western part of the province (best known by the Serbian name *Metohija* or *Rrafshi i Dukagjinit* in Albanian), where most *chiftliks* existed. After the end of Ottoman domination, many of these Gypsy agricultural labourers settled in nearby towns. Nowadays, in and around the towns of Gjakova (Djakovica) and Peja (Peć) but also in some other towns in Kosovo, *Ashkali* are found in fairly large numbers.[18] They clearly differentiate themselves from Gypsies and strictly adhere to Albanian customary law, par-

---

[16] Vukanović who has written an important book on the Gypsies in Yugoslavia (1983), does not write more than a few lines about these *Ashkali*. He states that they are nomadic Gypsies, of the Muslim faith, that they are by profession blacksmiths, kettle-menders and tinsmiths, and that their mother-tongue is the Romani language. They are affiliated to Albanian tribes, as Vukanović writes, and are in the process of transforming themselves into Albanians (1983:138). Not all of his qualifications seem to be correct, however. As far as I have experienced, *Ashkali* do not know Romani, or do so only inadequately. Albanian is their native language. Furthermore, they are sedentary, unlike nomadic Gypsies who are generally the least assimilated.

[17] Petrović assumes that the use of Gypsies as a work force on Turkish estates started soon after the Ottoman conquest (1976:55-6). Nonetheless, generally the fate of Gypsies living under the Ottomans was better than in Western Europe (Fraser 1992:173-8). For the *chiftlik* system, in particular for Kosovo, see Roux (1992:192-3).

[18] According to Vukanović there are 63,000 Gypsies whose native language is Albanian (1983:134). Officially, the number of (declared) *Romi* with Albanian as their native language (according to the census of 1981) is much smaller, fewer than 7,000 (Petrović 1992:120).

ticularly in family matters. Furthermore, they are strongly en-
dogamous and rarely marry other Gypsies. Because of their assimilated way of life, *Ashkali* claim a higher social status than
ordinary Gypsies.

Although the phenomenon of the Egyptians is primarily linked
to the *Ashkali*, at least in Kosovo, it is likely that also other Gypsy
groups are using the label. This may be the case among the *Arlije*,
a general designation for sedentarized Muslim Gypsies. Culturally
the *Ashkali* and *Arlije* are closely related; the *Ashkali* might be
seen as a sub-category of the *Arlije*, i.e. as 'Albanian' *Arlije*
(Heinschink 1978:12). In Macedonia the phenomenon seems to
be much more related to existing groups of 'Egyptians' as mentioned
by Tatomir Vukanović (1983). Since Vukanović wrote his book
on the Gypsies in Yugoslavia long before the rise of the current
Egyptian movement, he deals exclusively with local groups of
Edjup(c)i or 'Egyptians'. Mostly these groups seem to have been
sedentary and urban for many generations, using this label to
imply superiority over Gypsies. They claim to be from Egypt
(Vukanović 1983:140). Also in nineteenth-century Montenegro
the word 'Egyptian' was used as a 'euphemism' for the pejorative
term *Ciganjin* (Bogišić 1874:402); the same is true in contemporary
Albania (Cortiade 1991:3).[19]

For the moment we may conclude that the Yugoslav Egyptians
want to distinguish themselves from Gypsies because of cultural
and status differences. This particular way of marking themselves
off socially and ethnically seems to have a long tradition in parts
of former Yugoslavia and Albania. Although their background

---

[19] Cortiade wrote a very informative article about Gypsies in Albania, published
in Italian in 1992. Here I use the original (unpublished) English manuscript
(1991). According to him, the *Evgjit* or *Jevg* are not Gypsies; both terms 'refer
properly to a dark-complexioned social group of unclear origin' (1991:3). They
constitute a minor group of a few thousand people, living in Tirana and other
cities of central Albania, and their native language is Albanian: '[M]any of them
have reached great success especially in the arts, first of all in music and dancing,
but also in some administrative jobs and even in the army, in spite of some
prejudices related to their proverbial lack of courage' (1991:5). In the 1930s
Stuart Mann wrote: 'They stoutly deny any connexion with the Roms, and
to call them "Tsikán" is the worst possible insult. Their traditions seem to point
to an African origin. [...] One theory (I forget whose) is that the Jevgs are
descendants of Egyptian slaves who escaped from Greece and fled to Albania.
They are clean, honest, hard working, and fairly intelligent' (1933:2-3).

has not been clarified, it seems likely that they adapted themselves to, and consequently identified with, dominant Turco-Albanian culture, especially in the towns. During the Yugoslav censuses they mostly registered as Albanians. However, since 1990 some of them do not want to be Albanians anymore, but Egyptians. Why?

Ethnic mimicry among Gypsies

One may conclude from the foregoing, that the identification with Albanians was a free and 'positive' choice, at least in the post-war period. But it is often hard to distinguish between free and more imposed choices. At first sight, people appear to behave in a certain way voluntarily, but on closer inspection their conduct turns out to be affected by economic, social, political or other pressures. This is particularly the case among Gypsies, not least those who designate themselves as Egyptians. Here, concentrating mainly on the role of the Yugoslav census system, and its political implications, we seek to show that the Egyptians are affected by changing ethno-political conditions that explain why they were first 'Albanians' and now want to be 'Egyptians'. It seems not to be accidental that the Egyptians appeared shortly before the census of 1991. First, however, it is necessary to analyse the widespread reluctance among Gypsies to declare themselves as Gypsies.

It is common for them to declare themselves as non-Gypsies, especially during censuses, which makes it always very difficult to assess their exact number. This has been the case in the republics of (former) Yugoslavia as well. As the Serbian ethnologist Barjaktarović once slightly ironically remarked: 'Today in Yugoslavia we have the opportunity to meet Rumanians, Albanians, Turks, Slovenes, Serbs, Macedonians and others, but who have nonetheless an outstanding Gypsy physiognomy' (1970:748). Since World War II, this has been reflected in the Yugoslav census results (before that, Gypsies were not registered). The official figures for Gypsies have always been much lower than the unofficial estimates of specialists. According to Vukanović's calculations the number in (former) Yugoslavia exceeded 600,000, mostly in Serbia and Macedonia (1983:134). In 1977, the Commission for Human Rights of the United Nations presented an even higher figure of almost 750,000 (Mitrović 1990:19). Neverthe-

Gypsy musicians at a Croat wedding, Šašare, spring 1992.

less, during the census of 1981 only 168,000 respondents declared themselves as such (approximately 25 per cent of the total Gypsy population if the estimates are correct), other Gypsies being registered as Serb, Albanian, Macedonian or other.[20] In addition, the censuses have shown considerable fluctuations in the numbers of Gypsies; e.g. that of 1961 showed a dramatic fall compared to 1953 (except for Macedonia), while in 1981 their number doubled compared to the results of ten years before.[21]

The reasons for this ethnic 'mimicry' are equivocal.[22] Inner

[20] In Kosovo 34,000 people declared themselves to be Gypsies, in Macedonia 43,000 (census 1981). The real numbers are probably about four times higher.

[21] With regard to Gypsies the official census results after World War II show the following numbers: 72,736 (1948), 84,713 (1953), 31,073 (1961), 78,485 (1971) and 169,197 (1981) (Petrović 1992:116).

[22] Following some authors from the former Yugoslavia, I use the term 'mimicry' to designate the widespread tendency among Gypsies to camouflage their ethnic background with a more respectable identity that offers them better prospects of survival. Yet it seems that they are never fully incorporated or 'assimilated' into the groups with which they identify.

motives as well as external pressures – 'pull' as well as 'push' factors – are in play. Some observers speak affirmatively of the 'integration' of Gypsies, emphasising positive identification, while many others argue that it is the result of 'stigmatisation' and 'assimilation', involving the social and economic pressures of the dominant society. It depends on the observer's personal assessment influenced by ethnic affiliation or political orientation, whichever factor is stressed. A good illustration of diverging opinions is an article by Popov (1992) analysing the 'Turcomania' among Bulgarian Gypsies, who have increasingly identified with the Turkish minority and declare themselves *en masse* to be Turks. The former socialist governments explained this Turkicisation by pointing to 'nationalist Turkish propaganda' and 'religious fanaticism', while Popov's emphasis is much more on voluntary identification with another (more prestigious) minority. He calls the declared Turkish identity of many Gypsies their 'preferential ethnic conscience'.

For Yugoslavia, Ruža Petrović makes a similar distinction between ethnic origin and ethnic orientation (*etničko poreklo* and *etnička opredeljenost*). Usually they coincide but they may differ considerably, as with Gypsies. In the Yugoslav censuses only the latter has been registered, giving free play to alternative identities (1992:115). Petrović makes some interesting observations about the possible discrepancies between ethnic origin and ethnic orientation: they are most profound in the census results and least in the official death rates. Mostly people may change their identity during their lifetime, but they die as they were born, with the ironic result that in the former Yugoslavia 'Yugoslavs' almost never died: most families preferred to identify a deceased relative according to ethnic origin rather than ethnic orientation, and avoided the classification 'Yugoslav' (1992:122). Petrović argues that those Gypsies who do not declare themselves as such belong to the more developed strata of Gypsy society (1992:127). Prokić (1992) and Mitrović (1990) have come to similar conclusions. Prokić argues that ethnic mimicry usually results from upward social mobility (1992:104), since most Gypsies who have climbed the social ladder have ambivalent feelings about their Gypsy background (1992:113). Mitrović concludes that ethnic mimicry is particularly prevalent among agriculturists and highly qualified workers, as well as among traditional urban sedentary families and the elderly. According to Mitrović, negative experiences as well as social and economic pressures from the non-Gypsy environment are responsible for these processes of ethnic mimicry (1990:21-2, 28-9).

Censuses and ethnic strife: large groups swallow small ones

Censuses have always had important political backgrounds and implications. Benedict Anderson has characterised the census, in the context of colonial South-East Asia, as one of the institutions of colonial power, which 'profoundly shaped the way in which the colonial state imagined its dominion' (1991:164). He points out the changeability and arbitrariness of identity categories. Frequently, ethnic labels were not recognised by those who had been so categorised and subcategorised, but administrative penetration would make them increasingly real: 'The flow of subject populations through the mesh of differential schools, courts, clinics, police stations and immigration offices created "traffic-habits" which in time gave real social life to the state's earlier fantasies' (1991:169).

For Eastern Europe the manipulation of censuses has been demonstrated by Liebich (1992). Apart from the widespread falsification of data and coercion of respondents, states control census data by manipulating the classification system and by fragmenting, amalgamating, inventing or omitting groups. For instance Gypsies and Jews have been the main victims of the procedure of omission, while the invention of new ethnic designations was especially in vogue in Yugoslavia. When the Macedonian nation was established immediately after World War II, Tito's regime invented the categories of 'Yugoslavs' and 'Muslims' – 'an act of pure creativity' in Liebich's view (1992:34). It may be tempting to ridicule the creation of a Muslim nation, as Liebich does, but recent history has shown that so-called 'fictitious' categories can become bitter reality on the battlefield.

Especially since the 1960s, when Yugoslavia pushed its multicultural policy furthest, census results have always had political consequences. They have been used to justify the establishment of 'ethnic keys' connected particularly to the regional and local levels of administration. By means of these ethnic quotas, resources like jobs, houses, (key) positions in administration and scholarships were divided proportionally among the different nations and nationalities. Although the system was designed to guarantee the fair distribution of resources and reduce ethnic tensions, it did not always produce the intended results. In some poor, underdeveloped and ethnically mixed regions in the south it probably stimulated ethnic rivalry or at least kept it alive. The ultimate consequence was the creation (or perpetuation) of a political arena in which ethnic affiliation was of primary importance. The mechanism appears similar to what Anderson describes: when ethnic lines of division, fictitious or not, are of crucial importance in administration, they become increasingly 'real' because they are repeatedly reinforced.

However, this was not the only deficiency of the Yugoslav ethnic quota system. In addition, it was insufficiently safeguarded against abuse and nepotism. Many individuals in key positions favoured their own ethnic group to the detriment of others. Ethnic rivalry was further enhanced by the fact that the ethno-political balance changed drastically when Yugoslavia took steps in the direction of political and economic decentralisation in the 1960s. In Kosovo ethnic relations were turned upside down, causing frustration among Serbs and presenting an opportunity for revanchism among Albanians (Popović *et al.* 1990). A consequence of the ethnic quota system at the local level, was a tendency among representatives of the dominant nations and nationalities to 'assimilate' or incorporate statistically some of the minor ethnic groups, especially those of the same religion and cultural characteristics as themselves. Mostly, this was a 'natural' process in which coercion was largely unnecessary. Those who renounced their ethnic origin in censuses could count on certain social and economic favours or political protection. In this way a system of ethnic patronage developed, in which the main ethno-religious groups tried to absorb the small and powerless ones. This is illustrated by the well-known complaint of small ethnic and religious minorities: '*Mi smo u sendviču izmedju dva naroda; i zna se, sendvič se pojede*' ('We are being sandwiched between two nations; and it is well-known that a sandwich is always swallowed'). Consequently the official statistics do not accurately reflect the numbers of some of the smaller minorities, especially the most vulnerable. Certainly Gypsies have been 'eaten up' statistically. As their political rights have always been very limited, they were especially susceptible to attempts at statistical assimilation.

From the mid-1960s till the mid-1980s, when Milošević started his campaign to abolish Kosovo's autonomy, the Albanians were, as is well known, the most numerous ethnic bloc in Kosovo as well as in parts of western Macedonia. However, Albanians never achieved the same level of political dominance in Macedonia, as in the autonomous province of Kosovo. Their local numerical and economic predominance was counterbalanced by Macedonian political hegemony at the republican level. Nonetheless it is likely that Gypsies, through mechanisms of socio-economic and political control, were exposed to some kind of pressure to declare themselves Albanians. Serbs and Macedonians, as well as Gypsies themselves, have accused Albanians of urging them (and other Muslims) to do this during the censuses of 1971 and 1981, and it has even been claimed that Albanians falsified the census results. They are said to have made an appeal to common religious identity: 'We are all Muslims, so why not declare yourself as an Albanian?' These accusations have been made against Kosovo's Albanians by the Gypsy activist Slobodan Berberski, with much detailed evidence, especially over the 1971 census (1984).[23] In Macedonia the authorities made similar allegations in 1990, accusing the main Albanian party (the Party for Democratic Prosperity in Macedonia) of manipulating Gypsies through religion. Shortly afterwards the Macedonian Roma community called on all Gypsies to stop declaring themselves as Albanians (Poulton 1991:90).

It is clear that in the conflict between Serbs and Albanians many Gypsies have sided with the Serbs, although generally they have much more in common with the Albanians, in religion as well as culture.[24] Since the mid-1980s Gypsies have accused the

---

[23] In *Romano allav*, a local Gypsy journal in Prizren, such allegations were already being made in 1972, just after the census of 1971: 'The census surely does not give a realistic number of Romas, because they did not declare themselves for what they are. The reason for this is very strong public pressure from other nations to declare not as Romas but as Albanians and Turks. Of course, this suits the others. The more Albanians there are, the better it is for them. Turks [who are quite numerous in Prizren] also want to absorb as many Romas as possible, so that their own numbers will not become endangered. There was also pressure from nationalist Serbs, who wanted the Romas to be as numerous as possible so that other nations would be reduced in number. In that case, Serbs would play a much more significant role.' (Menekshe *et al.* 1972:36)

[24] Roux notes that Gypsies have had diverging positions in the recent past: some Gypsy groups have tended to be pro-Serb (even if they are Muslims)

Albanian majority in Kosovo of discriminatory attitudes, while Serbs, themselves a small minority in Kosovo, are praised for their 'tolerance'. Although this may not be completely untrue, it would seem that the identification with Serbs has much more to do with changed political conditions than with the tolerance attributed to them. Under the conditions existing at the time of writing, Gypsies were unwilling to put their money on the Albanian horse, only on the Serbian one; after all, Kosovo was again strictly under Serbian rule, Albanian autonomy had been abolished, and the Albanian aspirations for a republic of Kosovo had been violently suppressed.

This dramatic change in the ethno-political balance of power also explains the appearance of the Egyptians, or perhaps more precisely their emergence from identities that were previously only meaningful in local contexts. It was no longer advantageous to be Albanian: Serbs had taken over political hegemony and they were in control of all strategic institutions and key positions. Now they, and not the Albanians, were in the position to offer jobs or other 'favours'. Since 1990, when more than 100,00 Albanians were sacked from their jobs, Serbs employed Gypsies instead, some of them jobless for many years. Albanians lost power and were therefore unable to secure the 'ethnic loyalty' of minor groups as they did before. Because the Egyptians no longer want to be Albanians and are still less inclined to become Gypsies, they have drawn on an old alternative identity: the Egyptian one. This identity is again 'vacant' now that most Gypsies cherish India as their homeland. Furthermore, in the long term the Egyptian identity may be used to mobilise the political and economic support of Egypt. This outside support may result in an official status as a nationality – something which Gypsies have never attained.

The Serbs and the Macedonians have supported this shift in identity, obviously to weaken the Albanian numerical and political position as much as possible. It has been in their interest to detach

---

whereas others (like the *Ashkali*) were pro-Albanian (Roux 1992:282). However, on the basis of this case study, it seems that groups which were previously 'pro-Albanian' have shifted their loyalties. In the summer of 1998 the Kosovo Albanian press accused Gypsies of joining in the looting of Albanian houses by Serbian paramilitaries (see Fatmir Podrimaj, 'Romët u ndihmojnë paramilitarëve çetnik në djegje e plaçkitje', *Eurozëri*, 14 August 1998, p.22).

Muslim Gypsies from the Albanian bloc, politically and culturally. And if some of them do not want to be Gypsies, why not let them be Egyptians? It is also significant that the Serbian scholars mentioned above have re-labelled the Macedonian and Kosovan Egyptians as Christian Copts, which is one step further in the detachment of these Gypsies from the Muslim Albanian bloc. They are 'Christianised' and their unauthentic Islamic identity is changed into an 'original' Christian one. It is questionable whether the Serbian and Macedonian authorities are ready ultimately to grant substantial minority rights to the Egyptians, especially in the present conditions. Furthermore, in Macedonia under the leadership of Kiro Gligorov the position of Gypsies seems to have improved considerably (Poulton 1993; Barany 1995), which will probably prevent any further spreading of the phenomenon. In present-day Serbia the conditions for some minorities are not favourable, to say the least. For most leaders of the (former) Yugoslav Gypsy community, the phenomenon is an extreme example of political manipulation and juggling with figures, a 'pyramid of lies' as Rajko Djurić writes (1990). For them the Egyptians are Gypsies who have surrendered to the promises and enticements offered by Serbian and Macedonian politicians.[25] In their opinion the phenomenon is the result of the old practice of divide and rule of which Gypsies are once again the victims.

Ethnic identity is not something fixed, and nations and peoples are not isolated and self-confined entities. Since Fredrik Barth's pioneering work (1969) on ethnic groups and their boundaries, this insight has been widely accepted in the social sciences. Ethnic identities vary and change, they are manipulated, they are imposed and may in turn be rejected; they may slowly become lost; they may be discarded, revived or (re)invented. Identities, in the words of James Clifford, are conjunctural and negotiated.

The Egyptians in Kosovo and Macedonia are a clear case in point. Although at first sight they seem a coincidental and arbitrary creation, their emergence is closely connected to the political turbulence that occurred in Yugoslavia at the end of the 1980s:

[25] For Macedonia, Barany writes: 'Most Macedonian Roma consider the "*Egipcanis*'s" claim to be as ridiculous as it sounds and no more than a desperate attempt to acquire support from abroad' (1995:528).

the advent of Serbian nationalism and the rise to power of Slobodan Milošević. Milošević reversed the 'subordinate' position of Serbia within the Yugoslav federation – eventually at the cost of Yugoslavia itself – by abolishing Kosovo's autonomy, as well as by installing his supporters in other federal units. For the Albanians in Kosovo this meant a dramatic change for the worse. As has been argued above, the emergence of the Egyptians as a national identity emanates from this drastic shift in the ethnic balance of power to the Albanians' detriment. As a result, the Egyptians no longer wish to be Albanians, and moreover refuse to become Gypsies again. Their claims to an Egyptian identity have been supported by others, notably by Serbian and Macedonian academics and journalists, who regard the creation of an Egyptian identity as an instrument to affect the numerical predominance of the Albanians.

More generally this case clearly shows that political change may lead to shifts in identity, in particular among groups occupying a relatively weak position within the ethno-political arena. It also shows that the 'authenticity' and 'credibility' of claims of a new ethnic group trying to work out a distinct profile are not established mainly by the group itself, but are also determined by other more powerful actors. Although the impression may have been conveyed that the 'Egyptian' advent was a deliberate act of political manipulation and far-fetched invention, closer inspection of the material suggests that this Egyptian identity has a basis in existing groups and identities. However, they were purely local until recently: this notion of invention therefore only applies to the wider 'Yugo-Egyptian' identity and not to the 'grassroots' identities on which it is ultimately based. In order to explain their otherness, the Egyptian leaders have recycled an old and obsolete theory about the origins of the Gypsies.

Demonstrably, ethnic competition was inherent in the way the Yugoslav brand of communism tried to solve the national question. Whether this ethnic rivalry was the result of a deliberate communist policy of divide and rule, or perhaps the unintended outcome of a genuine attempt to overcome inter-ethnic problems, is a question still to be answered. In any case, instead of mitigating tensions, the census system and the related system of ethnic quotas kept ethnic rivalry alive. Particularly in the 1980s, when the Yugoslav economy collapsed under the burden of enormous debt and rocketing inflation, these institutional arrangements contributed considerably to the rise of local tensions; nationalism was then becoming the dominant paradigm in the political centres. In my analysis of this process of ethnic polarisation, I have tried to highlight the position and fate of small minorities. While Albanians, Serbs and Macedonians are trying to establish political and ethnic hegemony over what they consider their territories, small minorities have been caught figuratively – and in some other parts of former Yugoslavia literally – in the line of fire. With inventiveness they try, as we have seen, to make the best of it.

7

NAIM FRASHËRI'S *QERBELAJA*
RELIGION AND NATIONALISM
AMONG THE ALBANIANS

We have argued that religion is a major factor in processes of identification in the Balkans, and in most of the chapters, dealing with cases at the grass-roots level, this principle has been illustrated. In the last two chapters the locus of attention is shifted from the local to the national level, and I try to analyse the manner in which religion has influenced the ways in which the Albanian and the Serbian nations have been 'imagined' (Anderson 1991).[1] In both chapters the focus is on the attempts of nineteenth-century intellectuals and ideologists of both sides to incorporate religious elements in their respective nationalisms. As was mentioned earlier, nationalism, despite being a modern ideology, has often resorted to 'pre-modern' values and symbols, borrowed in particular from kinship and religion. A comparison of the development of Albanian and Serbian national ideology is of particular interest because in both cases there are attempts to use religious images to sacralise the nation, but within completely different contexts and with quite opposite results: unlike Serbian nationalism, where ethnic and religious identity have merged, Albanian nationalism nowadays lacks any strong religious attachments.

Nevertheless, at the turn of the century, there were some efforts in Albania to inject religious elements into Albanian national ideology. The Albanian national poet, Naim Frashëri, tried to

---

[1] I agree with Richard Jenkins (1997:107) that the 'cultural stuff' with which groups mark themselves off and define their identities is not irrelevant to an understanding of ethnic processes. See also Cora Govers and Hans Vermeulen, who note a renewed trend in ethnic studies towards the analysis of the *content* of ethnicity, i.e. of culture in the sense of collective representation. They have termed this shift in attention the constructionist turn in the study of ethnicity (1997:8).

make (Shi'ite) Bektashi symbols and myths part of Albanian national discourse. More specifically, he tried to promote the Kerbela myth (see Chapter 5) as a source of inspiration in the struggle against Ottoman domination, not unlike the way Serbian nationalists used the myth of Kosovo. Moreover, the Serbian-Orthodox myth about the Battle of Kosovo and the Shi'ite myth about the Battle of Kerbela are very similar to each other in content and style. In both the plot of the story is centred around a lost battle, which makes them examples of what Elias Canetti has called 'religions of lament': 'The legend around which they form is that of a man or a god who perishes unjustly. [...] This is the one death which should not have taken place, and the grief it arouses is beyond all measure. [...] His death is not recognised by the mourners. They want him alive again ... lamenting him, they feel *themselves* as persecuted. Whatever they have done, however they have raged, for this moment they are aligned with suffering' (Canetti 1962:143-5). Suffering, so ubiquitous in the Balkans, is an element which in one way or another has found expression in Balkan nationalism, and all too often it is in the name of this suffering that new crimes are committed.

Albanian nationalism and overcoming religious divisions

From the beginning the Albanian national movement has been confronted with a situation of strong internal religious divisions. The Albanians in the Balkans belong to three different faiths (Islam, Orthodoxy and Roman Catholicism), and if the Bektashis are added as a separate religious community – which *de facto* they have been – then we have a fourfold religious divide.[2] Although Albanian nationalist ideology claims that religion was never important – 'Albanianism' being the only true faith of the Albanians – religion has caused deep divisions within that society, raising a

[2] Although most Albanians (80-90% of all those in the Balkans) are Muslims, in Albania itself the predominance of Islam is slightly less pronounced, especially when one takes the traditionally strong Bektashi presence into account. Slightly more than half of the Albanians in Albania proper are Sunni Muslims (55%), while the rest of the population is divided between the Orthodox (20%), Bektashis (15%) and Catholics (10%). These figures, based on the 1942 census, are reproduced in Daniel (1990:2). One can safely assume that the basic proportions have remained more or less the same.

major obstacle to national unity at the end of the nineteenth century. The threat of internal cleavages along religious lines was reinforced by the fact that many higher ecclesiastics, Albanian as well as non-Albanian, tended to define the ethnicity of their believers in terms other than Albanian, thus inhibiting the development of an Albanian national consciousness: during the late Ottoman period, for instance, the Orthodox in the south were subjected to a process of Hellenisation, while Sunni Muslims were being defined as 'Turks' (Peyfuss 1992).[3]

There have thus been continuous attempts since the nineteenth century to neutralise the legacy of religious cleavages for the politics of Albanian national identity. Since none of the faiths was in the position to unite all Albanians on a religious platform, language became the main vehicle: being very distinct from the languages of its direct (Slav and Greek) neighbours, Albanian was the only factor that could bridge the differences between various religious and regional identities.[4] Religion as a source of communal identity was and is still being systematically played down. In present-day Kosovo, an area where the level of religiosity of the population was above the Yugoslav average, religion is almost irrelevant in official political life (but see Chapter 4). Although more than 90% of the Albanian population in Kosovo are Muslim, Islam has played no role of importance in political mobilisation, and Catholics

[3] At the end of the nineteenth century the Ottoman government strictly prohibited all publications in Albanian, which explains why most Albanian books were printed abroad. Also in schools, which were virtually all maintained by clergy, the language of instruction was usually not Albanian but Greek (in schools run by the Orthodox Church), Italian (Catholic schools), and Turkish (Muslim schools) (see Jacques 1995:276).

[4] Apart from their language it was hard for the Albanians to identify other markers of national identity or symbols of common history. Skanderbeg, the national hero, was probably one of the few historical figures who was sufficiently ambiguous or 'undetermined' in religious terms to be acceptable to all. Skanderbeg (like his father Gjon Kastrioti) changed religious allegiance several times during his lifetime: he was baptised as a Christian, raised as a Muslim, and became Christian again on his return to Albania. Although fifteenth-century European sources celebrated him as the 'Champion of Christianity' fighting against the rule of Islam, nineteenth-century Albanian intellectuals saw him mainly as the figure who liberated his countrymen from foreign domination. They pushed the religious (Christian) component of his resistance to the background (see Jacques 1995:236; Logoreci 1977:30-1; Skendi 1980; Skendi 1956:313-14).

have become as prominent members of the Albanian resistance against Serbian hegemony as their Muslim compatriots.

Because of this legacy of internal religious divisions Albanian nationalism is not clothed in religious terms, in striking contrast to Serbian, Croatian and Bosnian Muslim (Bosniac) nationalism which have clear religious overtones.[5] From the start, its proponents have propagated a kind of 'civil religion' of Albanianism, epitomised in Pashko Vasa's famous *O moj Shqypni* ('Oh poor Albania'), one of the earliest and most influential nationalist poems in Albanian literature, published in 1879-80 (Faensen 1980:148-51; Elsie 1995: 258-67). The author, who was of north Albanian Catholic background, lamented the country's fate, divided as it was along the lines of competing ethno-religious affiliations.

Shqyptar, me vllazën jeni t'u vra,	Albanians, you are killing each other,
Ndër nji qind çeta jeni shpërda;	You are divided into a hundred factions,
Sa thon kam fe, sa thon kam din,	Some say 'I believe in God', others 'I in Allah';
Njeni: jam turk, tjetri: latin	Some 'I am a Turk', others 'I am Latin'
Do thon: jam grek, shkje disa tjerë,	Some say 'I am Greek', others 'I am Slav',
Por jeni vllazën t'gjith more t'mjer!	But you are all brothers, you miserable people!
Priftnit e hoxhët ju kan hutue,	Priests and hoxhas have deceived you
Për me ju da e me ju vorfnue.	To divide you and to keep you poor.

Later he compares his country to a mother and a *zoj e rand* (grand lady) who has been raped and defiled by foreigners. Through this gendered image of the nation and an appeal to the patriarchal values and manly virtues of its men, he calls upon them to undo this disgrace. Again, towards the end of his poem he summons the Albanians to forget their religious differences:

Çonju, Shqyptar, prej gjumit çonju,	Awake, Albanians, wake from your slumber,
të gjith si vllazën n'nji bes shtërngonju,	Let us all, as brothers, swear an oath,
e mos shikjoni kish a xhamija;	Not to mind church or mosque,
feja e Shqyptarit asht shqyptarija!	The faith of the Albanians is Albanianism![6]

---

[5] The merger of religious and national identity can be seen in most of south-eastern Europe, in Orthodox countries like Greece and Serbia (cf. Ramet 1988), as well as in Catholic Croatia and Slovenia (Mojzes 1995).

[6] The Albanian original as well as a translation into English are provided by

The need to bury religious differences is a recurring theme in the literature of the Albanian *Rilindja* (Rebirth) era, especially around the turn of the century. Many prominent patriots of different religious background expressed this idea in some way (Maliqi 1997:122). For instance, after the annexation of Kosovo by the Serbs in 1912, in his poem 'The Voice of the Flag', the well-known Albanian poet Asdreni called upon his compatriots 'to end their religious quarrels and unite in order to save what remained of the country' (Mann 1955:58). This obsession with religious discord certainly shows that confessional differences mattered in Albania, despite the dominant Albanian discursive image that religious fanaticism or intolerance were less profound than in other parts of the Balkans. For several centuries religion had been the primary source of identification, and although nationalist rhetoric declared it to be unimportant (and religious fanaticism to be alien to the Albanian soul), the reality on the ground was sometimes quite different.

The case of the martyrs of Stublla is an obvious example of where these divisions could lead. Throughout the nineteenth century Muslims in Kosovo had the reputation of being quite conservative and fanatical, a phenomenon which cross-cut the ethnonational lines of division. Instances of religious violence against Catholic Albanians were noted by Edith Durham in her book *High Albania*, particularly near the town of Gjakova (Djakovica) (1985:246-8). Even though Catholic Albanians nowadays take an active part in the resistance to Serbian rule, their relations with Muslims have not always been friendly. Because of their 'atypical' religious identity, they have occupied a distinctive and sometimes intermediate social and ethno-political position between the Muslim Albanian majority and the Christian Orthodox Serbs. Even today Catholics rarely marry Muslims, and some are deeply suspicious of their Muslim compatriots, a feeling which is mixed with fear of Islamicisation and of homogenisation of all the Kosovo Albanians along religious lines.

In (proto-)ethnographic sources (mostly dating from the turn of the century) there are many other instances to be found of religious

---

Robert Elsie (1995: 263-7). My translation is based on Elsie's, with some slight alterations.

divisions among Albanians, which present-day Albanian historiography tends to ignore. Even a cursory look at these sources provides ample evidence of religiously motivated tensions, particularly in the towns, where religious leaders tended to guard orthodoxy and orthopraxy with the greatest strictness (Bartl 1968:94-5). Only in the tribal regions of the north did religious divisions seem to play only a minor role. There religious conflict only occurred between tribes of different religious background, and hence the religious divide was secondary to the tribal distinction (Bartl 1968:96). But in the rest of Albania religious difference counted a great deal. Apart from the Albanian-Slav and Albanian-Greek frontiers (in Kosovo, Macedonia and northern Epirus), where ethnic and religious difference overlapped, religious intolerance also existed between Albanians themselves: well-known examples are the Sunni hostility to the Bektashis in the south and the animosity between Catholics and Muslims in the north, as in the town of Shkodra.

Hyacinthe Hecquard, French consul in Shkodra in the midnineteenth century, vividly depicts the tensions between conservative Muslims and Catholics in Shkodra, the largest town in Albania at that time. 'Oppressed because of their fanaticism, or possibly fanatical because of their oppression, the Catholics of Shkodra seem to have been singled out for grievous measures. They were forbidden to build a wall around the cemetery. Situated as it was outside the city, Muslim hoodlums delighted in enraging the Catholics by breaking or overturning the headstones, sometimes even exhuming dead bodies. The intimidated Christians did not dare to make complaints, and the government took no punitive measures' (Hecquard 1858:340, translation by Jacques 1995:212). Until 1857 the market-day was on Sunday, forcing Christians to open shops or buy provisions on their day of rest because local Muslims opposed the change to another day. Only in 1857 was the market-day changed to Wednesday (Hecquard 1858:327-8; 337).

Bartl (1968:39-40) mentions several of Hecquard's contemporaries, who tell similar stories about Shkodra: until the middle of the nineteenth century local Catholic priests were not allowed to wear priestly garb, and the Catholic congregation did not possess a church. The town was divided into twelve Muslim and two Catholic *mahale* (quarters), and it was especially during

Ramadan, when Muslims were irritated at seeing Christians looking fat and well fed, that fights between them occurred, as the British consul in Shkodra, Wadham Peacock, wrote (1914:118-20). On the national level, the question of the Albanian alphabet provides a good example of the way religious divisions inhibited the attainment of unity; after the much-debated choice of the Latin alphabet (1908) strong opposition arose from conservative Muslims who favoured the 'Turkish' (i.e. Arabic) script (Skendi 1960; Peyfuss 1992:132).

However, it is also clear that the national issue slowly began to take the place of religious differences. New 'ethnic' cleavages emerged, especially within the religious communities, for instance within the Greek Orthodox community: in southern Albania, growing tensions between the Greek hierarchy and nationally minded Orthodox Albanian priests led to violence (Ramet 1998: 205-6). On the other hand, religious differences lost some of their importance among the Albanians. In Shkodra, the rift between Catholics and Muslims proved less deep than that between (Albanian) Catholics and the (Slav) Orthodox; despite their common Christianity, Albanians and Slavs despised each other deeply (Jacques 1995:230). Also during the period of the League of Prizren (1878-81) Albanian Muslims and Catholics worked closely together in the Shkodra committee (Bartl 1968:118). !8

The most radical attempt to eradicate religion from the political arena was made under communism. Enver Hoxha took Pashko Vasa's motto ('The faith of the Albanians is Albanianism') literally and made Albania the first 'atheist' state in the world. Under his regime, the fight against religious divisions evolved into a fight against religion *per se*, aiming to replace allegiances to various religious communities with one undivided loyalty to the Party. 'The regime continuously emphasised that Catholicism, Islam and Orthodoxy were alien philosophies introduced into Albania by foreign elements which essentially threatened the integrity of the

[7] For other examples of clashes between Muslims and Catholics in Shkodra see Jacques (1995:220).

[8] The rift between Muslims and Catholics has nevertheless continued, even up to the present day. As Bowers notes, in 1980 only 5% of marriages in the Shkodra district were 'mixed' (i.e. between people of different religious background) (1983-4:129).

nation. Priests and muftis were ridiculed as backward relics of the past, easily recruited as agents of foreign powers to undermine Albanian nationalism' (Vickers and Pettifer 1997:98). Finally, in 1967, the Albanian communists prohibited all religious practices, closing down numerous churches and mosques, and transforming them into cinemas, sports halls or warehouses. In spite of Enver Hoxha's radical Stalinist outlook, it was nationalism which provided the backbone of his policies: his harsh treatment of the religious communities should be seen primarily in this light (Fischer 1995: 45).[9] However, not all religious communities were treated in the same way: it was the Catholic church which was persecuted most rigorously, whereas the attack on Islam was much more restrained (Bowers 1983-4).

After the demise of communism, faith regained some of its importance in the lives of ordinary Albanians, to some extent reviving the old religious divisions. Intellectuals and politicians in Albania have been debating whether their country should find its main allies in the 'Muslim' Middle East or in the 'Catholic' West, and the former President Berisha's move to make Albania a member of the Organisation of the Islamic Conference in December 1992 sparked much controversy (Albania withdrew from it in January 1999). A contributing factor has been the tendency of Albania's (Orthodox) neighbours to perceive Albanian identity not only in ethno-linguistic but also in religious terms, and thus to label them as a 'Muslim' nation or as 'Muslim fundamentalists', a process which has put the secular character of Albanian identity under pressure (Draper 1997:141). Liberal Albanian intellectuals have tried to counteract these tendencies, propagating Albanian 'ecumenism' as the only remedy against internal religious divisions and attempts by one particular religion (Islam) to gain political

[9] Bernd J. Fischer stresses the nationalist character of Enver Hoxha's regime (1995). Since national consciousness in Albania developed relatively late, Hoxha saw his main task as being to forge a nation out of population divided by linguistic, religious, tribal and other 'traditional' allegiances. The Albanian scholar Arshi Pipa is even more outspoken: 'Hoxha was decisive in producing a cultural atmosphere totally dominated by a doctrinaire propaganda exalting nationalism. Linguistics, literature, history, geography, folklore, and ethnology have been cultivated, not only to give the people a sense of their own past, but also to spread and inculcate xenophobia, slavophobia, isolationism, ethnic compactness, and linguistic uniformity' (quoted in Fischer 1995:47-8).

predominance. As Shkëlzen Maliqi writes, 'If the emptiness that Communism left behind can be replaced by something, by some kind of national faith or conviction, then it is the creed that Albanians are a nation of ecumenism, carrying on the tradition of people like Naim Frashëri, Fan Noli and Gjergj Fishta (1997: 122).'

Frashëri's blend of Albanian nationalism and Bektashi doctrine

In spite of the continuous efforts to neutralise religion, there have nevertheless been attempts to give this Albanian 'ecumenism' a firm religious basis. This was exemplified by the attempts of Albania's national poet Naim Frashëri (1846-1900) to promote the Bektashi order as the religious pillar of an emerging Albanian national movement. He hoped that the heterodox and syncretist Bektashis could eventually transcend religious divisions in Albania and bridge the differences between Islam and Christianity. Naim Frashëri seemed to believe that only a bond founded on religion could forge unity among the Albanians, an idea he shared with many other Balkan nationalists of his time. A popular Albanian proverb says: 'Without faith there is no fatherland' (*Pa fe nuk ka atdhe*) (Qazimi 1996:161); and a Greek nationalist historian exclaimed at the end of the nineteenth century, 'Blessed is the nation that professes one and the same faith' (Arnakis 1963:115). For centuries religion had been the main repository of identity in the Balkans and the primary source of loyalty, which could not simply be pushed aside. Consequently, many Balkan nationalists realised that in order to be effective, new forms of identity and political loyalty needed to have the same religious component.

Naim Frashëri was above all a nationalist, whose main aim it was to unite the Albanians, and this dominant national orientation underlines most of his literary work.[10] Nevertheless, his religious

---

[10] Not only Naim but also his two brothers Abdyl and Sami Frashëri played a prominent role in the Albanian national movement. Abdyl was one of the organisers and leaders of the League of Prizren (1878-81), and Sami became the key advocate of Albanian independence at the turn of the century. All three were members of the Bektashi sect, which set them apart from the leaders of the more conservative and traditional Sunni majority (see especially Elsie 1995:226-48, Faensen 1980:99-112, and Bartl 1968:132-40).

writings should not be ignored, as has happened during most of the twentieth century.[11] In much of his work, especially in his pastoral poetry, he blended his passion for Albania's countryside and natural beauty (so characteristic of nineteenth-century romantic nationalism) with Bektashi pantheist ideas, adding a religious and mystical flavour to the former and thus 'sacralising' the landscape. Even more important, in some of his works he mobilised the anti-Sunni and Shi'ite orientation of the Bektashis to express opposition to Ottoman rule, and articulate a separate (Muslim) identity for the Albanians. He was thus trying to transmute the Bektashis' religious doctrine into a vehicle of national aspiration. This process took place against the background of Ottoman Islamic restoration under Sultan Abdulhamid, after the Tanzimat reforms had been terminated.

Naim Frashëri's Bektashi sympathies were evident throughout his life. He grew up in the village of Frashëri (in southern Albania), where he frequently visited the famous Bektashi monastery which later would become one of the main centres of the Albanian national movement (Clayer 1990:275-8).[12] There he was made familiar with the Shi'ite and pantheist beliefs of the sect, and through his education he developed an interest not only in the ideas of the Western Enlightenment but also in the traditions of

[11] In Marxist Albanian historiography and studies of Albanian literature, Naim Frashëri's religious sympathies are disregarded, or at best, criticised in tune with Stalinist dogma (see Shuteriqi *et al.* 1983:186). As Norris writes, Frashëri's Bektashi writings 'have proved difficult to appraise. Indeed, from the prevailing view in Marxist Albania, they had to be dismissed as a *cul-de-sac* and were only redeemable by the nationalist heartbeat still detectable in the content. Even so, much of that content was out of keeping with what was viewed as positive national aspirations, and without question was incompatible with current progressive ideas and ideology' (Norris 1993:168). Nevertheless among Albanian communists there seems to have been an understanding that because of its independent role and its resistance against Ottoman domination Bektashism had been the least damaging of all religious communities in Albania (See Clayer 1992:306-7). The religious (Muslim) dimension in Frashëri's work has only recently become the subject of research again (Qazimi 1996).

[12] The Frashëri lodge was one of the most influential Bektashi lodges in Albania. During the League of Prizren it was a major centre of nationalist activity, and at the beginning of the twentieth century dervishes from the Frashëri lodge went from village to village to make Albanian peasants, Muslim as well as Christian, more sensitive to the national cause (Clayer 1992:291).

the Orient, especially Persian poetry. 'His education made him a prime example of a late nineteenth-century Ottoman intellectual equally at home in Western and Oriental civilisation' (Elsie 1995: 229). After the suppression of the League of Prizren in 1881 he begin to play a role in the activities of the Albanian national movement, quickly becoming one of its key figures together with his younger brother Sami.[13] Naim contributed to the nationalist cause by writing patriotic poems, historical epics and textbooks for Albanian elementary schools. Most of his poetry, which was extremely popular among the very small minority of literate Albanians, was profoundly romantic in character, glorifying the natural beauties of Albania and the delights of rural existence, and expressing dislike for life in the city (a characteristic Naim Frashëri shared with many other nineteenth-century Romantics).[14] As Arshi Pipa has noted, Naim Frashëri was the first to introduce Albanian shepherds and peasants to the literary scene, describing their lives in idyllic terms and ignoring the hardships that were very much part and parcel of peasant life (Pipa 1978:105-8).

As has been noted by several authors, Naim Frasheri's writings were primarily patriotic in scope, while their religious element served to strengthen and deepen his nationalist ideals. Nevertheless, as he was a devout and religious person, Naim Frashëri hoped that Bektashism would one day become the national religion of all Albanians, bridging the religious differences between Islam and Christianity (Mann 1955:38; Elsie 1995:238). He tried to promote the Bektashi order in his *Fletore e Bektashinjet*, the 'Bektashi notebook' (1896), a 'sort of religious-cum-nationalist tract' (Logoreci 1977:44) which was his most direct testimony of Bektashi beliefs primarily meant for non-Bektashi consumption (Birge 1937: 171). It contains an introduction to the Bektashi faith with an

---

[13] Sami Frashëri expressed his political views most comprehensively in his manifesto *Shqipëria – Ç'ka qënë, ç'është e ç'do të bëhetë* (Albania – What was it, what is it and what will become of it, Bucharest 1899), in which he criticised the Ottomans for equating Muslim Albanians with Turks, and attacked the Greeks for their attempts to Hellenise Orthodox Albanians in the south. He proposed Albanian independence as the only way to prevent the division of the country between Slavs and Greeks (see also Bartl 1968:137-40).

[14] See for instance his pastoral poems *Bagëti e Bujqësija*, 'Herds and Pastures' (1886), and *Luletë e verësë*, 'The Flowers of Spring' (1890).

account of the religious doctrine, the organisation, the rituals and the practical ethics of the Bektashi order.[15] The Kerbela theme figures prominently in Frashëri's description of Bektashi ritual in which the main Bektashi feast is the Passion of Kerbela during the first ten days of the month *Muharrem*.[16] From Naim Frashëri's account it is clear that the Albanian Bektashi order held no allegiance to Orthodox Sunni Islam, which it saw as symbolising Ottoman domination over Albanian lands. Absent are references to the five pillars of Islam that are fundamental to Sunnite belief; instead most of the prayer and fasting rituals are centred around the tragedy at Kerbela, as Norris has noted (1993:170). The Albanian Bektashis do not observe the fast of Ramadan.

As Stuart Mann writes, the Bektashi Notebook 'was designed to attract Albanians to a liberal faith acceptable to Christians and Moslems alike, and so to remove one cause of national dissention' (Mann 1955:40). Naim Frashëri tried to capitalise on the non-sectarian and interfaith appeal of the order and depicted it in the most favourable terms. Apart from highlighting religious tolerance, he also stressed its national orientation as one of the central assets of the Bektashi doctrine: 'Not only among themselves but also with all men the Bektashi are spiritual brothers. They love as themselves their neighbours, both Mussulman and Christian, and they conduct themselves blamelessly towards all humanity. But more than all they love their country and their countrymen, because this is the fairest of all virtues' (quoted in Hasluck 1929, II:556). At the end of the text his ideal of promoting the Bektashi order as the national church of Albania shines through in his wish for Bektashis to co-operate with eminent Albanians and local authorities and to work for the salvation of Albania, i.e. to guide Albanians not only on their path to God, but also on their road to national unity (Clayer 1992:292). 'Together with the chiefs and notables let them encourage love, brotherhood, unity, and friendship among all Albanians: let not the Mussulmans be

---

[15] The first part of the Bektashi notebook was published in a German translation by Norbert Jokl (1926). For an English translation see Hasluck (1929).

[16] See especially Norris for a comprehesive treatment of the Kerbela theme in Bektashi ritual and the writings of Naim Frashëri (Norris 1993:169-88). See Degrand (1901:233-4) for a description of this ritual in the town of Kruja around the turn of the century.

divided from the Christians, and the Christians from the Mussulmans, but let both work together' (quoted in Hasluck 1929:526).

The Bektashis' response

It was Frashëri's ideal to establish an independent Bektashi order in Albania, and he put great effort in convincing Bektashi leaders of the need to form an Albanian Bektashi community, as well as to sever ties with the mother lodge in Turkey (Skendi 1967:123-4). He seems to have succeeded, judging from a statement by Margaret Hasluck: 'Latterly in Albania the tendency has been for the local *khalifehs* rather than the distant Akhi Dede [in Anatolia] to appoint abbots, an innovation due to the present Balkan rage for autocephalous Churches, which has so infected Albania that the Catholics of the north actually talk of disowning the supremacy of the Pope' (Hasluck 1925:602).[17] In addition to favouring the establishment of a separate Bektashi religious community, he also proposed purging Bektashi terminology of foreign loan words. Instead of using the Turkish expressions *baba* (sheikh) and *dede* (head of an order), he introduced the Albanian terms *atë* and *gjysh*, and for the term *dervish* (actually of Persian origin) he proposed an Albanian equivalent: *varfë*. As Jokl notes, his language reform was mainly targeted at Turkish loan words, whereas he did not seem to mind vocabulary absorbed from other languages (Jokl 1926:229).

It seems that the Bektashi order was greatly influenced by Naim Frashëri's plans, though there were some sheikhs within its ranks who, fearful of Ottoman authority, expressed reservations about identifying too closely with the nationalist movement (Clayer 1992:286). But, on the whole it is clear that the Bektashis accepted the national role Naim Frashëri had in mind for them. Much earlier, the Bektashis had already fought for looser ties with the Ottoman centre, especially during Ali Pasha's time (1790-1822) when it was one of his major allies (see Chapter 3). The order had been officially abolished by the Ottoman authorities in 1826, which strengthened its opposition to the Ottoman state. In the final decades of the nineteenth century, Albanian Bektashi lodges

[17] After Albania became independent, it was especially Zog (later King Zog) who supported the establishment of autocephalous ('national') churches in order to lessen foreign (especially Greek) influence (see Skendi 1982:253; Fischer 1995:37).

(often places of worship for Muslims and Christians alike) were generally known to be centres of Albanian nationalist activity. In addition, the order played a very important role in the establishment of clandestine schools and the distribution of Albanian books, as well as giving active support to armed nationalist bands.[18] It is noteworthy that the Bektashis, as far as the question of the Albanian alphabet was concerned, favoured adoption of the Latin script, unlike most other Muslims who supported the adoption of the Arabic script (Clayer 1992:287). Hasluck claims that at the time of the Young Turk Revolution (1908), the Albanian Bektashis hoped to establish a Bektashi state in Albania (1929:438).[19]

The prominent role of the Albanian Bektashis in the national movement led to an explosive growth of the order, though for historical reasons it never succeeded in extending its influence into the north.[20] However, in the south of Albania the number of lodges more than doubled (from twenty to fifty) between 1878 and 1912.[21] This remarkable growth in strength and popularity enhanced the self-consciousness of the order, which increasingly started to mark itself off from the Turkish Bektashis and Sunni Albanians, both of whom opposed Albanian independence (Clayer 1992:296). The growing independence of the Albanian Bektashis and their support for Albanian national goals expressed itself for instance in the composition of patriotic poems written in the traditional genre of Bektashi *nefes* (hymns),[22] and in the cultivation

[18] Clayer (1992), who is the foremost scholar on the history of Albanian dervish orders, gives a detailed picture of these nationalist activities, mainly using contemporary sources.

[19] Similarly, the Turkish Bektashis aligned themselves with Turkish nationalism. According to Ramsaur, they embraced the national idea and became the most 'Turkish' of all the dervish orders, using the vernacular and cultivating Turkish forms in their literature (1942:8; see also Birge 1937:16, 84).

[20] In the north there were only lodges in Prizren, Gjakova and Tetova (Kalkandelen). Since Ali Pasha's times, his rivals in the north (the Bushatli and Toptani families) regarded the order with suspicion (Jacob 1908:16–17; Ippen 1907:36; Hasluck 1929:2).

[21] There are parallels here with the rise of the Sanusi-order in Cyrenaica (in present-day Libya) which organised opposition against Italian colonial domination some years later. See the excellent account by Evans-Pritchard (1949).

[22] Clayer gives several examples of patriotic poems written by Bektashi sheikhs (1992:293–6).

of the Kerbela theme. In particular, the Kerbela epics written by members of the Frashëri family – *Hadikaja* by Dalip Frashëri (1842), and the *Myhtarnameja* ('Tale of Myhtar') by Dalip's brother Shahin Bey Frashëri (1868) – had a lasting influence.[23] Both works describe the events during the battle at Kerbela and their aftermath, and were recited during the *matem* ceremonies (the memorial services in honour of Husayn) in Albanian Bektashi lodges. These epics depicted (Sunni) Islam as corrupt and equated its representatives with the main adversaries of Husayn during the Kerbela battle. Instead of stressing Muslim unity throughout the Ottoman empire, greater importance was attached to good relations with other (Christian) Albanians. Since Dalip Frashëri's *Hadikaja* is perhaps the first and certainly the longest 'epic' known in Albanian literature, Kerbela was deeply rooted in not only the literature but also the consciousness of Albanians, as Norris has argued (1993:180-1). This epic generated a whole new genre of national epics and served as a model for recounting other historical themes of national importance.

Naim Frashëri made his major contribution to the epic genre with his *Histori e Skënderbeut*, 'History of Skanderbeg', and *Qerbelaja*, both published in 1898. Although the former work became much more famous (as the first epic account of Skanderbeg's fight against the Ottomans written by a Muslim), some Albanians consider his *Qerbelaja* to be more beautiful. The paramount theme of this epic, which contains twenty-five sections, is the lamentation of the martyrs of Kerbela, whose death is described in great detail.[24] Naim Frashëri describes the terrible thirst at the beginning of the battle, the heroism of its martyrs who are slaughtered one after another, Husayn's farewell to his womenfolk, his brave attack on his enemies, and his final death and decapitation. The tragic outcome of the battle is relayed in vision-like dreams, which highlight the divinely pre-ordained nature of Husayn's defeat. Husayn accepts his martyrdom: out of the two options offered to him – allegiance to Yazid which will make him a traitor, or resistance to Yazid

---

[23] They were not direct relatives of Naim Frashëri, though they came from the same village (Shuteriqi 1983:74). See Clayer (1992:279) for other examples of the *Hadika* tradition in Albanian Bektashi literature.

[24] Norris gives a very useful section by section summary of Naim Frashëri's *Qerbelaja* (Norris 1993:182-5).

which means he will be killed – he chooses the latter. There are many parallels here with the Serbian Kosovo myth (discussed in the next chapter): as in Tsar Lazar's tribulations in Kosovo, moral victory is achieved through actual defeat, suffering and martyrdom (Norris 1993:184). As in the Kosovo myth, the sacrifice of Husayn will lead to the redemption for the community of believers whose sacred duty it is to avenge his death.[25]

What is most interesting is that Naim Frashëri tried to translate this theme of Shi'ite suffering and redemption for a national audience. He was not only describing a (lost) battle in the first century of Muslim history, a battle which became the founding myth in Shi'ism, but he also used it as a symbolic tool for denouncing Ottoman (and Sunni) hegemony (Shuteriqi 1983:186). He was aiming at a national poem that would appeal to all sections of society and would provide a religious source of inspiration for the struggle against Ottoman domination (Norris 1993:182).[26] As with the nineteenth-century Serbian efforts to put the Kosovo myth at the heart of Serbian national ideology, Naim Frashëri seems to have tried to promote the Kerbela myth as one of the components of Albanian national ideology. It is possible that he found his 'inspiration' in the Serbian example: the Kosovo myth had played an important political and ideological role from the beginning of the nineteenth century, when the Serbs started to

---

[25] As Mahmoud Ayoub's study *Redemptive Suffering in Islam* (1978) shows, Shi'ite Islam puts great emphasis on keeping the memory of this tragic event alive through epic poetry, plays, processions, commemorative services (*taziyah*) and other mnemonic devices (see also Eickelman 1989:278-81). The use of very direct language and imagery, the re-enactment of suffering, and the constant repetition of ideas is meant to invoke sorrow and grief among believers, but also to arouse hatred and violent anger against those who killed Husayn. The most important effect of these Muharrem rituals is that men and women can relive these important and dramatic events of the past. As Ayoub puts it, through the commemoration of Husayn's martyrdom the 'now' of the Shi'ite community may be extended back into the past and forward into the future, and thus serve as a strong basis for identity and cohesion (1978:148). In the Shi'ite worldview it is a cosmic event around which history revolves, a universal drama which transcends the confines of time, space and human imagination (1978:145). The parallels with the Kosovo myth (and the so-called *Vidovdan* cult) are striking (see next chapter).

[26] See also Shuteriqi (1983:186).

stand up against Ottoman rule, and even more so after the country became independent in 1878 (Ekmečić 1991).

It is evident that Naim Frashëri's Kerbela epic had a patriotic message (much like his Skanderbeg epic): it was intended to offer a lofty example for the Albanians' fight for independence. Throughout the work Naim Frashëri appeals to the Albanians as a nation that must remember Kerbela and revere its heroes, such as in section XII where he describes the battle, and in section XVIII, where he comments on its significance:

O vëllezrë shqiptarë!	O brother Albanians!
Pa qasuni duke qarë,	Come closer while crying
dhe mbani zi këtë ditë,	and mourn this death
t'u xbresë nga Zoti dritë.	so the light from the Lord comes to you.
Pa kujtoni Qerbelanë!	Remember Kerbela![27]
(Frashëri 1978:201)	

At the very end of the epic, in sections XXIV and XXV, he turns fully towards national issues, urging Albanians to love their nation and country, to learn their own language which is given by God, and to become brothers and friends.

Pa qasuni, Shqipëtarë,	Come close, Albanians
Zot' i math e sjellë mbarë,	let God bring luck
të zëmë vëllazërinë,	let us be brothers
mirësin' e miqësinë,	let us be friends
jemi të gjithë një farë,	we are all of the same seed
e nukë jemi të ndarë,	we are not divided
vëllezrë të tërë jemi,	we are all brothers
një shpirt e një zëmrë kemi,	and have one soul and one heart
gjithë rrojmë me një shpresë,	we all live with one hope
dhe kemi gjithë një besë.	and we all have one faith.
(Frashëri 1978: 274-5)	

He finishes the epic in this undeniably nationalist fashion, linking the tragic events in Kerbela with the tribulations of Albanians under Ottoman rule, cursing contemporary *Yazids* for Albania's enslavement and suffering, and calling upon Albanians to find inspiration in the events of Kerbela in order to challenge Turkish domination.

---

[27] Thanks to Vjollca Henci who translated these (and the following) verses.

Zot i math! për Qerbelanë!
për Hysejn' e për Hasanë!
për ata të dymbëdhjetë!
që hoqn'aqë keq në jetë!

për gjithë ato mundime!
për gashërimënë t'ime!
Shqipërinë mos e lerë,
të prishetë e të bjerë (...)
(Frashëri 1978:288)

O God, for the sake of Kerbela,
for Hasan and Husayn
for the sake of the twelve Imams
who suffered as they did whilst they
    lived,
for all that suffering
for my deepest sadness
Do not let Albania fall nor perish.
Rather let it remain for ever and ever

Frashëri's failure to promote Bektashism as the national creed

In spite of his efforts to reframe Albanian national suffering in Shi'ite terms, Naim Frashëri's attempts had little impact. There are several reasons for this. In the first place the Kerbela myth had a direct appeal only to a small (Bektashi) minority of the population, and even then the myth was not part of any long folk tradition as was for instance the case with the Kosovo songs of the Serbs. *Qerbelaja* was much more the product of literary activity, or 'invention', than the Kosovo myth.[28] Secondly, the attempts by Naim Frashëri and the Bektashi order to promote the order as the 'national' church of Albania also failed because the Bektashis were in a much weaker position as a religious minority than was the Serbian Orthodox church, even though the Bektashi sect had a greater aura of nationalist respectability than any other religious community in Albania. Thirdly, one should bear in mind that it was not Naim Frashëri's first priority to promote the Bektashi order as such, but to propagate religious tolerance. The Bektashi order offered the most appropriate vehicle for that. However, in spite of their popularity, the Bektashis were unable to erase existing religious divisions and counteract the resilience of other, more powerful, religious communities. Finally, during the Balkan Wars and World War I, the Bektashis suffered

---

[28] The adoption of the Skanderbeg myth, which was also a literary invention, shows that such a project can nevertheless succeed. In Albania there were no songs about Skanderbeg; they existed only among the Albanians in Italy (Skendi 1982:250-1).

heavily from all the destruction, a shock which took the order much effort to overcome.[29]

After Albania received independence, religious divisions in Albanian society were played down in the name of common ethnicity. Albanian identity became profoundly non-religious in character (although the notion of 'suffering' remained an important element in nationalist ideology), and Albania became one of the few states in the Balkans with a strong secular character; no official state religion was proclaimed. Nevertheless, the Bektashi order continued to be one of the main pillars of the Albanian national movement. In the 1920s it introduced 'patriotic' elements into its rituals, such as the use of the Albanian flag during religious ceremonies and the use of Albanian as the official language of the Bektashi faith (Clayer 1992:303). Finally, in 1932, the Bektashi order was recognised as a *de facto* independent religious community, a sign of recognition of the important national role it had played.

[29] Between 1913 and 1916, the majority of Albanian lodges (about forty lodges), were destroyed, i.e. looted and burnt by Greek troops, and many Bektashis fled from Albania. It is worth mentioning that the Orthodox population in southern Albanian tried to protect Bektashi *babas* from Greek persecution (Clayer 1992:297).

8

THE KOSOVO EPIC
RELIGION AND NATIONALISM
AMONG THE SERBS

The previous chapter highlighted Naim Frashëri's fruitless attempts to inject a religious element into Albanian nationalism. Through the use of the (Shi'ite) Kerbela myth, Frashëri attempted to give a religious underpinning to the liberation struggle from Ottoman (Sunnite) domination. However, his endeavours had no lasting influence on mainstream nationalist thinking. Most intellectuals active in the Albanian national movement were determined to eliminate religion as a factor in the politics of national identity because it divided instead of united the Albanians. Since then, Albanian nationalism has evolved into one of the most secular nationalisms of south-eastern Europe.

Serbian nationalism has followed a different path: since the early nineteenth century, (Orthodox) religion and (Serb) national identity have fused, moving the Kosovo myth – a profoundly religious one – to the centre of Serbian nationalist discourse. During the nineteenth century, when Serbian identity was formulated, Orthodoxy became central to Serbianness, even though previously the religious allegiances of the Serbs had occasionally shifted, some Serbs adopting Catholicism (for instance in Dalmatia), others Islam (Bosnia). The central importance of Orthodoxy was the outcome of the Orthodox church's crucial role in preserving a kind of rudimentary Serbian identity during Ottoman times (Petrovich 1980:386-91).[1] When, therefore, in the nineteenth century modern concepts of nationhood developed, religion (or rather the religious imagery of Serbian Orthodoxy) became crucial in defining Serbian

[1] The reinstatement of the Serbian Orthodox patriarchate of Peć (1557-1766) was particularly important for the preservation of Serbian or Slav identity within an Orthodox *millet* increasingly dominated by Greeks.

national identity instead of language, a trait Serbs shared with other South-Slavs (Croats and Muslims).[2] This merger between national and religious identity was reinforced by the creation of several autonomous and autocephalous ('national') Orthodox churches in the newly established Balkan states.[3]

Since the first Serbian uprising against Ottoman rule (1804-13), the infant Serbian state and the Serbian church developed a relation of close co-operation and symbiosis. In the first decades of the nineteenth century many Serb Orthodox priests were actively and militantly involved in the Serbian insurrections against the Turks (Petrovich 1980:399). A rump Serbia acquired autonomy within the Ottoman empire in 1830, and in 1831 the Serbs acquired the right to choose their bishops. The now autonomous Serbian Orthodox church became autocephalous in 1879, one year after Serbia's independence (Arnakis 1963:135-6). Then, under the Serbian constitution of 1903, Orthodoxy was proclaimed the official state religion and all state and national holidays were celebrated with church ritual (Ramet 1988:233). This intimate link between state and church has induced the Serbian Orthodox church to adopt a direct political role, especially in times of crisis, eversince.

The fact that Serbian nationalism is grounded in religious mythology and symbolism has led some observers to explain the recent Serbian assault on the Bosnian Muslims and other non-Orthodox populations in the former Yugoslavia in religious terms. As Michael Sells states in his book on religion and genocide in Bosnia (1996), religion has been used as a justification for genocide and ethnic cleansing:

[2] Although throughout the nineteenth and twentieth century it was possible to be a Serb without being Orthodox (but for instance Catholic, Muslim, or Jew), there were always strong social, political, and church pressures to closely identify the two, rendering these groups or categories of non-Orthodox Serbs 'anomalous' or 'ambiguous'. Yet many nineteenth-century Serbian intellectuals (Vuk Karadžić and others) were initially hostile to the church and argued for a language-based definition of Serbian national identity, as in most other countries of Central and Eastern Europe.

[3] This process of compartmentalisation along ethnic lines met strong opposition from the Ecumenical Patriarch in Constantinople, who was the head of the Orthodox *millet*. The creation of autocephalous churches among the Orthodox nations of the Balkans was labelled 'filetism' or 'ethno-filetism' (a term derived from the Greek *file* or tribe) (Radić 1996:269).

Those organising the persecutions […] identified themselves and their cause through explicit religious symbols. The symbols appeared in the three-fingered hand gestures representing the Christian Trinity, in the images of sacred figures of Serbian religious mythology on their uniform insignia, in the songs they memorised and forced their victims to sing, on the priest's ring they kissed before and after their acts of persecution, and in the formal religious ceremonies that marked the purification of a town of its Muslim population (Sells 1996:15).

The thrust of his argument is that Bosnian Muslims, or 'Turks', as they are called by Bosnian Serbs, have been singled out for genocide by Serbian nationalists because of their role as 'Christ killers', i.e. killers of the Serbian prince and martyr Lazar during the Kosovo battle. Although in my view this analysis is flawed because Sells explains historical events exclusively in culturalist terms, I think it is important to look at this level of religious and nationalist discourse. I want to repeat here that the 'cultural stuff' with which nations mark themselves off and define their identities is not irrelevant to an understanding of ethnic processes (Jenkins 1997:107). We should be prepared to acknowledge that ideologies, religious doctrines and myths indeed shape people's cognition and perception and that they to some extent motivate or mould action, though any analysis of specific events always needs to take the economic, political and historical dimensions into account as well. Through the manipulation of myths and symbols, political programmes may be transmitted from the intellectual sphere to that of mass politics, inducing people to think, feel, and act collectively according to the political premises (Denich 1994:369). Myths and symbols can even help in breeding collective violence, through the creation of an ideological context in which violent acts are made thinkable.[4]

The theme of suffering

Not unlike Shi'ism, Serbian Orthodoxy is imbued with a strong sense of victimisation and suffering, which is traced back to the

[4] I am particularly inspired by the work of Stanley Tambiah (1986), who provides a combination of social, economic, political and cultural explanations for the violence in Sri Lanka, and the work of Bruce Kapferer (1988), who demonstrates how myths are invoked to create environments in which ethnic violence, including murder, becomes acceptable.

Kosovo battle when the Serbs were defeated by the Ottoman Turks (1389). The Serbian Orthodox church sees itself as a *suffering* church (Ramet 1988:232), an idea which was brought to its apogee in the first half of the twentieth century by the Serbian bishop and theologian Nikolaj Velimirović (Bremer 1992:112-60). Velimirović (together with the other major Serbian theologian of this century, Justin Popović) adapted this mindset of Serbian suffering to the modern conditions of the nation-state, transforming the suffering of the church into the suffering of the Serbs as a *nation*. World War II reinforced the notion of Serb suffering, with the destruction of hundreds of monasteries and churches, the liquidation of hundreds of Serbian Orthodox priests (including six of the church's top hierarchs), and an enormous number of civilian casualties. As the losses were huge both in human, material and psychological terms, the war had an equally traumatic effect on the Serbian Orthodox church (Ramet 1988:236-8). After the war, the church's suffering did not stop: under communism it was severely punished by the communists for its nationalist and reactionary stands in the pre-war period. It was marginalised in social and political life, its possessions were confiscated and Serbian Orthodox clerics were severely harassed (Ramet 1988:238-41).

In the early 1980s, in the wake of growing ethnic unrest and nationalism in the former Yugoslavia, the Serbian Orthodox Church made a come-back on the political scene. It started to revive the notion of a suffering Serbian nation by focusing on the problem of Kosovo. The growing conflict between Serbs and Albanians was presented as a clash between two opposing civilisations, a renewed battle between Christianity and Islam, in which Serbs were being threatened with extinction and 'genocide'. It was alleged that Albanian 'fundamentalists' were embarking upon a *jihad* attempting to ethnically cleanse Kosovo of its Serbian inhabitants.[5] By exploiting the Kosovo issue, the Serbian Orthodox church saw a chance to regain much of its political influence after forty years of forced submission to communist rule. It reclaimed

---

[5] In 1985 the Kosovo mindset was epitomised by the case of Djordje Martinović, a Serb peasant from Kosovo who claimed to have been raped and abused by two Albanians with a broken beer bottle. He immediately acquired the status of a martyr, an 'archetype of Serb suffering and Albanian (Muslim, Ottoman...) evil' (Thompson 1992:129).

its national role by using its pan-Serb church structure to strengthen Serbian unity in a federalised Yugoslav state, where the Serbian nation had been divided among several republics and autonomous provinces. It claimed that under communism it had been the only institution that had not betrayed the Serbian nation, unlike most Serbian communists who had 'sold out' Kosovo to the Albanians.[6] It was particularly the theologian (and later bishop) Atanasije Jevtić, a tough nationalist and prolific writer, who contributed most to the reactivation of the discourse of the 'suffering Serbian nation' (Jevtić 1987, 1990). He developed an entire Serbian theology out of Serb suffering in the centuries-old struggle for Kosovo (van Dartel 1997:145). Another major advocate of this idea was the controversial Montenegrin bishop Amfilohije Radović.

However, the cultivation of the theme of Serbian suffering did not remain confined to the church. In the second half of the 1980s, it became a leitmotif in politics and academia as well as in the mass media. The Kosovo problem, which had initially been presented as a human rights issue, was now being redefined as a Serbian national issue, a new Kosovo battle fought between the old enemies, the Orthodox Serbs and the 'Turks', i.e. Muslim Albanians. Eventually, this discourse was adopted by leading communist politicians. Slobodan Milošević sky-rocketed to power when he stood up to protect the Kosovo Serbs against further suffering, making his famous declaration, 'nobody should dare to beat you ...' during a visit to Kosovo in April 1987 (Magaš 1993).

The notion of Serb suffering (in a more secular version) was for the first time expressed in the Memorandum of the Serbian Academy of Sciences and Arts (1986), which presented the predicament of the Serbs in Kosovo in almost apocalyptic terms: 'The physical, political, legal and cultural genocide of the Serbian population in Kosovo and Metohija is a worse defeat than any experienced in the liberation wars waged by Serbia from the first Serbian uprising in 1804 to the uprising in 1941' (Mihailović and Krestić 1995:128). The document compares the 'genocide' in Kosovo to

---

[6] Church dissent with communist policy in Kosovo was for instance openly expressed in April 1982, when twenty-one priests signed an appeal to the authorities 'for the protection of the spiritual and biological existence of the Serbian nation in Kosovo and Metohija'. An English translation of this petition can be found in *South Slav Journal*, 5(3), 1982, pp.49-54.

the extermination of Serbs during World War II. It also claims
that the Serbs were discriminated against and under threat of
annihilation in other parts of Yugoslavia, particularly in Croatia
and Bosnia, hence painting a picture of a humiliated nation whose
cultural and spiritual integrity was trampled upon (Mihailović and
Krestić 1995:134). The document further claims that the Serbs
are subjected to 'physical annihilation, forced assimilation, conversion to a different religion, cultural genocide, ideological in-
doctrination, denigration and compulsion to renounce their own
traditions because of an imposed guilt complex. Intellectually and
political unmanned, the Serbian nation has had to bear trials and
tribulations that are too severe not to leave deep scars in their
psyche...' (Mihailović and Krestić 1995:138).

In 1989, on the eve of the 600th anniversary of the Kosovo
Battle, there was a further outburst of publications in which Serbian
history was portrayed as a succession of defeats and losses.[7] Even
in the mass media Serb suffering – particularly under the Ottoman
Turks and in World War II – became the focus of attention (Marković
1996). In the next two years, before the outbreak of the war,
counting the dead became a kind of 'national hobby' (Marković
1996:647), while nationalist politicians (for instance, the leader
of the Krajina Serbs, Jovan Rašković) started to refer to their
nation as 'the slaughtered people', giving more sinister meaning
to the notion of 'heavenly Serbia'. The dead bodies of Serbian
victims of World War II were exhumed and reburied in church
ceremonies which were frequented by nationalist politicians (Denich
1994; Hayden 1994; Bax 1997). Yet some nationalists underlined
the fact that suffering made the Serbs what they are and that they
should somehow be grateful for that: 'We are a lucky people ...yes,
we really are in a special way. The Turks hate us. Thank God.
[...] Everything of us that has any value came into being when
they oppressed and hated us most. Thanks to them we exist and

---

[7] The obsession with suffering and death is present in many literary works, for
instance in the works of writer-politicians like Vuk Drašković (*Nož*, 'Knife',
1983), Dobrica Ćosić (*Vreme smrti*, 'Time of Death' 1977-8), but also in the
poetry of Radovan Karadžić. For similar tendencies in academic historiography
see for instance Dimitrije Bogdanović's *Knjiga o Kosovu* (1986), *Le Kosovo-Metohija
dans l'histoire serbe* (Samardžić *et al.* 1990), and Bataković's *The Kosovo Chronicles*
(1992) which can all be read as chronicles of Serb suffering in Kosovo since
the Middle Ages, under Ottoman, Albanian and communist rule.

we know who we are. [...] Had they not existed, we would not have had our Kosovo....' (Danilo Radomirov, member of the nationalist party *Srpska Narodna Obnova*, 'Serbian National Renewal', quoted in *Vreme*, 8 May 1995, p.39).

The Kosovo myth

Central to this obsession with suffering is Kosovo, where a defeat by the Turks in 1389 led to the downfall of the Serbian medieval empire and the 'enslavement' of the Serbs for the next 500 years. It is this lost battle between the Christian (mainly Serbian) and Ottoman forces which has gained mythical proportions in Serbian history. Although the first reports of the battle proclaimed a Christian victory, in the next few decades the Christian armies failed to halt the Ottoman advance and almost all of the Balkans fell under Turkish rule. During the battle both army leaders died: Sultan Murad was killed by Miloš Obilić (so the legend goes), while the leader of the Christian forces, Lazar, was captured by the Turks and beheaded.

Almost immediately after the Kosovo battle, the writing of ecclesiastical sermons and hagiographies began, commemorating the battle and Prince Lazar's death (Zirojević 1995:9). Lazar was proclaimed a martyr who sacrificed himself for the Christian faith; his military defeat was seen as a consequence of his choice for a heavenly kingdom over an earthly one. Thus his downfall was turned into a moral and spiritual victory.[8] Later, these monastic texts about Kosovo became the substance of songs, which were composed and sung in the courts of the Serbian aristocracy (Koljević 1980). However, with the advance of the Ottoman Turks and the destruction of Serbian feudal society, this oral poetry mainly became the property of peasants. Since the (Serbian) Orthodox church enjoyed a privileged position within the Ottoman *millet* system, it was compelled (at least officially) to suppress the memory

---

[8] For early samples of hagiographic work on Prince ('Tsar') Lazar, see: Holton and Mihailovich 1988:22-8. The central theme of the Kosovo myth, Lazar's choice of the heavenly kingdom ('Better a praiseworthy death than a life in scorn') was formulated soon after the battle in the poem 'Narration about Prince Lazar' (1392) (Holton and Mihailovich 1988:25).

Prince ('Tsar') Lazar.

of Kosovo (Skendi 1954:76).[9] But it was kept alive in epic songs performed by *guslars* (singers of folk epics) to the accompaniment of their *gusle* (one-stringed instruments played with a bow), who retold the tragic events of Kosovo and also sung about their own heroes and fights with the Turks.[10]

There is clear evidence of continuous transmission and development of Kosovo songs from the earliest years after the battle (Malcolm 1998:78). However, these songs focus on the principle characters of the Kosovo legend (such as Prince Lazar and Miloš Obilić), their martyrdom and the downfall of the Serbian kingdom and feudal society rather than the destiny of the Serbs as a nation. This shift in meaning occurred only in the nineteenth century, when the Kosovo theme evolved into a national myth, providing a source of inspiration to avenge its loss, to resurrect the nation and to recover the national homeland. Prince Lazar became a national saint and martyr whose *živo telo* (living body) became the most important Serbian national relic.

Vuk Stefanović Karadžić was instrumental in retrieving the Kosovo songs from Serbian popular tradition and standardising them into a coherent story.[11] Between 1814 and his death in 1864, he collected numerous epic songs, of which the songs about the Kosovo battle formed a major part. By collecting and compiling them into a whole he 'canonised' the Kosovo myth and thus provided Serbian national ideology with its mythical cornerstone.

---

[9] By the seventeenth century the monastery of Ravanica (Lazar's burial place) was the only location where the cult of St Lazar was celebrated (Malcolm 1998:78).

[10] The heartland of epic songs seems to be the mountainous terrain of Bosnia, the Sandžak, Montenegro and northern Albania. One of the major functions of these songs has been to make important historical events known, or to spread the news about recent events among an illiterate population. Ugrešić has aptly called it '*gusle* journalism' (Ugrešić 1994).

[11] Vuk Karadžić was a pivotal figure in this formative period of the Serbian national idea: among other things he was responsible for the standardisation of the Serbian vernacular language and the development of the Serbian Cyrillic script, both key steps in the process of Serbian nation-building. In 1815 he produced a Serbian grammar, and three years later a Serbian dictionary. He published his first collection of Serbian poetry in 1814. His famous six-volume *Srpske narodne pjesme*, published between 1844 and 1866, became the classic anthology of traditional Serbian oral poetry.

In taking the popular Kosovo songs as his source, he also made a great step forward in bridging the gap between the nationalist intelligentsia and popular culture (Ekmečić 1991:335). Perhaps the most important episode of the Kosovo cycle (which consists of a number of songs describing the events before, during and after the battle[12]) is Prince Lazar's choice of a heavenly kingdom, as a result of which the Serbian army lose the battle against the Turks. It is described in the poem below, *The Fall of the Serbian Empire*, which is central to Serbian national ideology.

Poletio soko tica siva	From that high town, holy Jerusalem,
od svetinje od Jerusalima,	There comes flying a grey bird, a falcon,
i on nosi ticu lastavicu.	And in his beak a small bird, a swallow.
To ne bio soko tica siva,	Yet this grey bird is not just a falcon;
veće bio svetitelj Ilija;	It is our saint, the holy Saint Elijah.
on ne nosi tice lastavice,	And the swallow is not just a swallow,
veće knjigu od Bogorodice;	But a message from the Holy Virgin.
odnese je caru na Kosovu,	The falcon flies to Kosovo's flat field.
spušta knjigu caru na koleno,	The message falls in the lap of the Tsar;
sama knjiga caru besedila:	For Tsar Lazar is the message destined:
'Care Lazo, čestito koleno,	'O Tsar Lazar, Prince of righteous lineage,
kome češ se privoleti cartsvu?	which of the two kingdoms will you embrace?
Ili voliš cartsvu nebeskome,	Would you rather choose a heavenly kingdom,
ili voliš carstvu zemaljskome?	Or have instead an earthly kingdom here?
Ako voliš carstvu zemaljskome,	If, here and now, you choose the earthly kingdom,

---

[12] Of special importance are the episodes that predict or announce the coming battle and its tragic outcome (such as dreams or quarrels between Serbian knights), the events at the eve of the battle – especially Prince Lazar's supper which is modelled on Christ's Last Supper (Zirojević 1995:10) – as well as the aftermath of the battle seen through the eyes of the women that remain behind. The main characters are Prince Lazar Hrebeljanović, Miloš Obilić and Vuk Branković. While Lazar embodies devotion to the Christian faith (figuring even as a kind of Christ reincarnated), Miloš Obilić primarily represents the virtues of loyalty and bravery: according to the Kosovo legend he infiltrates the Ottoman camp and kills Sultan Murad. Vuk Branković is the third main figure, the traitor or Judas figure. He enters into an agreement with the Sultan in return for the preservation of his position. He is basically blamed for the loss of Kosovo. The most important women are the Kosovo girl who tends the dying warriors with wine and water and the mother of the Jugovići who loses all her nine sons in the battle. All these figures have become 'the archetypes of Serbian virtue and villainy' (Thompson 1992:144).

sedlaj konje, priteži kolane!　　　　　saddle horses, tighten the saddles' girths,
Vitezovi sablje pripasujte,　　　　　　let all the knights put on their mighty swords,
pa u Turke juriš učinite:　　　　　　and launch you then assault against the Turks.
sva će turska izginuti vojska!　　　　Then their army, all the Turks, shall perish.
Ako l' voliš carstvu nebeskome,　　　But if, instead, you choose the heavenly
　　　　　　　　　　　　　　　　　kingdom,
a ti sakroj na Kosovu crkvu,　　　　　Then you must build a church at Kosovo.
ne vodi joj temelj od mermera,　　　　Do not build it upon a marble base,
već od čiste svile i skerleta,　　　　But on pure silk and costly scarlet cloth,
pa pričesti i naredi vojsku;　　　　And give your host orders to Holy Mass.
sva će tvoja izginuti vojska,　　　　For every man, all soldiers, will perish,
ti češ, kneže, s njome poginuti.'　And you, their prince, will perish with your
　　　　　　　　　　　　　　　　　host.'

A kad care saslušio reči,　　　　　When Tsar Lazar has heard the whole message,
misli care, misli svakojake:　　　Lazar is vexed; he ponders, he thinks much:
'Mili Bože, što ću i kako ću?　　'O my dear Lord, what shall I ever do?
Kome ću se privoleti carstvu:　　And of the two, which kingdom should I
　　　　　　　　　　　　　　　　choose?
da ili ću carstvu nebeskome,　　　Shall I now choose the promised heavenly
　　　　　　　　　　　　　　　　kingdom,
da ili ću carstvu zemaljskome?　Or shall I choose an earthly kingdom here?
Ako ću se privoleti carstvu,　　If I do choose, I embrace the latter,
privoleti carstvu zemaljskome,　If I do choose the earthly kingdom here,
zemaljsko je za malena cartsvo,　Then what I choose is but a transient kingdom;
a nebesko uvek i doveka.'　　　　The eternal one is that promised in heaven.'

Car volede carstvu nebeskome,　　Lazar chooses the promised heavenly
　　　　　　　　　　　　　　　　kingdom;
a negoli cartsvu zemaljskome,　　he refuses the earthly kingdom here.
pa sakroji na Kosovu crkvu:　　　So he has built the church of Kosovo.
ne vodi joj temelj od mermera,　He does not build upon a marble base,
već od čiste svile i skerleta,　But on pure silk and costly scarlet cloth.
pa doziva srpskog patrijara　　　He calls to him the Serbian patriarch;
i dvanaest veliki vladika,　　　　Beside him stand twelve great Serbian bishops.
te pričesti i naredi vojsku.　　The whole army comes to take communion.
(Arsenijević 1989:257)　　　　　(Holton and Mihailovich 1988: 95-6)

The stanza, Prince Lazar's oath (first published in 1815 and part of the poem *Musić Stefan* in the Kosovo cycle), in which Lazar curses those Serbs who refuse to join him on the Kosovo battlefield, became a battle cry of the national movement:

Ko je Srbin i srpskoga roda	Whoever is a Serb of Serbian blood,
i od srpske krvi i kolena,	Whoever shares with me this heritage,
a ne doš'o na boj na Kosovo:	and he comes not to fight at Kosovo,
ne imao od srca poroda,	May he never have the progeny
ni muškoga ni devojačkoga!	his heart desires, neither son nor daughter;
od ruke mu ništa ne rodilo,	Beneath his hand let nothing decent grow
rujno vino ni šenica bela!	Neither purple grapes nor wholesome wheat;
Rdom kap'o dok mu je kolena!	Let him rust away like dripping iron
(Stojković 1987:204)	Until his name shall be extinguished!
	(Sells 1996:39)

These two poems became central to the *Vidovdan* cult: the first depicts the Serbs as a chosen nation which has signed a Covenant with God, while the second calls on all Serbs not to forsake their duty of defending their nation in times of crisis.

Kosovo in the Active Mood

Vuk Karadžić collected the Kosovo songs and other heroic songs at a time when the first Serbian uprising against Ottoman domination was in full swing (1804-13). The ideological underpinnings of Serbia's liberation struggle, i.e. revenge for the loss of Kosovo and the resurrection of the medieval Serbian empire, were already emerging at that time (Judah 1997:51). In the first half of the nineteenth century Serbian writers, especially those living in areas under Hapsburg control, took the Kosovo battle as the subject of their work, for instance Zaharija Orfelin (Holton and Mihailovich 1988:62-4) and Jovan Sterija Popović (Holton and Mihailovich 1988:72). In 1828 Popović wrote *Boj na Kosovu* (The Battle of Kosovo) and a drama based on the same theme, *Miloš Obilić*, which were performed for many decades in small towns all over Serbia (Ekmečić 1991:334). Serbian romantic poets wrote poems that vilified the Turks and praised the joys of Serbian peasant life, whereas the style of the epic song came to dictate most literary expression.

In more concrete political terms, the Kosovo myth was harnessed to a programme of territorial expansion and the recovery of the great medieval Serbian kingdom. The figure who combined both elements (the poetic and the political) was Petar Petrović Njegoš, who ruled over Montenegro in the middle of the nineteenth century. The work that is most relevant to our theme is his epic drama *Gorski Vijenac* (The Mountain Wreath) which is considered a masterpiece in Serbian and Montenegrin literature. This work is interesting not only because of its unusual combination of genres, but also because of the wider political context in which it was written: when Montenegro and Serbia were involved in a struggle for independence against the Ottoman empire. The play is dedicated to the leader of the first Serbian uprising, Karadjordje, who 'roused people, christened the land, and broke the barbarous fetters, summoned the Serbs back from the dead, and breathed life into their souls' (Njegoš 1989:2)'. Its overriding theme is the struggle against the Turks, and as such *Gorski Vijenac* can be read as Njegoš's answer to the tragedy of Kosovo (Ekmečić 1991:335). Holton and Mihailovich have named it 'Serbia's epic', and 'the emblem of her identity' (1988:147). Borrowing Fischer's terminology with regard to the Kerbela myth, I would argue that Njegoš's *Mountain Wreath* is the first major example of 'Kosovo in the Active Mood', i.e. using the myth to trigger revolutionary (political) action and avenge Kosovo.[13]

The Mountain Wreath, which is a play written in epic verse, is based on a pseudo-historical event known as the extermination of the Turkish converts, which is said to have taken place on Christmas Eve at the beginning of the eighteenth century. The basic theme of the work is the fight against those Montenegrins who became Muslim, thereby switching allegiance to the Turkish occupiers. The main plot of the play – the extermination of Muslims who refuse to convert back to Christianity – expresses Njegoš's main ambition: to free Montenegro from Turkish domination and Islam. Kosovo takes a central position in *The Mountain Wreath*: Njegoš refers several times to the Kosovo tragedy, cursing the figure of Vuk Branković, and depicting Miloš Obilić as the only true Serb, 'a mighty military genius, a terrific thunder that shatters crowns'. Although contempt for the Muslims as these 'Turkish turncoats', 'loathsome degenerates' and 'filthy breed of dogs' (to

---

[13] Some have presented this work as a blueprint for genocide (Sells 1996:51; see also Judah 1997:241; Mojzes 1995:38). Although the poem can certainly act as a source of inspiration for those who want to start a 'holy war' against Islam and want to expel Muslims from the Balkans, we should be cautious in drawing a straight line of causation from a literary text to the occurrence of genocidal practices.

mention only a few labels applied in the poem) is tremendous, they are offered the choice of reconversion to Christianity. As Vojvoda Batrić (one of the main heroes) says:

Turci braćo, – u kam udarilo! –
što ćemo vi kriti u kučine?
Zemlja mala, odsvud stiješnjena,

s mukom jedan u njoj ostat može
kakve sile put nje zijevaju;
za dvostrukost ni mislit ne treba!
No primajte vjeru praedovsku,
da branimo obraz otačastva.
Ćud lisičja ne treba kurjaku!
Što jastrebu oće naočali?
No lomite munar i džamiju,

pa badnjake srpske nalagajte
i šarajte uskrsova jaja,
časne dvoje postah da postite;

za ostalo kako vam je drago!
Ne šćeste li poslušat Batrića,
kunem vi se vjerom Obilića
i oružjem, mojijem uzdanjem,
u krv će nam vjere zaplivati, –

biće bolja koja ne potone!
Ne složi se Bajram sa Božičem!

Je l' ovako, braćo Crnogorci?

'Turkish brothers – may I be forgiven! –
we have no cause to beat around the bush.
Our land is small and it's pressed on all sides.
Not one of us can live here peacefully,
What with powers that are jawing for it;
for both of us there is simply no room!
Accept the faith of your own forefathers!
Guard the honor of our fatherland!
The wolf needs not the cunning of the fox!
Nor has the hawk the need for eyeglasses.
Start tearing down your minarets and mosques
Lay the Serbian Christmas-log on the fire,
Paint the Easter eggs various colors,
Observe with care the Lent and Christmas fasts.
As for the rest, do what your heart desires!
If you don't want to listen to Batrić,
I do swear by the faith of Obilić,
and by these arms in which I put my trust,
that both our faiths will be swimming in blood.
Better will be the one that does not sink.
Bairam cannot be observed with Christmas!

Is that not so, Montenegrin brothers?'
(Njegoš 1989:31)

However, the Montenegrin 'brothers' who became Muslims refuse to reconvert. Since they do not want to be baptised with water, they have to be baptised with blood, as the expression in *The Mountain Wreath* has it, and the long-awaited battle with these Montenegrin 'Turks' ensues. After the victorious battle, which avenges the loss of Kosovo, Abbot Stefan (an Orthodox priest) calls upon all Montenegrins to commemorate the heroes of the Kosovo battle, saying: 'This day will be the most priceless to them; since Kosovo there's never been such day' (Njegoš 1989:96). Kosovo and the martyrs of Kosovo have been avenged, their souls can rest, and the honour of the Montenegrins has been restored.[14] At the end of the epic, messengers bring the good news of other Montenegrins following the example of the uprising, killing and slaughtering Turks and levelling mosques and Turkish buildings to the ground.

The notion of avenging the Kosovo tragedy and 'liberating' Kosovo once and for all also became a main preoccupation of Serb politicians, especially in the middle of the nineteenth century. The Kosovo cycle evolved into the ideological instrument of a nation under construction and an expanding Serbian state, justifying the reconquest of 'Serb' lands from the 'Turks'. In the 1860s Ilija Garašanin, prime minister and minister of foreign affairs in Serbia's government, made Kosovo an integral part of Serbian national thought (Judah 1997:58-9). In his *Načertanije* ('Draft', 1844) he justified the recovery of Serb lands from the Ottoman empire as a restoration of the medieval Serbian empire; this document was aimed primarily at the annexation of Bosnia and Kosovo, union with Montenegro, and having an outlet to the Adriatic sea (Jelavich 1983-I:331). Since then, the liberation of territories under Ottoman control has been a kind of sacred duty, an obligation to avenge the injustices of Kosovo.

Although the Kosovo myth came under attack in the late 1860s, in particular by Serbia's main socialist thinker Svetozar Marković (1846-75), it nevertheless became a crucial element in justifying Serbian aims for territorial expansion. This period marks the beginning of the *Vidovdan* (St Vitus Day) cult which was fostered by the state (Ekmečić 1991:336). It provided ideological ammunition for the numerous wars Serbia fought after 1876, and it was continually revitalised by writers, poets, politicians and ecclesiastics. In the second half of the nineteenth century it showed its mobilising power during the Bosnian peasant insurrection (1875): Ekmečić states that '[a]n invitation sent to villages to join the rural uprising was almost a carbon copy of Prince Lazar's oath in verse' (Ekmečić 1991:337). Finally, on St Vitus Day (28 June) 1876, Serbia declared the war on Turkey that was to lead to Serbia's independence. During these years the *reconquista* of Kosovo became a Serbian obsession, and when the Serb armies conquered

---

[14] It is the patriarchal Montenegrin moral concept of vengeance – 'Vengeance is holy' (*Osveta je sveta*), and 'Only the avenger can be consecrated' (*Ko se ne osveti, taj se ne posveti*) – which is at work here (Brkić 1961:147).

and temporarily occupied parts of Kosovo in January 1878 the mood was euphoric.[15]

At the end of the nineteenth century, 28 June (Vidovdan) was integrated into the calendar of the Serbian Orthodox church as the commemorative day of the battle of Kosovo (Malcolm 1998:78). Special efforts were then made by the Serbian government to turn the 500th anniversary of the battle into a huge national commemoration, the first of this kind in Serbia. Indeed, in 1889, Vidovdan was massively celebrated, with the main commemoration ceremonies in Kruševac (Lazar's former capital) and Ravanica (the monastery where Lazar's remains were kept). As Ekmečić writes: 'It was a day of national mourning with black flags on roofs, the national standard at half-mast, and invitations for the evening commemorations printed with black margins' (1991:338). In 1890, one year after the 500th anniversary of the Kosovo battle, Vidovdan became a state holiday (Zirojević 1995:16). At the beginning of the twentieth century, with the advent of mass nationalism, it became a festival on an even grander scale with commemorations under the open sky and gatherings at churches (Ekmečić 1991:334).

During the First Balkan War (1912) Kosovo was finally avenged: the Serbs 'liberated' Kosovo, making an end to the long period of humiliation under Turkish and Albanian hands. When the Serbian army marched into Kosovo, illiterate soldiers knelt and kissed the soil (Thompson 1992:145). Two years later, on 28 June 1914, World War I was triggered by the assassination of Archduke Franz Ferdinand by Gavrilo Princip. Again the Kosovo heroes served as a model for this new generation of freedom fighters. Princip, and most of the members of the Young Bosnia group who carried out the assassination, had been inspired by the heroic deeds of Miloš Obilić, and thus were literally re-enacting the Kosovo myth (Judah 1997:64, 97; Ekmečić 1991:340).

There are other historical events in which the Kosovo myth played a role. In March 1941 the 'spirit of Kosovo' ideologically shaped the military coup against the Serbian government which had succumbed to Hitler's threats and signed up to the Axis Tripartite Pact. Patriarch Gavrilo, who had been staunchly against the signing, clearly saw the coup in terms of the Kosovo ethic.

---

[15] One of the places which the Serbs took was the monastery of Gračanica.

On the radio he said: 'Before our nation in these days the question of our fate again presents itself. This morning at dawn the question received its answer. We chose the heavenly kingdom – the kingdom of truth, justice, national strength and freedom. That eternal idea is carried in the hearts of all Serbs, preserved in the shrines of our churches, and written on our banners' (Judah 1997:113). Even under communism Vidovdan kept its emotional appeal. According to-Milovan Djilas, the reception of the Cominform Resolution against Yugoslavia on 28 June 1948, 'cut into the minds and hearts of all us Serbs. Though neither religious nor mystical, we noted, with a certain relish almost, this coincidence in dates between ancient calamities and living threats and onslaughts' (Djilas 1985: 201).

Folk poetics and populist politics

Like the Kerbela myth in Shi'ite Islam, the Kosovo myth is about a lost battle between the righteous forces of good against the victorious forces of evil. In both cases the main heroes of the story refuse to surrender and they know this will inevitably lead to their defeat and death. In both examples the main hero's sacrifice is the central event of the legend, providing a powerful and emotional theme of martyrdom and resistance. And in both cases the myth enjoins people to be patient and accept suffering as a necessary step towards redemption, but it also inspires them to rise up in revolt against tyranny even in the face of overwhelming odds.

If we confine ourselves to the content and 'messages' of the Kosovo myth, it teaches the Serbs lessons about themselves, their identity, and the moral principles they have to live up to. The following summarises the myths primary teachings: (1) God required Lazar to make a choice between the earthly and the heavenly kingdom. Lazar's choice of the heavenly kingdom created a special bond between God and the Serbian people; (2) The Serbs are no ordinary nation but a 'chosen' people whose destiny flows from this covenant with God: He is on our side and our cause is a divine and righteous one;[16] (3) Because we

[16] Some Serbian nationalists have gone as far as declaring God to be a Serb, e.g. a recent song of the turbo-folk star Baja-Mali Knindža contains the line:

are a chosen people, we should never compromise our dignity and principles for the sake of earthly benefits; (4) We should defy our enemies and never give in to foreign domination, even if defeat is inevitable; (5) This requires personal sacrifices: one needs to be prepared to die for these principles; (6) The inevitable consequence is loss and suffering, but that is central to Serbian identity – only through suffering do we achieve moral perfection; (7) This is the fate of a small nation like the Serbs which is surrounded by powerful enemies and empires, but it also comprises its greatness; (8) In the end there is the final prospect of justice and liberation: God will reward the Serbs, the kingdom that was lost will once be resurrected and accounts with the Muslim enemy will be settled.

The Kosovo epic offers Serbs a mental framework; it clearly fits Durkheim's notion of *collective representations*, which are sanctioned and enacted in rites that figure prominently in public debate and are used for demarcating the boundaries of the group (Durkheim 1925:13-14). As in other national myths the Kosovo myth establishes continuity with the past and projects a predestined future. As a narrative it formulates certain values and oppositions which are fundamental to the community and are personified in the main characters of the story. The Kosovo myth is therefore a kind of 'enacted ideology or philosophy', and because of this it is of 'transcendental' importance (Allcock 1993:162).

Another important aspect of myths is their a-historical character. As Evans-Pritchard has written: '[Myth] is not so much concerned with the succession of events as with the moral significance of situations, and is hence allegorical or symbolic in form. It is not encapsulated, as history is, but is a re-enactment fusing present and past. It tends to be timeless, placed in thought beyond, or above historical time; and where it is firmly placed in historical time, it is also, nevertheless, timeless in that it could have happened at any time, the archetypal not being bound to time or space' (1961:8). The past, the present and the future are fused, and 'there is a sense that centuries are no more than a few years; the distant past is like yesterday' (Mojzes 1995:50). The pan-chronistic

---

Bog je Srbin, ne boji se Srbine ('God is a Serb, so do not be afraid, Serb'). (The song is *Neće biti granica na Drini* – 'There will be no border on the Drina river', the tape *Pobediće istina* – 'The truth will win', 1994).

character of myths makes them play havoc with historical truth. Not only do events of different periods merge, but many folk epic characters from different periods mingle. As will be shown, there are constant and direct equations made between the main protagonists of the Kosovo legend and present-day political and military players.

What has made the Kosovo myth so extremely powerful is its rootedness in popular culture, which has made it possible to translate moral concepts, 'higher' values and political principles into the language of ordinary people. Serb nationalist politicians have plugged into this electrifying world of popular culture in order to mobilise the masses, to legitimate political actions, or to explain the puzzling political landscape in simple and understandable terms, i.e. in terms of 'we' against 'them'. They are usually assisted by *gusle* singers or their modern counterparts, (turbo-)folk singers, who put both historical and current events into a meaningful mythical context. This already happened in Vuk Karadžić's times, when epic folk singers sang heroic songs not only about Kosovo but also about contemporary battles against the Turks.[17] Dubravka Ugrešić has aptly called these songs 'the glue of the nation', and a 'collective remembrance reduced to sound'; because of their mass appeal, 'they are the most potent means of sending political (war) messages' (1994:12-16).

One of the main functions of myth is to create order out of chaos, especially in times of crisis and war. During World War I, epic ballads could be heard from the lips of Serbian soldiers, as a British contemporary noted:

Thus the Serbian soldier of today has a rich store of national history in his songs and knows far more of the tradition, the triumphs, and the struggles of his own people than does his English brother-in-arms. [...] To the Serbs the old heroes are familiar characters, some of whom, like St Sava and Kralyevitch Marko, will appear in moments of national crisis to lead their people to victory. In the hour of disaster and trial, too, these chants are the solace of the long-martyred race. A French

---

[17] As Malcolm has noted: 'It has long been the practice of Serb folk-poets to turn events almost immediately into poetry. [...] One memorable example of this was the poet-peasant Ante Nešić, who was a member of the Serbian National Assembly in 1873-4. He would emerge each day from the Assembly and convert the entire debate into blank verse for an admiring audience...' (Malcolm 1998:69).

doctor, who went through the terrible retreat in 1915, describes how the last act of some Serbian soldiers, before retiring from Kralyevo towards exile and probable death, was to gather round a blind *gousla*-player and to listen once more to the national epic. Nor are all the *pesme* by any means ancient. The Serbs have sung the story of this war, of their retreat, of Corfu, and of the present campaign. Unsophisticated, primitive folk find it natural to express themselves in poetry. Lieut. Krstitch tells me that during the campaign many of his soldiers write home to their wives or parents in song and describe the details of their lives in verse (Laffan 1989:23-24).

Within this epic context every Serb can feel himself a living link in a great drama that is being played out across the centuries (Laffan 1989:24-5). The power of this epic literature is its strong moral overtones and its compelling story lines which have had a great impact, particularly among the (illiterate) peasant masses.

The ethno-linguist Ivan Čolović has extensively written about recent Serbian war propaganda, not its direct political forms, but rather its folklorised and 'popular' ones – slogans, proverbs, songs. He has shown how contemporary Serbian nationalism is markedly populist in character, as it borrows from folk culture and uses epic formulas to mobilise and homogenise the masses (Čolović 1993).[18] The Kosovo myth is also expressed through 'para-literary' forms (in slogans, songs, etc.) which explicitly or implicitly refer back to the original myth. Nationalist politicians, church leaders and other self-appointed defenders of the Serbian nation embellish their militant speeches with quotations from national songs and proverbs and references to those past national heroes and enemies who provide models of patriotic and treasonable behaviour. Čolović has also pointed out the 'sacral' or 'religious' character of the political mass meetings at the end of the 1980s, when nationalist myth was expressed and acted out. The social-psychological function of these meetings was to produce a feeling of solidarity among participants, to be absorbed by the collective and speak with one voice (1995:27). This folklorism in politics is effective because its very form suggests that these messages are in harmony with the deepest feelings of the people, representing the *vox populi* instead of *his master's voice* (1994:8-9). It creates the illusion that

[18] Another major contribution to the study of Serbian populism is Nebojša Popov's *Srpski populizam* (1993).

the specific interests of warlords and political leaders are identical with the interests of the nation, and that war is part of an eternal mythical conflict between good and evil, an extra-temporal conflict that stands outside the sphere of politics, economics and history. Through the ages, the heroes and enemies have been the same: behind their current incarnations hide the ancient figures of Tsar Lazar, Miloš Obilić and Vuk Branković (1994:9).

The recent political use of the myth

Since the mid-1980s Serbian nationalist propaganda has interpreted events according to the narratives provided by folk epics. Serbian nationalist politicians constructed a 'story' from these epic narratives which was constantly repeated and rehearsed before the war broke out, and then, as soon as the violence started, used to create order out of the chaotic reality of war, imbuing it with a higher national or transcendental meaning. The grim realities of war were transformed to align with epic narratives as actors and events were 'edited' according to the logic of myths. The main protagonists of the Kosovo epic were resurrected. Reality was simplified, messages were sharpened and nuances pruned away; content was polarised and contrasts were emphasised.

As stated earlier, it was the Serbian Orthodox church which took the lead in revitalising the Kosovo myth after Tito's death (1980). Church dignitaries started to criticise Serb communists for giving up Kosovo to the Albanians, and they later gained the support of Serbian intellectuals, and eventually, communist hardliners. In the mid-1980s, when Kosovo had become a major political issue, communists started to talk about Serbia as being the defender of 'Europe' and 'Christianity' against Islam. The explosive language used by Serbian ecclesiastics, intellectuals and nationalists, and the adoption of the same rhetoric by the mass media (as soon as Milošević came to power), was starting to produce a dangerous atmosphere:

In the late 80s a collective hysteria about Kosovo gripped Serbia and Montenegro. It was an official hysteria, disseminated by politicians, intelligentsia, and media. The Kosovars were accused of every imaginable crime. Mass rallies of Serbs and Montenegrins, transported with grief and yearning for Christian vengeance, demanded a day of judgement. Scholars did their bit by extolling the medieval Serbian empire that allegedly (not actually) met its end here at the battle of Kosovo in 1389, and praising the glorious Serbian monuments that still stand here. The clergy called for Orthodox churches and nuns to be saved from the Muslims (Thompson 1992:129). After years of propaganda Serbs finally 'understood' that they were the 'victims'. The only thing that was left was somebody to bang on the table and say: 'It can't go on like this!' (Marković 1996:653). And this was the way Milošević came to power, promising the Serbs an end to their humiliation. Immediately, a personality cult developed around him, accompanied by suitable songs and jingles. As Čolović writes, he became a figure who stands outside historical time, who is blessed with supernatural power and is the last in a long series of heroes such as Obilić, Tsar Dušan and Karadjordje (1994:25-6). New songs were composed about Milošević as the saviour and unifier of the holy Serbian lands, who would liberate the country from 'Turks' and Ustaše:

Mila braćo, došlo novo doba,	My dear brothers, a new era has started,
Rodio se Milošević Sloba,	Milošević 'Slobo' is born,
Heroj pravi, duša od čoveka,	a true hero, with a great heart,
Bori se za Srbiju dvadesetog veka.	he fights for twentieth-century Serbia.

(quoted in Čolović 1994:26)[19]

In this period (1988-9) relations between the state and the church improved considerably; for instance church dignitaries began to attend important political meetings and ceremonies, inconceivable only a few years before. The Serbian Orthodox church organised a big Lazar procession, which began in Belgrade on Vidovdan 1988; Lazar had been buried in the Orthodox Cathedral forty-six years earlier (Zirojević 1995:10). His remains were carried around Serbia and eastern Bosnia, through churches and monasteries, ending up in the monastery of Gračanica where the procession was welcomed on the eve of the 600th anniversary of the battle. It was during this parade that the concept of a 'Heavenly Serbia' was reiterated by bishop Jovan of Šabac-Valjevo. On the arrival of Lazar's remains in his diocese, he wrote: 'From the times of prince Lazar and Kosovo, Serbs have first of all built Heavenly Serbia, which nowadays has surely grown into the largest heavenly state. If only we take together all the innocent victims of the last

[19] For other examples see Pavković (1995:29-31).

war, millions and millions of Serbian men and women, children
and the weak, those killed and tortured in most appalling pains
or thrown into caves by Ustaše criminals, then we can comprehend
how large the Serbian empire in heaven is' (Radić 1996:278).

Nationalist hysteria was at its height during the early summer
of 1989, with an avalanche of books, films and plays commemorating the battle. At the end of June hundreds of thousands of Serbs
(Serbian estimates even run up to two million) gathered on the
Kosovo battlefield and in Gračanica. It was the first time since
the communist era that Vidovdan was celebrated as a Serbian
public holiday. 'Slobo' was revered by the masses as a hero and
a saint, and in tune with his new role as modern-day saviour,
he was flown in to the ceremony by a helicopter, literally descending
from Heaven. His portrait could be seen on thousands of buses,
next to images of Serbia's other heroes from the past (such as
Karadjordje and Lazar). For some people the adoration of 'Slobo'
took the form of outright veneration: they made crosses in front
of his portrait before kissing it. Serbia was reborn and the defeat
of six centuries ago had been avenged. Milošević had a clear
message for other Yugoslav nations: 'Six centuries after the battle
of Kosovo Polje we are again engaged in battles and quarrels.
These are not armed battles, but the latter cannot be ruled out
yet.'

It is in this period that (turbo-)folk singers started to produce
new epic and popular songs about present-day 'heroes' and 'villains'.
Of the contemporary politicians besides Milošević, the leader of
the Bosnian Serbs, Radovan Karadžić, was often made the subject
of these new songs.

Radovane, čovječe od gvodja	Radovan, you man of iron
Prvi vožde posle Karadjordja	Our first leader after Karadjordje
Odbrani nam slobodu i vjeru	Defend our freedom and faith
na studenom Ženevskom jezeru[20]	On the cold Geneva Lake...

[20] Similar to the surrogate truths produced by this turbo-folk culture, Radovan
Karadžić claims to have common blood and genetic traits with 'the most famous'
Karadžić, Vuk Karadžić. He is proud of being a poet himself, of being born
in a famous *hajduk* and *guslar* family where he absorbed the Kosovo myth as
the 'ideal model for practical life and behaviour'. See the documentary *Serbian
Epics* by Paul Pawlikowski, Bookmark, BBC 2, 16 December 1992.

In many of these songs present-day politicians and (para-)military leaders are compared and identified, implicitly or explicitly, with the primary characters of the Kosovo myth. Thus it has become a habit to use the label 'Vuk Branković' for those Serbs who are believed to have betrayed the Serbian interests during the war. Vuk Drašković was one man who received this label when he was advocating an anti-war stand (Pavković 1995:87), while the numerous young Serb men who left Serbia at the beginning of the war because they refused to fight were labelled the 'descendants' of Vuk Branković.[21] Women who lost husbands and sons during the war were glorified as they were compared to the Mother of the Jugovići, the epic heroine whose nine sons died at Kosovo. Through this image present-day mothers are called upon to accept their sons' deaths as a sacrifice for Serbia. As Wendy Bracewell has noted, 'Even efforts to reward and encourage motherhood that are not overtly linked to the imperatives of war carry dark undertones of the sacrifice that will eventually be expected. In a ceremony in Priština on Vidovdan, 28 June 1993 [...], dignitaries of the Serbian Orthodox Church honoured Serbian mothers of more than four children with medals called after the Mother of the Jugovići, the mother who raised nine sons only to see them die in battle – presumably without intending any irony' (Bracewell 1996:29-30).

The central heroes of the Kosovo epic have been resurrected as 'super-Serbs' like the paramilitary leader, nationalist politician and suspected war criminal Arkan (Željko Ražnatović). In songs and poems he was restyled as the new Miloš Obilić.[22] An example can be found in the poem *Srbin samo Arkanu veruje:*

---

[21] See the poem *Pesma srpskim dezerterima* by Simo Bozalo, which was first published in the Serbian *Oslobodjenje*, and was again published in *Vreme* (26 June 1995, p.38). Throughout the war the independent weekly journal *Vreme* published samples of new 'heroic' poetry and songs, written by self-appointed poets, soldiers, businessmen, politicians, and academics, under the rubric *'pesnici'* (poets). A selection of these poems was published by Vasa Pavković (1995).

[22] Dubravka Ugrešić has called this process *gusle* laundering, i.e. the transformation of murderer into hero through epic songs: 'After *gusle* laundering, contemporary Serbian war criminals gleam with the pure glow of national heroes!' (1994:34). After the war Arkan founded his own football team named after the main Kosovo hero, *Obilić*. He was assassinated in Belgrade in January 2000.

Molim Boga, molim Obilića	I pray to God and Obilić
Oj Srbijo rodi mladjeg Tića	Oh Serbia, give birth to a younger Bird
Da pomogne u Bosni Srbima	So he can go and help the Serbs in Bosnia
Oj, Srbijo, da li takvog ima	Oh, Serbia, is there somebody like him
Iznenada s nebeskih visina	Suddenly from the heavenly heights
Bog nam posla Arkana svog sina	God sent us Arkan, his son
Srce srpsko a̓ hrabrost do neba	With a Serbian heart and a sky-high bravery .
U ratu je gde najviše treba	He is in the war where we need him most
...	...
Srpska truba ponovo se čuje	One can hear the Serbian bugle again
Srbin samo Arkanu veruje	Serbs only believe Arkan
Oj Kosovo od Kosovskog boja	Oh Kosovo, since the time of the battle
Takvog nisi imala heroja	You did not have such a great hero

(cited in: Pavković 1995:88-9)[23]

It is significant in this context that Arkan had close links with the Serbian Orthodox church, particularly with bishop Amfilohija (a nationalist hard-liner); during the war he stated that for him the Serbian Orthodox patriarch, Pavle, was his main commander. The high point of the adulation of Arkan came in February 1995 when he married Ceca (Svetlana Veličković), Serbia's most popular turbo-folk diva, thereby creating a literal marriage of politics and folklore. The wedding, which was broadcast direct by Serbian state television, was presented in mythic and epic dimensions. The nationalist magazine *Duga* wrote that the bond between Arkan and Ceca was no ordinary bond 'but a mythical bond, the roots of which lie in Kosovo! The bond between Ceca and Arkan is

---

[23] The poem was previously published in *Vreme* (6 September 1993, p.56). Other Serb paramilitary leaders were also compared with Miloš Obilić, e.g. Šešelj (see *Vreme* 6 March 1995, p.43). Some of these leaders, like Dragoslav Bokan, identify themselves with medieval Serbian historical figures. Bokan is an intellectual and a cineast who was the commander of the paramilitary group *Beli Orlovi* (White Eagles), very active in ethnic cleansing operations in Bosnia. He has presented his 'White Eagles' as the present-day incarnation of medieval crusaders for a Greater Serbia. The Dutch journalist Frank Westerman wrote: 'He murders in the name of prince Lazar, no: he thinks he is the reborn Lazar himself' (Westerman 1993:26).

the bond between the Kosovo girl and the Kosovo hero...' (quoted in *Vreme*, 27 February 1995:41).

Republika Srpska as the realm of the Kosovo spirit.

When Milošević came to power, relations between church and state were cordial for a while. But this did not continue for long, as the church became agitated by Milošević's arrogance and persistent 'socialist' posture. As early as the Kosovo festivities of 1989 Serbian ecclesiastics were disappointed in Milošević for failing to turn up at the memorial service at the Serbian Orthodox church in Gračanica: this caused much resentment in circles close to the Patriarchate (Radić 1996:285). In 1992 criticism by the church of Milošević's policies became more and more open and frequent, and in 1994 relations reached a low point when Milošević broke ties with the Serbs in Republika Srpska. Nationalists in Republika Srpska and Serbia started to call him a traitor (a reincarnation of Vuk Branković).

Since then, Republika Srpska is the only place where the Serbian Orthodox church has been recognised as an important moral force, where state symbols like the flag and the hymn are clearly Orthodox, where leading politicians go to church and where religious education has been introduced in schools (Radić 1996: 296). Currently the traditional symbiosis between Orthodoxy and Serbian statehood has been realised most extensively in Republika Srpska (Radić 1996:295-300). From the very beginning the Kosovo mythology has played a role in legitimating war by presenting the Serbian war efforts in Bosnia as an attempt to avenge Kosovo. Although the experiences of World War II have filled the imaginary space of Serb suffering in Bosnia much more than Kosovo, Muslims have persistently been labelled '*Turci*', the direct descendants of the Turkish oppressors, while the war was constantly understood in terms of a battle between Christianity and Islam. As Judah has noted, '[w]hen Serbian peasants from villages surrounding Sarajevo began to bombard the city they did so confusing in their minds their former Muslim friends, neighbours and even brothers-in-law with the old Ottoman Turkish viziers and pashas who had ruled them until 1878' (Judah 1997:xi).

The important role of the Kosovo myth as a force of legitimisation in Republika Srpska was most poignantly expressed in the

adoption of Vidovdan as the Bosnian Serb Army's official holiday
and patron's day at the beginning of the war (1992). It also
emphasised General Ratko Mladić's position (as seen by many
ordinary Bosnian Serbs) as a modern-day Lazar, as their saviour
who led his troops against the 'Turks'. During the war his popularity
acquired almost mythical dimensions. When in the Serbian Orthodox church of Bijeljina Mladić made *acte-de-présence* at the
Vidovdan ceremony of the Bosnian Serbian Army in 1995, 'he
was mobbed by adoring fans. Old women cried and tried to hug
him. Babies were held up for him to touch' (Block 1995). There,
in Bijeljina, days before the Army of the Republika Srpska would
open the attack on the safe area of Srebrenica, he spoke to his
soldiers about the importance of the Battle of Kosovo: 'Prince
Lazar gave his army the sacrament, and bowed for the Heavenly
Empire, defending fatherland, faith, freedom and the honour of
the Serbian people. We have understood the essence of his sacrifice
and have drawn the historical message from it. Today we are a
victorious army, we do not want to convert Lazar's offering into
a blinding myth of sacrifice' (Bulatović 1996:154). Srebrenica was
taken, thousands of 'Turks' were killed, and a huge cross was
carved out in the forests on a hill behind Srebrenica.

9

CONCLUSION

As I am writing these lines in January 1999, war is once again raging in Kosovo after a short winter break. As in Bosnia the violence seems to forestall hope of coexistence between Serbs and Albanians, if there was any chance of that after so many years of ethnic polarisation and segregation. In 1990, a year before war in the former Yugoslavia broke out, Kosovo already exemplified the paradigm of a segregated society, where ethnic communities live entirely separated, in parallel worlds, with as little contact as possible. Similar processes of ethnic unmixing and national homogenisation were soon repeated elsewhere, albeit in a much more violent fashion, leading to results that seem to be irreversible: Bosnia-Hercegovina has been practically divided into three, Croatia has driven out almost all Serbs, and Serbia has expelled most Croats and many of its other non-Serbian inhabitants.

These developments have led to great human suffering, and it is this suffering that has given new impetus to feelings of national victimisation at the hands of neighbours or more distant political forces (such as the old Hapsburg and Ottoman empires in previous times, or the world's superpowers today). Serbian nationalism is most paranoid in this respect, but it is certainly not unique: Albanian nationalist politicians and activists from Kosovo have also presented their people to the outside world as a wronged and victimised nation which has been the object and never the subject of history. Each nation and ethnic group in the former Yugoslavia has its own catalogues (often quite literally) of victims, atrocities, destruction and endured injustices, but none seems to have the capacity to grieve for the hurts of others. As two journalists exclaimed: 'To work in former Yugoslavia is to enter a world of parallel truths. Wherever you go, you encounter the same resolute conviction that everything that has befallen the region is always someone else's fault, except one's own side. [...] Each nation has embraced a separate orthodoxy in which it is uniquely the victim and never the perpetrator' (Silber and Little 1993:390-1). Although these myths of suffering reflect real historical experiences – of oppression and exploitation, of violence and existential insecurity and of peoples' lack of control over their own lives – they are exploited politically in order to justify further violence, making people insensitive to the suffering they inflict upon others.

I certainly do not want to play down the amount of suffering that has been the fate, in particular, of the Albanians in Kosovo: for most of this century, and especially in the last ten years, it is the Albanian population which has been at the receiving end of political oppression, police violence and grave human rights violations. For almost a year their villages have been destroyed and many have been killed or expelled from their houses. Yet it would be incorrect to blame only the Serbs for what went wrong in the province or to say that the Kosovo conundrum has caused suffering only among Albanians. Serbs, Croats, Montenegrins, Turks, Muslims, and Gypsies (whose daily misery in terms of social and economic deprivation and discrimination is mostly deemed irrelevant by the main parties) have had their share as well. It is just as incorrect and dangerous to maintain, as nationalist Serbian politicians and media have done since the second half of the 1980s, that it is only they who suffer. The hate campaign in the Serbian media directed against the Kosovo Albanians – who were accused of raping Serbian women, of waging a demographic war against the Serbs, of ethnically cleansing the province and committing genocide – and later against the Croats and Muslims, prepared some Serbs to repay in kind.

In the end many of Kosovo's problems are not ethnic in origin, but have been ethnicised by politicians who want easy political gain and by populations who have learned to be deeply suspicious of 'others', especially if these 'others' belong to a different ethnic group. Although ethnic and nationalist discourses lead to self-fulfilling prophesies, it is my view that most of Kosovo's problems need primarily to be understood in political, social and economic terms if one wants to solve anything at all (Horvat 1988). One of the most urgent problems is the lack of a democratic political culture, both among the Albanians in Kosovo and the Serbs in Serbia. Among the Albanians nationalist discipline and internal factionalism has led to political and ethnic intolerance; the establishment of a genuine pluralist democratic culture will be the main and most difficult task after the Kosovo issue is solved, whatever the solution is. In Serbia the situation seems to be even worse: Milošević's regime has transformed Serbia into a country dominated by populism, nationalist resentment, paranoia, xenophobia and the readiness to use violence.

The Kosovo myth seems to have lost much of its power, especially after the end of violence in Bosnia. Even with regard to present-day events in Kosovo, where the use of the myth is most appropriate (at least in theory), its rhetoric appears bleak and exhausted. Its extensive political exploitation at the end of the 1980s and the beginning of the 1990s has solved nothing and has only brought Kosovo's secession nearer. As some Serbian intellectuals have remarked, the myth has become grotesque: Serbs in Serbia are not willing to sacrifice themselves for Kosovo, and Serbs in Kosovo sell their land and houses to Albanian buyers, yielding to the high prices offered to them (see for instance Krstić 1994:162-74). Widespread corruption among Serbian authorities in Kosovo, and the fact that many Serbian officials have benefited from 'co-operating' with Albanian businessmen, has made the Kosovo myth – especially where it calls on Serbs to sacrifice earthly values for the sake of higher principles – more or less hollow. The myth has been discredited by those who have utilised and manipulated it most. Recent events, which have only accelerated the Serb exodus from Kosovo, have made the failure of official Serbian policy in Kosovo complete.

While almost all Serb politicians share the idea that Serbian rule over the province is an almost inalienable and sacrosanct right – even among the liberal Belgrade opposition and the leaders of the student movement this idea is predominant – it is my own experience that many ordinary Serbs appear to be less adamant and more pragmatic. They are indifferent to the 'teachings' of the Kosovo myth, they are too much occupied with their daily struggle to survive, and they do not really care what will happen to Kosovo: they only know they do not want to go and fight there. These are predominantly the urban and more moderate and democratically minded segments of Serbian society, which have lost all hope after the mass demonstrations against Milošević's regime in the winter of 1996-7 ended in huge disappointment. Now they have become apathetic, invisible and voiceless. A huge number of educated young people have voted with their

feet and left the country, a braindrain which has continued un-
abatedly and which in the end will have much more serious
consequences for Serbia than the exodus of Serbs from Kosovo.
One of the lessons that may be gleaned from these events is
that the political utility and productivity of myths such as the
Kosovo one is limited. While myth can provide a considerable
mobilising and homogenising force in periods of crisis, the capacity
to captivate the masses diminishes after they fail to provide guidance
when circumstances do not change for the better. As we see in
Serbia certain segments of the population may turn away from
these nationalist myths and look in other directions. As Fredrik
Barth writes, individuals usually participate in several and often
discrepant 'universes of discourse' at the same time, with varying
intensity or depth (Barth 1989:130), and this seems to offer some
hope for the future. Until recently the Kosovo myth has dominated
political discourse in Serbia, yet it has certainly not been the only
one on offer: there are several other accounts – of what Serbia
was, what Serbia is and what Serbia will be –which will one day
surface and compete for political space. The idea of a modern
and democratic Serbia is one of them.

I am not arguing here against myth *per se*, but against particular
myths that propagate revenge and exclusivism, which sacralise
the nation and demonise others. People cannot do without myths:
even in the West, where politics is supposedly based on rational
and secular principles, myths play an important role (Hosking
and Schöpflin 1997). They are not merely 'untruthful' fabrications
or 'false' representations of reality; they also serve positive functions,
i.e. they create order out of chaos and show us what direction
to take. As myths are an indispensable part of society we should
adopt a much more nuanced and appreciative approach to modern-
day (political) myths. We should study them comparatively, and
judge them on the basis of universalist values like compassion
and tolerance.

In this book I have not only analysed Balkan myths, but have
challenged dominant Western myths *about* the Balkans, particularly
those pertaining to the phenomena of ethnic conflict and violence
in the region. Although most chapters could be read as ethnographic
'snapshots' of processes of identification in peripheral places and
among marginal populations, together they shed light on larger
issues. In the first place they show that the common Western

view of the wars in the former Yugoslavia as conflicts evolving around ancient and irreconcilable animosities, between fixed and clearly demarcated ethnic groups, is largely illusory. This image of old and 'tribal' hatreds has to be seen with great scepticism: people are constantly (trans)forming their identities, they tend to unite (or hide) behind various and ever changing banners, often disregarding and cross-cutting other boundaries. As Jenkins has formulated it, '[h]uman society is best seen as an ongoing and overlapping kaleidoscope of "group-ness", rather than a "plural" system of separate groups' (Jenkins 1997:51). In periods of political change people may shift their identity, or – more fundamentally – reformulate the ways they form groups and identify with others. Particular identities (such as ethnic or religious ones) are significant one day and insignificant the next, depending on political, historical and other circumstances. As some authors have rightfully argued (see for instance Sorabji 1993:33 and Denitch 1994:6), the West has only identified and acknowledged the ethnic ones. By understanding the conflict in the former Yugoslavia exclusively in ethnic terms, it has contributed to the triumph of nationalist forces and has encouraged the use of ethnic principles in organising political and social life.

Another lesson to be learned is that ideas of connectedness, oneness and coherence which are often attached to the concept of culture, and the essentialist and relativist understanding of 'cultures' as bounded, unique and permanent (which is most poignantly expressed in Huntington's notion of clashing civilisations, see Huntington 1993) is not very appropriate ethnographically. As can be seen in this book, cultural praxis in the Balkans can best be described as mixed, heterogeneous, contradictory, fragmented and incoherent (or 'creolised' to use the most fashionable post-modern term), at least from the point of view of national and religious orthodoxies. The centres of political and religious power have tried to overcome this situation: they have attempted to eradicate these elements of mixture and multiple ethnic and religious 'orientations', and have pressed for clear-cut single identities, with or without violent means, and mostly with varying and limited success. It seems that our Western concept of identity, denoting personal 'integrity' and 'oneness' which is stable and fixed, is not the rule but rather the exception; it is probably the

result of a long historical process of societal integration and nation-state formation.

In many parts of the former Yugoslavia ethnic and religious
identities have been ambivalent and unstable until quite recently,
and the recent wars have been attempts to eliminate these ambiguities. The third lesson to take note of is that instead of seeing
the violence in the Balkans as irrational, as tribal, as archaic, as
something that is ingrained in the culture and psyche of Balkan
inhabitants, I would like to suggest that the violence has profoundly
rational dimensions and is primarily 'European' in origin: it is a
European ideal, that of the nation-state, which has been the ob-
jective of most of this violence, of 'ethnic cleansing' and other
forms of 'ethno-demographic engineering', which were practised
in all parts of the former Yugoslavia. From this point of view
the most brutal and so-called 'irrational' violence can be explained
rationally, as Todorova notes. Even if there has been a level of
irrationality involved on the part of the actual perpetrators – who
have often been convicted criminals or hooligans recruited into
paramilitary units to do the 'dirty' work (Čolović 1996) – this has
been made functional at a higher (political or military) level. In
Bosnia people were scared away by extreme violence and the
cleansing of 'undesired' populations was swift and efficient
(Todorova 1997a:137-8).

In other respects as well, the violence had rational dimensions:
it served to homogenise the population, by establishing undivided
loyalties, unambiguous identities and clear boundaries out of a
situation of mixture perceived by many nationalists as one of
'impurity' and 'contamination'. Violence draws clear boundaries,
and as Bax has noted for western Hercegovina, it substitutes locally
and regionally based identities with national ones: violence is thus
not simply a sign of disintegration and 'barbarisation', but also a
force of integration (Bax 1998). My own research in Letnica has
shown that through violence the ambiguities and complexities of
local identities are pushed to the background and that 'ethnoscapes'
are simplified in the course of this process (cf. Karakasidou 1997).
Gellner vividly described this process:

...consider the history of the national principle; or consider two ethnographic maps, one drawn up before the age of nationalism, and the
other after the principle of nationalism had done much of its work.
The first map resembles a painting of Kokoschka. The riot of diverse

points of colour is such that no clear pattern can be discerned in any detail, though the picture as a whole does have one. A great diversity and plurality and complexity characterizes all distinct parts of the whole: the minute social groups, which are the atoms of which the picture is composed, have complex and ambiguous and multiple relations to many cultures; some through speech, others through their dominant faith, another still through a variant faith or set of practices, a fourth through administrative loyalty, and so forth. When it comes to painting the political system, the complexity is not less great than in the sphere of culture. Obedience for one purpose and in one context is not necessarily the same as obedience for some other end or in some other season. Look now instead at the ethnographic and political map of an area of the modern world. It resembles not Kokoschka but, say, Modigliani. There is very little shading; neat flat surfaces are clearly separated from each other, it is generally plain where one begins and another ends, and there is little ambiguity or overlap. Shifting from the map to the reality mapped, we see that an overwhelming part of political authority has been concentrated in the hands of one kind of institution, a reasonably large and well-centralized state. In general, each such state presides over, maintains, and is identified with, one kind of culture, one style of communication, which prevails within its borders and is dependent for its perpetuation on a centralized educational system supervised by and often actually run by the state in question, which monopolizes legitimate culture almost as much as it does legitimate violence, or perhaps more so (Gellner 1983:139-40).

I think that this (as well as much of my own research) should remind us that the idea that fragmented and creolised identities in this era of globalisation are 'new' and 'post-modern' somehow distorts the picture (cf. Jenkins 1997:51). A view from the Balkans shows that they are not new, that they are also or perhaps primarily 'pre-modern', and that the modernist project of creating nation-states is still a very important force in the world.

I hope that I have shown the kind of contribution anthropology – and particularly ethnography – can make in understanding the events in Kosovo and the rest of the former Yugoslavia. The anthropological approach applied in this study is identifiable in the perspective 'from below', looking at wider developments from the viewpoint of small communities which have been affected by events and decisions that are far beyond their control. Because of its method of participant observation and its focus on the grassroots level of social life, anthropology is capable – more than other disciplines – of uncovering the important local dimensions of larger events. It can thus offer a healthy corrective to the top-down approach that characterises many studies of South-East European politics, and it is able to question models produced by Western scholars and indigenous intellectuals. In this book the anthropological imagination is also visible in the attention paid to phenomena that are often regarded as 'unusual' and 'marginal': in this respect my approach is quite different from mainstream studies on Kosovo, which usually adopt the basic Serbian-Albanian opposition as the main framework of reference. I have chosen not to follow these well-trodden paths and to concentrate on topics that usually escape the attention of those authors. I believe that anthropology can offer many additional insights – simply by entering small and unknown side-paths – which in the end will open up new perspectives on old problems.

REFERENCES

Ahmeti, Šerif. 1979. 'Kosovska pseudo učenja tesavufa'. *Glasnik vrhovnog islamskog starješinstva u SFRJ*, XLII (3), pp.282-5.

Allcock, John. 1993. 'Kosovo: The heavenly and the earthly crown' in Ian Reader and Tony Walter (eds), *Pilgrimage in popular culture*. Basingstoke: Macmillan, pp.157-78.

Anderson, Benedict. 1991. *Imagined communities: Reflections on the origin and spread of nationalism*. Rev. edn, London: Verso.

Arnakis, E. 1963. 'The role of religion in the development of Balkan nationalism' in Charles and Barbara Jelavich (eds), *The Balkans in transition: Essays on the development of Balkan life an'd politics since the eighteenth century*. Berkeley: University of California Press, pp.115-44.

Arsenijević, Vesna. 1989. *Kosovo, zemlja živih* – 1389-1989: *u znaku Časnoga Krsta i slobode zlatne*. Beograd: Manastir svetog Stefana, Čelija Piperska.

Atiya, A.S. 1986. 'Kibt' in C.E. Bosworth *et al.* (eds), *Encyclopaedia of Islam*. New ed., Leiden: Brill & Luzac. Vol. 5, pp.90-5.

Ayoub, Mahmoud. 1978. *Redemptive suffering in Islam: A study of the devotional aspects of 'Ashura' in twelver Shi'ism*. The Hague: Mouton.

Badone, Ellen (ed.). 1990. *Religious orthodoxy and popular faith in European society*. Princeton University Press.

Baerlein, Henry. 1922. *A difficult frontier: Yugoslavs and Albanians*. London: Leonard Parsons.

Bakić-Hayden, Milica, and Robert M. Hayden. 1992. 'Orientalist variations on the theme "Balkans", and symbolic geography in recent Yugoslav cultural politics'. *Slavic review*, 51(1), pp.1-15.

Banks, Marcus. 1996. *Ethnicity: Anthropological constructions*. London: Routledge.

Barany, Zoltan. 1995. 'The Roma in Macedonia: Ethnic politics and the marginal condition in a Balkan state'. *Ethnic and racial studies*, 18 (3): 515-31.

Baretić, Renato. 1993. 'Kosovoski autobusi bez voznog reda'. *Nedjeljna Dalmacija*, 1 September 1993.

Barjaktarović, Mirko R. 1950. 'Dvovjerske šiptarske zadruge u Metohiji'. *Zbornik radova* (Etnografski Institut, SANU, Belgrade), IV, pp.197-209.

——. 1970. 'Cigani u Jugoslaviji danas'. *Zbornik filozofskog fakulteta* (Belgrade), IX(1), pp.743-8.

Barnes, J.A. 1994. *A pack of lies: Towards a sociology of lying.* Cambridge University Press.

Barth, Fredrik. 1969. Introduction in Fredrik Barth (ed.), *Ethnic groups and boundaries: The social organisation of culture difference.* London: Geo. Allen & Unwin, pp.9-38.

———. 1989. 'The analysis of culture in complex societies'. *Ethnos,* 54(3-4), pp.120-42.

Bartl, Peter. 1967. 'Kryptochristentum und Formen des religiösen Synkretismus in Albanien'. *Grazer und Münchener balkanologische Studien* (Beiträge zur Kenntnis Südosteuropas und des Nahen Orients), pp.117-127.

———.1968. *Die albanische Muslime zur Zeit der nationalen Unabhängigkeitsbewegung (1878-1912).* (Albanische Forschungen 8.) Wiesbaden: Otto Harrassowitz.

Bartlett, C.N.O. 1980. 'The Turkish minority in the Socialist Autonomous Province of Kosovo'. *Co-existence,* 17, pp.193-97.

Bataković, Dušan 1992. *The Kosovo chronicles.* Belgrade: Plato.

Bax, Mart. 1987. 'Religious regimes and state-formation. Toward a research perspective'. *Anthropological quarterly,* 60(1), pp.1-11.

———.1995. *Medjugorje: Religion, politics, and violence in rural Bosnia.* Amsterdam: VU University Press.

———. 1997. 'Mass graves, stagnating identification, and violence: A case study in the local sources of "The War" in Bosnia-Hercegovina'. *Anthropological Quarterly,* 70(1), pp.11-19.

———. 1998. 'Maria en de mijnwerpers van Medjugorje. De dynamiek van etnische zuivering in ruraal Bosnië-Hercegovina'. *Amsterdams sociologisch tijdschrift,* 25(3), pp.371-94.

Ben-Ami, Issachar. 1990. *Culte des saints et pèlerinages judéo-musulmans au Maroc.* Paris: Maisonneuve-Larose.

Berberski, Slobodan. 1984. 'Romi i iredenta na Kosovu'. *Naše teme* 28(7-8), pp.1335-47.

Birge, John Kingsley. 1937. *The Bektashi order of dervishes.* London: Luzac.

Black-Michaud, Jacob. 1980 (1975). *Feuding societies.* Oxford: Basil Blackwell.

Block, Robert. 1995. 'The madness of general Mladić'. *New York Review,* 5 October 1995, pp.7-9.

Blok, Anton. 1977. *Antropologische perspectieven.* Muiderberg: Coutinho.

Bogdanović, Bogdan. 1994 (1993). 'The city and death' in Joanna Labon (ed.), *Balkan blues. Writing out of Yugoslavia.* Evanston, IL: Northwestern University Press, pp.36-73.

Bogdanović, Dimitrije. 1986. *Knjiga o Kosovu.* Belgrade: SANU.

Bogišić, B. 1874. 'Die slavisirten Zigeuner in Montenegro'. *Das Ausland* 47 (21): 401-6.

Boissevain, Jeremy (ed.). 1992. *Revitalizing European rituals*. London: Routledge.

Boulay, Juliet du. 1976. 'Lies, mockery and family integrity' in J.G. Peristiany (ed.), *Mediterranean family structures*. Cambridge University Press, pp.389-406.

Bowers, Stephen R. 1983-4. 'The Islamic factor in Albanian politics'. *Journal of the Institute of Muslim Minority Affairs*, 5(1), pp.123-35.

Božović, Rade. n.d. 'Kulturno-religijski obrasci "Makedonskih Egipćana"'. unpubl. ms. (written 1990 or 1991).

Bracewell, Wendy. 1992. *The uskoks of Senj: Piracy, banditry, and holy war in the sixteenth-century Adriatic*. Ithaca, NY: Cornell University Press.

———. 1996. 'Women, motherhood, and contemporary Serbian nationalism'. *Women's Studies International Forum*, 19(1-2), pp.25-33.

———. 2000. 'Rape in Kosovo: Masculinity and Serbian nationalism'. *Nations and Nationalism*, (in press).

Brandenberg, Ton, *et al.* 1992. *Heilige Anna, grote moeder: de cultus van de Heilige Moeder Anna en haar familie*. Nijmegen: SUN.

Bremer, Thomas. 1992. *Ekklesiale Struktur und Ekklesiologie in der Serbische Orthodoxen Kirche im 19. und 20. Jahrhundert*. Würzburg: Augustinus-Verlag.

Brkić, Jovan. 1961. *Moral concepts in traditional Serbian epic poetry*. The Hague: Mouton.

Brubaker, Rogers. 1995. 'Aftermaths of empire and the unmixing of peoples: Historical and comparative perspective'. *Ethnic and Racial Studies*, 18(2), pp.189-218.

Bulatović, Ljiljana. 1988. *Prizrenski proces*. Novi Sad: Književna Zajednica Novog Sada.

———.1996. *General Mladić*. Belgrade: Nova Evropa.

Büschenfeld, Herbert. 1991. *Kosovo. Nationalitätenkonflikt im Armenhaus Jugoslawiens*. Cologne: Aulis Verlag/Deubner.

Canapa, Marie-Paule. 1986. 'L'islam et la question des nationalités en Yougoslavie' in Olivier Carré and Paul Dumont (eds), *Radicalismes islamiques*. Paris: L'Harmattan, Vol.2, pp.100-150.

Canetti, Elias. 1962 (1960). *Crowds and power*. London: Gollancz.

Ćehajić, Džemal. 1986. *Derviški redovi u jugoslovenskim zemljama sa posebnim osvrtom na Bosnu i Hercegovinu*. Sarajevo: Orijentalni institut.

Choublier, Max. 1927. 'Les Bektashis et al Roumélie'. *Revue des études islamiques*, I, pp.427-53.

Clayer, Nathalie. 1990. *L'Albanie, pays des derviches. Les ordres mystiques-*

musulmans en Albanie à l'époque post-ottomane (1912-1967). Wiesbaden: Harrassowitz.

———. 1992. 'Bektachisme et nationalisme albanais' in Alexandre Popovic and Gilles Veinstein (eds), *Bektachiyya. Etudes sur l'ordre mystique des Bektachis et les groupes relevant de Hadji Bektach.* Istanbul: ISIS, pp.277-308.

Clébert, Jean-Paul. 1967. *The Gypsies.* Harmondsworth: Penguin.

Clifford, James. 1988. *The predicament of culture: Twentieth-century ethnography, literature, and art.* Cambridge, MA: Harvard University Press.

Cohen, Anthony P. 1985. *The symbolic construction of community.* London: Routledge.

Cole, John W. 1977. 'Anthropology comes part-way home: Community studies in Europe'. *Annual Reviews in Anthropology,* 6, pp.349-78.

———. 1981. 'Ethnicity and the rise of nationalism' in Sam Beck and John W. Cole (eds), *Ethnicity and nationalism in Southeastern Europe.* Amsterdam: Antropologisch-Sociologisch Centrum Universiteit van Amsterdam, pp.105-134.

Čolović, Ivan. 1993. *Bordel ratnika. Folklor, politika i rat.* Belgrade: Biblioteka XX vek.

———. 1994. *Pucanje od zdravlje.* Belgrade: Beogradski krug.

———. 1995. *Jedno s drugim.* Novi Pazar: Damad.

———. 1996. 'Fudbal, huligani i rat' in Nebojša Popov (ed.), *Srpska strana rata. Trauma i katarza u istorijskom pamćenju.* Belgrade: BIGZ, pp.419-44.

Connell, R.W. 1996. 'New directions in gender theory, masculinity research, and gender politics'. *Ethnos,* 61(3-4), pp.157-76.

Cortiade, Marcel. 1991. 'The Romanis in Albania: An historical-social outline'. Unpubl. ms.

Damnjanović, Jevrem. 1990. 'Kojim jezikom govori Tot-Tot'. *Ilustrovana politika,* 13 November 1990, pp.36-7.

Daniel, E. Valentine. 1996. *Charred lullabies: Chapters in an anthropography of violence.* Princeton University Press.

Daniel, Odile. 1990. 'The historical role of the Muslim community in Albania'. *Central Asian Survey,* 9(3), pp.1-28.

Dartel, Geert van. 1997. 'A Catholic response to the Serbian Orthodox view on Kosovo' in Duijzings, Ger, Dušan Janjić and Shkëlzen Maliqi (eds), *Kosovo – Kosova: Confrontation or coexistence.* Nijmegen: Peace Research Centre, pp.142-149.

Davison, Roderic H. 1973. *Reform in the Ottoman empire, 1856-1876.* New York: Gordian Press.

Dawkins, R.M. 1933. 'The crypto-Christians of Turkey'. *Byzantion – revue internationale des études byzantines,* 8, pp.247-75.

Degrand, A. 1901. *Souvenirs de la Haute-Albanie*. Paris: Welter.

Denich, Bette. 1974. 'Sex and power in the Balkans' in Z.M. Rosaldo and L. Lamphere (eds), *Women, culture and society*. Stanford University Press, pp.243-62.

——. 1994. 'Dismembering Yugoslavia. Nationalist ideologies and the symbolic revival of genocide'. *American Ethnologist*, 21(2), 1994, pp. 367-90.

Denitch, Bogdan. 1994. *Ethnic nationalism: The tragic death of Yugoslavia*. Minneapolis: University of Minnesota Press.

Despot, Sanja. 1997. 'Janjevci u Kistanjama. Budučnost ili prevara'. *Tjednik*, 29 March 1997, pp.14-18.

Djilas, Milovan. 1985. *Rise and fall*. San Diego: Harcourt Brace Jovanovich.

Djordjević, Miloš. 1990. 'Faraon pod Prištinom. Kako je gotovo preko noći na Kosovu i Metohiji od Roma stvoreno oko 100,000 Egipćana?' *Dnevnik*, 28 October 1990.

Djordjević, Tihomir. 1984 (1930-4). *Naš narodni život*. Belgrade: Prosveta.

——. 1984a(1914). 'Čime se Cigani drže kao narod in T. Djordjević, *Naš narodni život*, vol.3, pp.7-12.

——. 1984b (1932). 'Dva biblijska motiva u predanju naših Cigana in *Naš narodni život*, vol.3, pp.87-101.

Djurić, Rajko. 1987. *Seoba Roma. Krugovi pakla i venac sreće*. Belgrade: BIGZ.

——. 1990. Romi iz Makedonije. Nova piramida laži. *Intervju*, 26 October 1990, p.15.

Djurić, Sladjana S. 1998. *Osveta i Kazna. Sociološko istraživanje krvne osvete na Kosovu i Metohiji*. Niš: Prosveta.

Djuričić, Milutin. 1994. *Običaji i verovanja Albanaca*. Belgrade: M. Djuričić.

Draper, Stark. 1997. 'The conceptualization of an Albanian nation'. *Ethnic and Racial Studies*, 20(1), pp.123-44.

Driessen, Henk. 1992. *On the Spanish-Moroccan frontier: A study in ritual, power and ethnicity*. New York: Berg.

Duijzings, Ger, Dušan Janjić and Shkëlzen Maliqi (eds). 1997. *Kosovo -Kosova. Confrontation or coexistence*. Nijmegen: Peace Research Centre.

Durham, M. E. 1904. *Through the lands of the Serbs*. London: Edward Arnold.

——. 1985 (1909). *High Albania*. London: Virago Press.

Durkheim, Emile. 1925 (1912). *Les formes élémentaires de la vie religieuse. La système totémique en Australie*. Paris: Alcan.

Eade, John, and Michael J. Sallnow (eds). 1991. *Contesting the sacred: The anthropology of Christian pilgrimage*. London: Routledge.

Eickelman, Dale F. 1989. *The Middle East: An anthropological approach.* 2nd edn. Englewood Cliffs, NJ: Prentice-Hall.

Ekmečić, Milorad. 1991. 'The emergence of St. Vitus Day as the principal national holiday of the Serbs' in Wayne S. Vucinich and Thomas Emmert (eds), *Kosovo – legacy of a medieval battle.* Minneapolis: University of Minnesota Press, pp.331-42.

Elsie, Robert. 1995. *History of Albanian literature.* 2 vols, East European Monographs, CCCLXXIX. New York: Columbia University Press.

Eriksen, Thomas Hylland. 1993. *Ethnicity and nationalism: Anthropological perspectives.* London: Pluto Press.

Evans, A. 1901. 'Mycenean tree and pillar cult'. *Journal of Hellenic studies,* 21, pp.99-104.

Evans-Pritchard, E.E. 1949. *The Sanusi of Cyrenaica.* Oxford: Clarendon Press.

———.1961. *Anthropology and history: A lecture.* Manchester University Press.

Faensen, Johannes. 1980. *Die albanische Nationalbewegung.* Wiesbaden: Otto Harrassowitz.

Filipović, Milenko S. 1951. 'Kršteni Muslimani'. *Zbornik radova Etnografskog Instituta* SANU (Belgrade), II, pp.120-8.

Fine, John V.A. 1983. *The early medieval Balkans: A critical survey from the sixth to the late twelfth century.* Ann Arbor: University of Michigan Press.

Fischer, Bernd J. 1995. 'Albanian nationalism in the twentieth century' in Peter F. Sugar (ed.), *Eastern European nationalism in the twentieth century.* Washington, DC: American University Press, pp.21-54.

Fischer, Michael M.J. 1980. *Iran: From religious dispute to revolution.* Cambridge, MA: Harvard University Press.

Fraser, Angus. 1992. *The Gypsies.* Oxford: Blackwell.

Frashëri, Naim. 1978 (1898). *Qerbelaja. (Naim Frashëri: Vepra,* vol. 4). Prishtinë: Rilindja.

Friedman, Victor A. 1985. 'The sociolinguistics of literary Macedonian'. *International journal of the sociology of language,* 52, pp.31-57.

———. and Robert Dankoff. 1991. 'The earliest known text in Balkan (Rumelian) Romani: A passage from Evliya Çelebi's Seyahat-name'. *Journal of the Gypsy Lore Society,* 1(1), pp.1-20.

Gellner, Ernest. 1983. *Nations and nationalism.* Oxford: Blackwell.

Gilsenan, Michael. 1982. *Recognizing Islam: An anthropologist's introduction.* London: Croom Helm.

Gjergji, Gjergj. 1972. 'Formimi i shkollave në dioçez të Prizrenit'. *Drita,* 3 (1), pp.4-5 and 8.

Gjergji-Gashi, Gjergj. 1988. *Albanski mučenici u razdoblju 1846-1848. Skopska Crnagora u skopsko-prizrenkoj biskupiji tijekom XIX. stoljeća. Peć*: Župni ured Peć.

Gjini, Gasper. 1986. Skopsko-prizrenska biskupija kroz stoljeća. Zagreb: Kršćanska Sadašnjost.

Goffman, Erving. 1959. *The presentation of self in everyday life*. New York: Doubleday Anchor Books.

Govers, Cora, and Hans Vermeulen (eds). 1997. *The politics of ethnic consciousness*. Basingstoke: Macmillan.

Grémaux, René. 1994. 'Woman becomes man in the Balkans' in Gilbert Herdt (ed.), *Third sex, third gender: Beyond sexual dimorphism in culture and history*. New York: Zone Books, pp.241-81 (endnotes pp.548-54).

Hadúzibajriïc, Fejzulah. 1979. 'Tesavuf, tarikat i tekije na području Starješinstva IZ BiH danas'. *Glasnik vrhovnog islamskog starješinstva u SFRJ*, XLII(3), pp.271-277.

———. 1990. 'Djelatnost tarikatskog centra u Sarajevu'. *Šebi arus, godišnjak tarikatskog centra* (Sarajevo), 12, pp.17-33.

Hadži-Vasiljević, Jovan. 1924. *Muslimani naše krvi u Južnoj Srbiji*. Bel-grade: Štamparija Sv. Sava.

———. 1939. 'Arnauti naše krvi'. *Bratstvo*, 30(50), pp.107-45.

Hann, C.M. 1995. *The skeleton at the feast. Contributions to East European anthropology*. Canterbury: Centre for Social Anthropology, University of Kent.

———. 1997. 'Ethnicity, language and politics in North-east Turkey' in Cora Govers and Hans Vermeulen (eds), *The politics of ethnic consciousness*. Basingstoke: Macmillan, pp.121-56.

Hasluck, F.W. 1929. *Christianity and Islam under the sultans*. Edited by M.M. Hasluck. 2 vols. Oxford: Clarendon Press.

Hasluck, Margaret M. 1925. 'The nonconformist Moslems of Albania'. *Contemporary review*, 127, pp.599-606.

Hastings, Adrian. 1997. *The construction of nationhood: Ethnicity, religion, and nationalism*. Cambridge University Press.

Hayden, Robert M. 1994. 'Recounting the dead: The rediscovery and redefinition of wartime massacres in late and post-communist Yugo-slavia' in Rubie S. Watson (ed.), *Memory, history, and opposition under state socialism*. Santa Fe: School of American Research Press, pp.167-201.

Hecquard, Hyacinthe. 1858. *Histoire et description de la Haute Albanie ou Guégarie*. Paris: Bertrand.

Hedl, Drago. 1993. 'Prokleti dodjoši. Nakaze demografskog inženjeringa'. *Feral Tribune*, 17 November 1993, p.7.

Heffening, W. 1993. 'Murtadd' in *The Encyclopaedia of Islam*. Leiden: E.J. Brill. VII, pp.635-6.

Heinschink, Mozes. 1978. 'La langue tsigane parlée en Autriche et en Yougoslavie'. *Études tsiganes*, 24: 8-20.

218   *References*

Holton, Milne and Vasa D. Mihailovich. 1988. *Serbian poetry from the beginnings to the present*. Columbus, OH: Slavica Publishers.

Horvat, Branko. 1988. *Kosovsko pitanje*. Zagreb: Globus.

Horvat, Domagoj. 1995. 'Vodite nas odavde. Žrtve repatrijacije kako su Hrvati s Kosova dovabljeni u zapadnoj Slavoniji, a potom izigrani'. *Feral Tribune*, 13 February 1995.

Hosking, Geoffrey, and George Schöpflin (eds). 1997. *Myths and nationhood*. London: Hurst.

Huntington, Samuel P. 1993. 'The clash of civilizations?' *Foreign affairs*, 72(3), pp. 22-49.

Hutchinson, John. 1994. *Modern nationalism*. London: Fontana Press.

Ippen, Theodor A. 1902. 'Das religiöse Protektorat Österreich-Ungarns in der Türkei'. *Die Kultur. Zeitschrift für Literatur und Kunst* (Vienna), 3, pp.298-310.

———. 1907. *Skutari und die nordalbanische Küstenebene*. Zur Kunde der Balkanhalbinsel 5. Sarajevo.

Jacob, Georg. 1908. *Beiträge zur Kenntnis des Derwisch-Ordens der Bektaschis*. Berlin: Mayer & Müller.

Jacques, Edwin E. 1995. *The Albanians: An ethnic history from prehistoric times to the present*. Jefferson: McFarland.

Jelavich, Barbara. 1983. *History of the Balkans*. 2 vols. Cambridge University Press.

Jenkins, Richard. 1996. *Social identity*. London: Routledge.

———. 1997. *Rethinking ethnicity. Arguments and explorations*. London: Sage.

Jevtić, Atanasije. 1987. *Od Kosova do Jadovna*. Belgrade: Glas crkve.

———. 1990. *Stradanja Srba na Kosovu i Metohiji od 1941. do 1990*. Prishtina: Jedinstvo.

Jevtić, Miroljub. 1989. *Džihad. Savremeni džihad kao rat*. Belgrade: Nova Knjiga.

Jireček, Konstantin. 1990. *Istorija Srba*. Reprint of 1951 edition, prepared by Jovan Radonić. 2 vols. Belgrade: Zmaj.

Jokl, Norbert. 1926. 'Die Bektaschis von Naim Be Frashëri'. *Balkan Archiv*, 2, pp.226-56.

Judah, Tim. 1997. *The Serbs: History, myth and the destruction of Yugoslavia*. New Haven: Yale University Press.

Kadare, Ismail. 1994. 'Préface' in Ibrahim Rugova, *La question du Kosovo. Entretiens avec Marie-Françoise Allain et Xavier Galmiche*. Paris: Fayard, pp.7-29.

Kaleshi, Hasan. 1971. 'Albanische Legenden um Sari Saltuk'. *Actes du premier congrès international des études balkaniques et sud-est européennes*, VII, pp. 815-28. Sofia.

Kapferer, Bruce. 1988. *Legends of people, myths of state: Violence, intolerance, and political culture in Sri Lanka and Australia*. Washington: Smithsonian Institute Press.

Karakasidou, Anastasia N. 1997. *Fields of wheat, hills of blood: Passages to nationhood in Greek Macedonia 1870-1990*. University of Chicago Press.

Karan, Milenko. 1985. *Krvna osveta*. Belgrade: Partizanska Knjiga.

Kasumi, Haki. 1988. *Bashkësitë fetare në Kosovë 1945-1980*. Prishtinë: Instituti i historisë së Kosovës.

Kissling, Hans J. 1962. 'Zum islamischen Heiligenwesen auf dem Balkan, vorab im thrakischen Raume'. *Zeitschrift für Balkanologie*, 1, pp.46-59.

Koljević, Svetozar. 1980. *The epic in the making*. Oxford: Clarendon Press.

Kostić, Petar. 1928. *Crkveni život pravoslavnih Srba u Prizrenu i njegovoj okolini u XIX veku (sa uspomenama pisca)*. Belgrade: Grafički institut 'Narodna misao'.

Kostović, Ivica, and Miloš Judaš (eds). 1992. *Mass killing and genocide in Croatia 1991/92: A book of evidence (based upon the evidence of the Division of Information, the Ministry of Health of the Republic of Croatia)*. Zagreb: Hrvatska Sveučilišna Naklada.

Kovačić, A. 1995. 'Janjevci našli novi dom. Kako su se u Daruvarskoj okolici snašli izbjegli Hrvati s Kosova'. *Večernji list*, 17 October 1995, p.10.

Kramer, Martin (ed.). 1987. *Shi'ism, resistance and revolution*. Boulder, CO: Westview Press.

Krasnići, Mark. 1957. 'Orahovac: antropogeografska monografija varošice'. *Glasnik muzeja Kosova i Metohije*, 2, pp.87-138.

———. 1958. 'Manastirske vojvode u Kosovsko-Metohiskoj oblasti'. *Glasnik muzeja Kosova i Metohije* (Prishtina), 3, pp.107-28.

Krstić, Branislav. 1994. *Kosovo izmedju istorijskog i etničkog prava*. Belgrade: Kuća vid.

Laffan, R.G.D. 1989 (1918). *The Serbs. The guardians of the gate*. New York: Dorset Press.

Lazović, Bojan. 1990. 'Šta da uradi čovek napadnut od svoje senke'. *Svet*, 31 October 1990, p.82.

Lazović, Bojan, and Aleksandar Nikolić Pisarev. 1990. 'Politički meningitis'. *Svet*, 18 April 1990, pp.56-7.

Lévi-Strauss, Claude. 1977. *L'identité*. Paris: Presses Universitaires de France.

Lewis, I. M. 1971. *Ecstatic religion: An anthropological study of spirit possession and shamanism*. Harmondsworth: Penguin.

Liebich, André. 1992. 'Minorities in Eastern Europe: Obstacles to a reliable count'. *RFE/RL research report*, 1(20), pp.32-9.

Liégeois, Jean-Pierre. 1986. *Gypsies: An illustrated history*. London: Al Saqi.

Le livre noir. 1993. *Le livre noir de l'ex-Yougoslavie. Purification ethnique et crimes de guerre* (Documents assembled by *Le Nouvel Observateur* and Reporters Sans Frontières). Paris: Arléa.

Ljubisavljević, Milorad. 1990. 'Nismo ptice selice'. *Svet,* 22 August 1990, pp.34-5.

Lockwood, William G. 1985. 'An introduction to Balkan Gypsies'. *Giessener Hefte für Tsiganologie,* 2(1), pp.17-23.

Logoreci, Anton. 1977. *The Albanians: Europe's forgotten survivors.* London: Gollancz.

Loizos, Peter. 1981. *The heart grown bitter: A chronicle of Cypriot war refugees.* Cambridge University Press.

Lopasic, Alexander. 1994. 'Islamization of the Balkans with special reference to Bosnia'. *Journal of Islamic studies,* 5(2), pp.163-86.

Lucassen, Leo. 1990. *'En men noemde hen zigeuners'. De geschiedenis van Kaldarasch, Ursari, Lowara en Sinti in Nederland.(1750-1944).* Amsterdam: Stichting Beheer IISG/SDU.

Lučić, Dejan. 1988. *Tajne albanske mafije.* Belgrade: Kosmos.

Lukinović, Andrija. 1986. *Naša Gospa Voćinska.* Zagreb-Voćin: Kršćanska sadašnjost i župni ured Voćin.

Mach, Zdzislaw. 1993. *Symbols, conflict, and identity: Essays in political anthropology.* Albany: State University of New York Press.

Magaš, Branka. 1993. *The destruction of Yugoslavia: Tracking the break-up, 1980-92.* London: Verso.

Majetić, Roman. 1993. 'Crkveni fond svetog Izidora preselio je 4000 Hrvata s Kosova u napuštene srpske kuće u zapadnoj Slavoniji'. *Globus,* 3 December 1993, pp.8-9.

Malaj, Vinçenc. 1990. 'Apostolic and educational work of the Fransciscan order among the Albanian people'. *Albanian Catholic Bulletin* (San Francisco), 11, pp.23-54.

Malcolm, Noel. 1994. *Bosnia: A short history.* London: Macmillan.

——. 1997. 'Crypto-Christianity and religious amphibianism in the Ottoman Balkans: The case of Kosovo'. Paper presented at the conference 'Religion in the Balkans', SSEES/SOAS June–July 1997.

——.1998.*Kosovo: A short history.* London: Macmillan.

Maletić, Mihailo *et al.* 1973. *Kosovo, nekad i danas/Kosova, dikur e sot.* Belgrade: Ekonomske politike.

Maliqi, Shkëlzen. 1997. 'Albanians between East and West' in Duijzings, Ger, Dušan Janjić and Shkëlzen Maliqi (eds), *Kosovo – Kosova. Confrontation or coexistence.* Nijmegen: Peace Research Centre, pp.115-22.

Mann, Stuart E. 1933. 'Albanian Romani'. *Journal of the Gypsy lore society,* 12 (1), pp.1-32 (part 1) and 147-152 (part 2).

———.1955._Albanian literature: An outline of prose, poetry, and drama_. London: Bernard Quaritch.

Marcus, George E. and Michael M.J. Fischer. 1986. _Anthropology as cultural critique: An experimental moment in the human sciences_. University of Chicago Press.

Marković, Zoran M. 1996. 'Nacija, žrtva i osveta (prema revijalnoj štampi u Srbiji 1987-1991)'. _Republika_, 1-15 May 1996, pp.I-V.

Marmullaku, Ramadan. 1975. _Albania and the Albanians_. London: Hurst.

Meier, Viktor. 1984. 'Immer mehr jugoslawische Muslime studieren in arabischen Ländern'. _Frankfurter Allgemeine Zeitung_, 10 August 1984, p.3.

Meijers, Daniel. 1989. _De revolutie der vromen: ontstaan en ontwikkeling van het Chassidisme, waarin is opgenomen het verslag van reb Dan Isj-Toms reis door de eeuwigheid_. Hilversum: Gooi & Sticht.

Menekshe, Shaip, _et al_. 1972. 'Položaj Roma u Socijalističkoj samoupravnoj pokrajini Kosovo'. _Romano allav_ (Prizren), 1, pp.35-43.

Mihailović, Kosta, and Vasilije Krestić. 1995. 'Memorandum of the Serbian Academy of Sciences and Arts. Answers to criticisms'. Belgrade: Serbian Academy of Sciences and Arts.

Mitrović, Aleksandra. 1990. _Na dnu. Romi na granicama siromaštva_. Belgrade: Naučna knjiga.

Mojzes, Paul. 1995. _The Yugoslavian inferno: Ethnoreligious warfare in the Balkans_. New York: Continuum.

Momen, Moojan. 1985. _An introduction to Shi'i Islam: The history and doctrines of Twelver Shi'ism_. New Haven: Yale University Press.

Mufaku, Muhammad. 1993. 'The Serbian view of Islam in the 1980s' in H.T. Norris (ed.), _Islam in the Balkans: Religion and society between Europe and the Arab world_. London: Hurst, pp. 295-8.

Mustapić, Andjelka. 1995. 'Kosovski bum u zapadnoj Slavoniji. U posjetu Voćinu, mjestu naseljenom kosovoskim Hrvatima'. _Nedjeljna Dalmacija_, 27 January 1995, pp.2-3.

Neimarlija, H. 1978. 'Primitivizam koji bruka i boli'. _Preporod_ (Sarajevo), 20 August 1978, p.7.

Njegoš, P.P. 1989. _The mountain wreath_. Transl. and ed. Vasa D. Mihailovich. Belgrade: Vajat.

Nopcsa, Franz Baron. 1907. _Das katholische Nordalbanien_. Wien: Gerold.

Nordstrom, Carolyn, and Antonius C.G.M. Robben (eds). 1995. _Fieldwork under fire: Contemporary studies of violence and survival_. Berkeley: University of California Press.

Norris, H.T. 1990. 'Muslim Albanian cultural identity in modern Kosovo: The personal impressions of a contemporary Arab reporter'. _South Slav Journal_, 13(1-2), pp.38-54.

———.1993. *Islam in the Balkans: Religion and society between Europe and the Arab world*. London: Hurst.

Nušić, Branislav. 1902. *S Kosova na sinje more. Beleške s puta kroz arbanase 1894. godine*. Belgrade: Električna štamparija P. Ćurčića.

Oberoi, Harjot. 1994. *The construction of religious boundaries: Culture, identity and diversity in the Sikh tradition*. Delhi: Oxford University Press.

Okely, Judith. 1983. *The traveller-Gypsies*. Cambridge University Press.

Oršolić, Marko. 1978. 'Štovanje Marije kod bosanskohercegovačkih muslimana' in Adalbert Rebić (ed.), *Bogorodica u hrvatskom narodu. Zbornik radova Prvog hrvatskog mariološkog kongresa, Split 9. i 10. rujna 1976*. Zagreb: Kršćanska sadašnjost, pp.26-30.

Osvald, Janez. 1989. 'Škof Gnidovec graditelj cerkva in drugih cerkevnih stavb' in Edo Škulj (ed.), *Gnidovćev simpozij v Rimu*. Celje: Mohorjeva družba, pp.141-50.

Pavković, Vasa. 1995. *Korovnjak. Srpske junačke poezije novog doba*. Belgrade: Vreme knjige.

Pavlowitch, Stevan K. 1988. *The improbable survivor: Yugoslavia and its problems, 1918-1988*. London: Hurst.

Peacock, Wadham. 1914. *Albania: The foundling state of Europe*. London: Chapman & Hall.

Petrović, Djurdjica. 1976. 'Društveni položaj Cigana u nekim južno-slovenskim zemljama u XV i XVI veku'. *Jugoslovenski istorijski časopis*, 1-2, pp.45-66.

Petrović, Ruža. 1992. 'Demografske osobenosti Roma u Jugoslaviji' in Macura (ed.), *Razvitak Roma u Jugoslaviji. Problemi i tendencije*. Belgrade: SANU, pp.115-27.

Petrovich, Michael B. 1972. 'Yugoslavia: Religion and the tensions of a multi-national state'. *East European quarterly*, 6, pp.118-35.

———. 1980. 'Religion and ethnicity in Eastern Europe'. In Sugar (ed.), *Ethnic diversity and conflict in Eastern Europe*. Santa Barbara, CA: ABC-Clio, pp.373-417.

Peyfuss, Max Demeter. 1992. 'Religious confession and nationality in the case of the Albanians' in Donal A. Kerr (ed.), *Religion, state and ethnic groups: Comparative studies on governments and non-dominant ethnic groups in Europe, 1850-1940*. New York University Press, vol.II, pp.125-38.

Pick, Daniel. 1993. *War machine: The rationalisation of slaughter in the modern age*. New Haven: Yale University Press.

Pipa, Arshi. 1978. *Albanian literature: Social perspectives*. Munich: Rudolf Trofenik.

Pope, Barbara Corrado. 1985. 'Immaculate and powerful: The Marian revival in the nineteenth century' in Clarissa W. Atkinson, Constance

H. Buchanan and Margaret R. Miles, *Immaculate and powerful. The female in sacred image and social reality.* Boston: Beacon Press, pp.173-200.

Popov, Nebojša. 1993. *Srpski populizam. Od marginalne do dominantne pojave.* Special supplement of *Vreme*, 24 May 1993.

Popov, Vesselin. 1992. 'La conscience ethnique préférentielle des Tsiganes'. *Études tsiganes* 38(2), pp.38-43.

Popovic, Alexandre. 1985. 'The contemporary situation of the Muslim mystic orders in Yugoslavia' in Ernest Gellner (ed.), *Islamic dilemmas: Reformers, nationalists and industrialization: The southern shore of the Mediterranean.* Berlin: Mouton, pp.240-54.

——. 1986. *L'Islam balkanique. Les musulmanes du sud-est européen dans la période post-ottomane.* Wiesbaden: Otto Harrassowitz.

——. 1991. 'Les derviches balkaniques II: les Sinanis'. *Turcica*, 21–23, pp.83-113.

——. 1994. *Les derviches balkaniques hier et aujourd'hui.* Istanbul: ISIS.

Popović, Janićije. 1927. *Gračanica manastir.* Belgrade: Mlada Srbija.

Popović, Srdja, Dejan Janča and Tanja Petovar. 1990. *Kosovski čvor. Drešiti ili seći? Izveštaj nezavisne komisije.* Belgrade: Chronos.

Popović, Tatyana. 1988. *Prince Marko: The hero of South Slav epics.* Syracuse University Press.

Poulton, Hugh. 1991. *The Balkans: Minorities and states in conflict.* London: Minority Rights Publications.

——. 1993. 'The Roma in Macedonia: A Balkan success story?' *RFE/RL research report*, 2(19), pp.42-5.

——. 1995. *Who are the Macedonians?* London: Hurst.

—— and Suha Taji-Farouki (eds). 1997. *Muslim identity and the Balkan state.* London: Hurst.

Prokić, Milutin. 1992. 'Socijalno-ekonomske karakteristike Roma u Jugoslaviji' in Miloš Macura (ed.), *Razvitak Roma u Jugoslaviji. Problemi i tendencije.* Belgrade: SANU, pp.97-114.

Qazimi, Qazim. 1996. *Ndikime orientale në veprën letrare të Naim Frashërit.* Prishtinë: Këshilli i Bashkësisë Islame të Gjilanit.

Qosja, Rexhep. 1995. *La question albanaise.* Paris: Fayard.

Radić, Radmila. 1996. 'Crkva i "srpsko pitanje"' in Nebojša Popov (ed.), *Srpska strana rata. Trauma i katarza u istorijskom pamćenju.* Belgrade: BIGZ, pp.267-304.

Radonić, Jovan. 1950. *Rimska kurija u južnoslovenske zemlje od XVI do XIX veka.* Belgrade: SANU.

Ramet, Pedro. 1988. 'The Serbian Orthodox church' in Pedro Ramet (ed.), *Eastern Christianity and politics in the twentieth century.* Durham, NC: Duke University Press, pp.232-48.

Ramet, Sabrina. 1998. *Nihil Obstat: Religion, politics, and social change in East-Central Europe and Russia.* Durham, NC: Duke University Press.

Ramsaur, Ernest. 1942. 'The Bektashi dervishes and the Young Turks'. *The Moslim world*, 32, pp.7–14.

Risteski, Stojan. 1991. *Narodni prikazni, predanija i obichai kaj Egipkjanite. Egjupcite vo Makedonija.* Ohrid: Nikola Kosteski (Nezavisni izdanija 8).

Rizaj, Skënder. 1987. *Kosova gjatë shekujve XV, XVI dhe XVII (administrimi, ekonomia, shoqëria dhe lëvizja popullore).* Tirana: 8 Nëntori.

———.1992.*Kosova dhe Shqiptarët. Dje, sot i nesër / Kosova and the Albanians. Yesterday, today and tommorow.* Prishtina: Academy of Albanian Intellectuals of Sciences and Arts.

Rosen, Georg. 1866. *Geschichte der Türkei von dem Siege der Reform im J.1826 bis zum Pariser Traktat vom J.1856.* 2 vols. Published in series *Staatengeschichte der neuesten Zeit.* Leipzig.

Ross, Dan. 1982. *Acts of faith: A journey to the fringes of Jewish identity.* New York: St Martin's Press.

Roux, Michel. 1992. *Les Albanais en Yougoslavie. Minorité nationale territoire et développement.* Paris: Éditions de la Maison des Sciences de l'Homme.

S.R. 1979. 'Boli me kada vidim umjesto islama'. *Preporod* (Sarajevo), 15–31 January 1979, p.9.

Sabalić, Ines. 1991. 'Kosovski terezijanski otpor'. *Start* (Zagreb), 5 January 1991, pp.24–30.

Sallnow, M.J. 1981. 'Communitas reconsidered: The sociology of an Andean pilgrimage'. *Man* (N.S.), 16, pp.163–82.

———.1987.*Pilgrims of the Andes: Regional cults in Cusco.* Washington, DC: Smithsonian Institution.

Samardžić, Radovan, *et al.* 1990. *La Kosovo-Metohija dans l'histoire serbe.* Lausanne: L'Age d'Homme.

Schwandner-Sievers, Stephanie. 1999. *The Albanian Aromanians' awakening. Identity politics and conflicts in post-communist transition.* ECMI Working Paper 3. Flensburg: European Centre for Minority Issues.

Scott, James C. 1990. *Domination and the arts of resistance: Hidden transcripts.* New Haven: Yale University Press.

———. 1995. 'State simplifications. Nature, space, and people. Great development disasters'. Sixth Wertheim Lecture. Amsterdam: CASA.

Sells, Michael A. 1996. *The bridge betrayed. Religion and genocide in Bosnia.* Berkeley: University of California Press.

Shuteriqi, Dhimitër S. 1983. *Historia e letërsisë shqiptare që nga fillimet deri te lufta antifashiste nacionalçlirimtare.* Tiranë: Akademia e shkencave e RPS të Shqipërisë, Instituti i gjuhësisë dhe i letërsisë.

Silber, Laura, and Allen Little. 1996. *The Death of Yugoslavia.* 2nd edn. London: Penguin and BBC Books.

Skendi, Stavro. 1954. *Albanian and South Slavic oral epic poetry*. Philadelphia: American Folklore Society.

———. 1956. 'Religion in Albania during the Ottoman Rule'. *Südost-Forschungen*, 13, pp.159-99.

———. 1960. 'The history of the Albanian alphabet. A case of complex cultural and political development'. *Südost-Forschungen*, 19, pp.263-85.

———. 1967. 'Crypto-Christianity in the Balkan area under the Ottomans'. *Slavic Review*, 26, pp.227-46.

———. 1980. 'Skenderbeg and Albanian national consciousness'. *Balkan cultural studies* (East European Monographs, Boulder). New York: Columbia University Press, pp.205-10.

———. 1982. 'The *Millet* System and its contribution to the blurring of Orthodox national identity in Albania' in Benjamin Braude and Bernard Lewis (eds), *Christians and Jews in the Ottoman empire: The functioning of a plural society*. London: Holmes and Meier, pp.243-57.

Slijepčević, Djoko. 1983 (1974). '*Srpsko-arbanaški odnosi kroz vekove sa posebnim osvrtom nanovije vreme*. 2nd edn. Himmelsthür: Štamparija Ostrog.

Smith, Grace M. 1982. 'Some türbes/maqams of Sari Saltuq; an early Anatolian Turkish Gazi-saint'. *Turcica*, 14, pp.216-25.

Sofos, Spyros, A. 1996. 'Inter-ethnic violence and gendered constructions of ethnicity in former Yugoslavia'. *Social Identities*, 2(1), pp.73-91.

Sopi, Marko. 1989. 'Briga biskupa Gnidovca o ljaramanima' in Edo Škulj (ed.), *Gnidovčev simpozij v Rimu*. Celje: Mohorjeva družba, pp.177-86.

Sorabji, Cornelia. 1989. 'Muslim identity and Islamic faith in socialist Sarajevo'. Ph.D. diss. University of Cambridge.

———. 1993. 'Ethnic war in Bosnia?' *Radical Philosophy*, 63, pp.33-5.

———. 1995. 'A very modern war: Terror and territory in Bosnia-Hercegovina' in Robert A. Hinde and Helen E. Watson (eds), *War, a cruel necessity? The bases of institutionalized violence*. London: I.B. Tauris, pp.80-95.

Soulis, G.C. 1961. 'The Gypsies in the Byzantine empire and the Balkans in the late Middle Ages'. *Dumbarton Oaks Papers* 15, pp.142-65.

Stadtmüller, Georg. 1956. 'Das albanische Nationalkonzil vom Jahre 1703'. *Orientalia Christiana Periodica*, 22, pp.68-91.

Stewart, Charles, and Rosalind Shaw (eds). 1994. *Syncretism/anti-syncretism: The politics of religious synthesis*. London: Routledge.

Šufflay, Milan. 1990(1925). *Srbi i Arbanasi (njihova simbioza u srednjem vijeku)*. Sarajevo: Kultura.

Šuvak, Dragica. 1994. 'Migracije stanovništva na slatinskom području'. *Zavičaj. Glasilo za kulturu, znanost i umjetnost* (Virovitica), 4(5-6), pp.4-5.

Tambiah, S.J. 1986. *Sri Lanka: Ethnic fratricide and the dismantling of democracy*. University of Chicago Press.

Thompson, Mark. 1992. *A paper house: The ending of Yugoslavia*. London: Hutchinson Radius.

Todorova, Maria. 1997a. *Imagining the Balkans*. New York: Oxford University Press.

———. 1997b. 'Identity (trans)formation among Pomaks in Bulgaria' in László Kürti and Juliet Langman (eds), *Beyond borders. Remaking cultural identities in the New East and Central Europe*. Boulder, CO: Westview Press, pp.63-82.

Tomasic, Dinko. 1948. *Personality and culture in Eastern European politics*. New York: George W. Stewart.

Tomitch, Iov. 1913. *Les Albanais en Vieille-Serbie et dans le Sandjak de Novi-Bazar*. Paris: Hachette.

Turk, Alojz. 1973. *Letnica. Marijansko hodočasničko svetište Ekumenski centar na Kosovu. Majka Božja Crnagorska. Letnička Gospa Zoja Cërnagore*. Belgrade: Blagovest.

———1992. *Škof Janez Gnidovec*. Celje: Mohorjeva družba.

Turner, Victor. 1974. *Dramas, fields and metaphors: Symbolic action in human society*. Ithaca, NY: Cornell University Press.

———. and Edith Turner. 1978. *Image and pilgrimage in Christian culture: Anthropological perspectives*. Oxford: Basil Blackwell.

Ugrešić, Dubravka. 1994. 'Balkan blues' in Joanna Labon (ed), *Balkan blues. Writing out of Yugoslavia*. Evanston, IL: Northwestern University Press, pp.2-35.

Urošević, Atanasije. 1933. 'Katolička župa Crna Gora u Južnoj Srbiji (Letnička župa)'. *Glasnik skopskog naučnog društva* (Skopje), 13, pp. 159-70.

———.1993(1935). *Gornja Morava i Izmornik*. Priština: Jedinstvo. Originally published in *Srpski etnografski zbornik* (Belgrade), Naselje, knjiga 28.

Veer, Peter van der. 1994. *Religious nationalism: Hindus and Muslims in India*. Berkeley: University of California Press.

Verdery, Katherine. 1994. 'Ethnicity, nationalism, and state-making. "Ethnic groups and boundaries": past and future' in Hans Vermeulen and Cora Govers (eds), *The anthropology of ethnicity: Beyond 'ethnic groups and boundaries'*. Amsterdam: Het Spinhuis, pp.33-58.

Vickers, Miranda. 1998. *Between Serb and Albanian: A history of Kosovo*. London: Hurst.

——— and James Pettifer. 1997. *Albania: From anarchy to a Balkan identity*. London: Hurst.

Vryonis, Speros. 1972. 'Religious changes and patterns in the Balkans, 14th-16th centuries' in Henrik Birnbaum and Speros Vryonis (eds),

Aspects of the Balkans: Continuity and change. The Hague: Mouton, pp.151-76.

Vukanović, Tatomir (T.P.) 1966. 'Gypsy pilgrimages to the monastery of Gračanica in Serbia'. *Journal of the Gypsy Lore Society*, 45, pp.17-26.

——.1983.*Romi (Cigani) u Jugoslaviji.* Vranje: Nova Jugoslavija.

——.1986.*Srbi na Kosovu.* 3 vols. Vranje: Nova Jugoslavija.

Weber, Eugen. 1976. *Peasants into Frenchmen: The modernization of rural France, 1870-1914.* Stanford University Press.

Westerman, Frank. 1993. 'De witte negers van Europa. Servië tegen de rest van de wereld'. *Intermediair*, 19 March 1993, pp.26-33.

Willems, Wim. 1995. *Op zoek naar de ware zigeuner. Zigeuners als studieobject tijdens de Verlichting, de Romantiek en het Nazisme.* Utrecht: Van Arkel.

Wilson, Thomas M., and Hastings Donnan. 1998. 'Nation, state and identity at international borders' in Wilson and Donnan (eds), *Border identities: Nation and state at international frontiers.* Cambridge University Press, pp.1-30.

Winstedt, Eric Otto. 1909-10. 'The Gypsies of Modon and the Wyne of Romeney'. *Journal of the Gypsy Lore Society*, 3, pp.57-69.

Wolf, Eric (ed.). 1991. *Religious regimes and state-formation: Perspectives from European ethnology.* Albany, NY: State University of New York Press.

Yuval-Davis, Nira. 1997. *Gender and nation.* London: Sage.

Zagorin, Perez. 1990. *Ways of lying: Dissimulation, persecution, and conformity in early modern Europe.* Cambridge MA: Harvard University Press.

Zirojević, Olga. 1995. 'Kosovo u istorijskom pamćenju (mit, legende, činjenice)'. *Republika*, 1-15 March 1995, pp.9-24.

Zürcher, Erik J. 1993. *Turkey: A modern history.* London: I.B. Tauris.

Zurl, Marino. 1978. *Krvna osveta u Kosovu.* Zagreb: August Cesarec.

First Balkan War (1912), 83, 101, 191
Balkans: 2n, 11, 17, 19, 22, 27, 32, 35, 65, 95, 103n, 106, 158, 177, 182, 206-9; Ottoman rule, 27-8, 79-80, 95-6; existential insecurity, 6-7, 34; as religious frontier, 13-14, 84; religious symbiosis, 2, 84; intertwining of ethnic and religious identities, 21, 28-9, 31, 157, 165; ambiguity of identity, 13; 'ancient ethnic hatreds', 8, 13, 207
Banja Luka, 55n
Barth, Fredrik, 23, 154, 206
Bastaji, 56, 62
Bataković, Dušan, 9, 181n
Bax, Mart, 4n, 20, 27, 35n, 126n, 208
Bektashi, 36n, 80-4, 114, 116, 158, 162, 165-9 *passim*, 169-71, 174-5; and Albanian national movement, 80-1, 83, 165, 166n, 168, 169-71, 175; as a bridge between Islam and Christianity, 80-1, 165, 167, 168; tolerance towards Christians, 66, 82-3, 171; usurpation of Christian shrines, 81-3; Shi'ite orientation, 121, 166; Sunni-Bektashi hostility, 162, 168, 171, 172; Bektashi in Turkey, 170
Belgrade, 18, 34, 49, 77, 132, 133, 143, 197, 205
Beli orlovi (White Eagles), 200n
Berberski, Slobodan, 152
besa, 72n
Bijeljina, 202
Binçë, 89, 94n
Bitola, 140, 144n
blood feuds: 7, 42, 126, 127; sheikhs as mediators, 126-7; Catholic priests as mediators, 127n
Bogdanović, Dimitrije, 9, 181n
Bokan, Dragoslav, 200n
Bosnia-Hercegovina: 2, 10, 13, 14, 15, 17, 37, 59n, 97n, 106, 110, 116, 128, 203; Ottoman rule, 116; Bosnian peasant insurrection (1875), 190; religion as marker of ethnic identity, 10, 30-1; ethnic violence, 33, 208; Bosnian War, 34n, 45, 109-

10n, 177-8, 200n, 201-2; Serb view of war as clash between Islam and Christianity, 201; western Hercegovina, 208; eastern Bosnia, 197
Bosnian language, 31n
Bosnian Muslim (Bosniac) nationalism, 160
Bosnian Muslims: 2n, 10, 15n, 33n, 37, 77, 106, 107, 108, 109, 128, 130-1, 177, 178, 201; recognition as nation, 19n, 30-1n, 129-30, 150; cultural gap with Albanian Muslims, 128-30; conversion to Orthodoxy in Bosnian War, 35
Bosnian Serb Army, 202
Bošnjaci (Bosniacs), 31n, 160
Boutros-Ghali, Boutros, 133
Božović, Rade, 143-4
Branković, Vuk, 185n, 188, 196, 199, 201
Britain, 94, 96
Bucciarelli, Dario, 94n
Bulgaria, Bulgarians, 16n, 17, 27n, 28, 29, 51, 149
Bushatli family, 170n
Byzantium, 14, 135

Canetti, Elias, 158
Carev, Fulgentius, 100
Çelebi, Evliya, 137-8n
Ćeralije, 56, 62
Cetinje (Orthodox) diocese, 78
Chetniks, 54, 67n, 73
Chiftliks, 145
Christian Orthodox, the: 15n, 28, 39n, 44n, 79, 89, 159, 160n, 175n, 177n; conversion to Catholicism, 44n
Christian Orthodox church: 28, 30, 159n, 176, 182; role in nationalist movements, 28; autocephalous churches, 169, 177; 'ethno-filetism', 177n
Christian Orthodox millet: 28n, 176n, 177n; Ecumenical Patriarch, 16n, 177n
Christian Orthodoxy, 14, 43n, 158, 163, 176, 177, 201
Christianity, 9, 103, 105, 137, 159n, 163, 165, 167, 179, 188, 189, 196, 201